Life and Living TOOLBOOK

Presented by Supernoetics™

A New Kind Of Life Awaits You Inside...

Keith Scott-Mumby MD, MB ChB, HMD, PhD

Life and Living TOOLBOOK
Presented by Supernoetics™

Published by:
Supernoetics Inc.
PO Box 19452,
Reno, NV 89511
USA

10 9 8 7 6 5 4 3 2 1

ISBN: 978-0-9968786-0-9

A catalogue record for this book is available from the Library of Congress, Washington.

Disclaimer

Dr. Keith will not be held responsible if this book changes your life dramatically, nor if you become so stirred to revitalization and change that your former friends abandon you!

He accepts no responsibility for new relationships, improved working conditions, increased financial success, visions, dreams, insights or new energetic focus.

It's your life, Pal!

Caution: there are stimulating mind exercises in this text for healthy people to refresh, review and revize their attitude and points of view. If you suffer from clinical depression, anxiety or other mental illness, they may not be appropriate for you.

Consult with a licensed medical practitioner or certified clinical.

Dedication

This book is dedicated to all good people, who care about the world and cherish those around them. May you find happiness, peace and love!

Your work is going to fill a large part of your life, and the only way to be truly satisfied is to do what you believe is great work. And the only way to do great work is to love what you do. If you haven't found it yet, keep looking. Don't settle. As with all matters of the heart, you'll know when you find it.

- Steve Jobs (1955- 2011)

Table Of Contents

Me To The Max. Supernoetics™ Explained

The word Supernoetics™ means the best of mind and Being (Me to the Max, if you like). It's a bigger idea than you could ever guess.

We have some unique systems of thinking for you. This is not indoctrination or "brain-washing"; you are free to adopt these ideas as you choose. But everyone who walks this path finds these dynamic explorations of the exact mechanisms of thought and the accompanying life hacks to be innovative, clever and extremely useful. Lots of "nifty ideas", as one member described his encounter with our superb and helpful programs.

Further along we have what amounts to viewpoint engineering. It's about discovering new states of being and new viewpoints from which to craft your approach to life. The most immediate benefits are:

- Improved emotions

- better outcomes

- enriched creativity and

- a new presence of mind that has been described as an intensity of serene joy that is even more exciting than "The Flow".

All you have to do to get started is study some exciting propositions, try them, practice them a little, and you'll find they work! Life gets better from then on.

The whole journey is a process of exploration and discovery—finding new places on the map of YOU.

Teaching Platform
Supernoetics™ has several important aspects, among which is the fact that it is a teaching platform. It puts historic educational methods in the shade.

Learning doesn't just mean gathering knowledge; it changes who you are, how you think and how you behave. True knowledge is restorative and very healing. It salves wounds and diminishes hurt. We take it as a sacred obligation to offer love, wisdom, kindness and experience.

Propelled by brilliant study techniques and what we call embodiment learning, Supernoetics™ can transform your life in as little as hours or days.

Just remember, finding yourself is the journey of a lifetime. You are the journey!

Evolution of Consciousness
Supernoetics™ is the newest evolution along the path of human evolution. Our aim is to discover, create and implement the tools for the purposeful reinvention of Humankind. We are researching the highest levels of conscious awareness, love and extended intelligence, thus resulting in the most effective long-term survival behaviors. It is a learning path and a reinvention of education. It didn't arise in a vacuum—it's built on existing methodology, much like the latest computers are not "new" but solid and tested improvements on previous models, which make our systems and techniques the best there are at this time.

Unquestionably, Supernoetics™ surpasses older ambiguous philosophies and what is laughably called psychology, by incorporating the latest science, methods and discoveries, as well as deep spiritual insights and detailed experimental research into the nature of mind and Being.

We have something for YOU in aspects of living as diverse as health, business, out-of-body sensory awareness, extended (or non-locational) mind and spiritual conversations with the Higher Self. Ever been curious about remote viewing or reincarnation?

We have a science of living and Being that is filled with surprises on the road to Truth we call **The Golden Path**.

This little book is to help introduce you to some of our basic concepts.

Fast Learning Framework

10-Steps To Maximize Learning Ability And Retention
In a time of drastic change it is the learners who inherit the future. The learned usually find themselves equipped to live in a world that no longer exists! Make sure you are a competent learner; it's a science, not an art.

The gateway to success is learning. You need to acquire new knowledge. That makes you a student. Be humble, as a student should be. One of the silliest barriers to learning is the attitude of knowing it already. If there is one thing that characterizes winners in all walks of life, it is that they are avid seekers of new and practical knowledge.

Even in the famous court case where there was an attempt to prove that Henry Ford was ignorant and therefore unworthy, he famously retorted that college learning wasn't important--- he could hire people to give him the facts he needed--- but never for a moment did he take the arrogant standpoint that he didn't need more knowledge, just because he was already hugely successful in commerce.

Remember the saying: knowledge is power. But knowledge has to be acquired.

To set the stage and help you get the best out of this learning process, here is a basic study strategy that you can use to extend your understanding of this or any other text.

1. Read Through What You Judge To Be A Reasonable-Sized Thought-Bite (sentence, paragraph, rule, axiom or whatever).
Traditional study is often just reading, no more. But that's not enough, as we shall see.

The exact amount you bite off for each chunk depends on many factors, including your own abilities and the pace and style of the author, or speaker if you are listening to an instruction tape.

We just want you to take in a complete thought or concept.

For text you can take the opportunity to high-light certain aspects of the text as revision points. Do not do as some people do and highlight 80- 90% of the text. This becomes self-defeating; highlights are supposed to stand out--- when everything is highlighted, there is nothing but a blur.

If you are not allowed to mark the text (a library book, for example) make notes which indicate key headings etc. or use "post-it" stickers on the page.

2. Ask Yourself: Are There Any Words I Don't Fully Understand. Look Them Up In A Competent Dictionary.
NEVER NEVER NEVER let yourself pass words you do not understand. Look them up in a dictionary. Words are the building blocks of ideas. Human consciousness is based around language. If you don't have the words; you don't have the concept. Even if you are not quite sure of a word, look it up anyway. You will find it remarkable how clearing up word haziness can focus your understanding of what is being said.

To omit this step is not merely folly—you are virtually guaranteed to fail in your life mission. No IFs and BUTs; it's a promise. You will never access the stock-pile of facts, techniques and expertise you need to succeed without a mastery of words and meanings.

You Don't Believe This?
Try the following simple test; you can do it as what Einstein called a "thought experiment" if you are really lazy:

Take a page of any text you are not fully familiar with and photocopy it. Now go through with a felt-tip pen and blank out twenty or so words on the page, so that you cannot read them. Getting someone else to do this step for you is even more revealing.

Now read the text, without filling in the word blanks from your imagination, and see what sense you can make of what is being said on the page. None at all, probably.

Now do you see the importance of clearing up word meanings as you go along?

If you haven't got a dictionary, go out and buy one---NOW! Close this manual and don't try to continue to read it without a competent dictionary to hand.

Rinky Dink Dictionaries
Don't be tempted to buy a cheap rinky-dink edition; these don't define words but associate them---so "old" might be written off as "ancient". Then you look up ancient and it says "very old"! This is useless.

For British readers, there is nothing better than the current Chamber's Dictionary or for US English, Webster's Comprehensive International Dictionary. Invest in a new copy of one or the other; it's important to have all the very up-to-date words defined. Try to get a slang or "buzz words" dictionary too, if you can.

Be on the lookout for specialist dictionaries related to your own sphere of interest (Dictionary of Archeology, Computing, Medical terms etc.)

Beware Idioms
You must also be alert for idiomatic phrases. English is particularly rich in them. Idioms are groups of words that have a specially recognized meaning, such as "hair of the dog that bit you". It is unlikely that you would guess the true meaning of "once bitten twice shy" simply by looking up the individual words (after being hurt once you will be doubly careful in future).

"Let's call it a day" is another example – meaning "We're done". See if you can jot down 10 such idiomatic expressions. Try looking one up in a dictionary: it's unlikely you'll find the phrase listed.

Ideally you need a dictionary of idioms. Cambridge produce a good paperback one (Cambridge International Dictionary of Idioms).

3. Then Ask Yourself: Do I Understand What I Have Just Read?
If not, you need to go back to step 2. You almost certainly have words and thought fragments that you still haven't exactly duplicated. These will block your understanding of the whole. Until you have experienced it for yourself, just believe that clearing up failed words will revive the material you are trying to assimilate and bring it back to life.

Don't worry in the least about "remembering". That's stuff and nonsense you learned at school and look where it got you! It got you through school of course. But the endless river of facts you were expected to "learn" were of little consequence out here in the big wide world.

The brilliant educator Michel Thomas made plain that trying to memorize information is not merely a waste of time but is stressful to the student and has a negative effect on the assimilation process.

Understanding is what we prize, not parroting (being able to spout it back) or what is called rote learning.

4. Can I Sum Up What Is Being Said In My Own Words?

Say it out loud, as if explaining it to somebody else. Switch into teacher mode and dish it out. There is an old saying that you learn most by teaching it. No need to be coy. In any case, winners do not care what other people think. Do it in private if you have to. But do it. There is no success without effort and commitment; mastering reticence is a must. Learning the tools of your trade is important-- in this case doubly important, because they are the tools for all of living.

So who cares what spectators think?

The important point here is to be able to say it in your own words. Do not simply re-arrange the writer's or speaker's words and commit them to memory. That's the shallow learning standard used at school and it's not good enough.

5. Ask Yourself: Does It Make Sense?

Does this follow, logically, from what I have studied so far? It should, unless the educator is very flawed (and some are undoubtedly really bad).

Then ask yourself, does this align with my own personal experience?

Be careful. If it doesn't fit the prejudice you have been saddled with during formal education years, it may nevertheless be true. You don't reject it just because it sounds unusual or challenging. Instead, go carefully and take steps 6 and 7 more thoroughly, until you are sure.

Remember: almost all new and revolutionary ideas meet what is called a "cultural lag". It takes most of the population years to follow behind the leaders and catch onto what they are trying to say. It's a balancing act: don't be rigid in your approach and don't be gullible either.

The worst mistake you can make is to accept data simply because some big shot said it or you read it in a book (or, even worse, the newspapers!) That's what they taught you to do at school and you must unlearn this whole blighting attitude.

Learning must cease to be mere assimilation of other peoples' data; you are to acquire your own knowledge and being able to exercise judgment and choice is part of that process.

6. Think Up Several Examples That Appear To Support The Text Or Lecture

The text you are using may offer supporting examples. But it is better if you can identify your own reinforcing experiences.

Actually, you will find with good life-orienting data—the kind you will find in our programs—that there is a certain comfortable "Yes, I sort of knew that..." feeling that will help you along.

Pure scientific and philosophical knowledge is around everywhere, embedded in the set up of the universe, if you like. So the chances are you have encountered some of these principles and either consciously or unconsciously assimilated them is quite high.

Just remember that sort of familiar feeling is very useful when studying because it speeds you up!

Play With The Reality
Here is a short catechism you can memorize and use in all your studies:

* Has this happened to me?

* Can I think of an example that illustrates this?

* Does it seem real to me?

* Can I now think up an example that shows it from history, fiction, TV or movies?

* Can I create (invent) a situation in which this might be applicable or useful?

If it is worthwhile learning and you have grasped it, examples should come to mind.

7. Be Willing To Think Up Examples That Might Disprove It.
In science philosophy there is a concept called "falsifiable", introduced by British philosopher Sir Karl Popper. It just means could the opposite be true? If so, it's a valid possibility. You just have to find out if can be proved wrong. Then make up your mind.

We don't go that deep but the principle is really just everyday common-sense:

Is it possible to think something different to what the writer or speaker says? Does something you have first-hand experience of seem to contradict it? If you can't find exceptions, this is obviously persuasive. But often the apparency of an exclusion increases our understanding of the workings of a theory we are studying.

Remember the saying: the exception proves the rule. While in physics there should be no exceptions to a law (otherwise it is not a law), in every day matters the fact that exceptions are found to be very rare make it a useful "rule".

Steps 6 and 7 are not about trying to be a "know-all": remember you are a student. But mental agility and thinking through the facts is something that is essential to true learning as opposed to mere schoolroom-style rote. Parroting is for parrots, not human beings.

8. Make Up Your Mind, On The Balance Of Evidence And Logicality, Whether You Accept Or Believe What Is Being Said.
If you are developing an affinity with the subject and gaining a pattern of integrated knowledge, you will soon form an opinion

Question everything; that's the motto. Including question what is being revealed to you in this manual.

Hopefully you will like what you read here. We can take plenty of scepticism and scrutiny. We are strong because all these ideas have been extensively road-tested. If you don't think they are for you, that's your problem.

9. If You Do, Decide To Have This Knowledge For Your Own Mind-Set.
Making knowledge your own, as we say, is something alien to the Western educational scene. The learning culture is simply that we accept what we are taught by our mentors or "betters".

To hell with that; once you grasp the way our society is being oppressed and enslaved through destructive and unworkable education, you will want out straight away. The secret to becoming truly educated is to know how to go about acquiring real knowledge for yourself. The truth is out there, you need to be able to select it from the chaff of opinions and dogma.

What we do INSIST on is that you make up your own mind. As Buddha said: "If it's true for you, then it is true". That's one of the greatest philosophical teachers of all time speaking. And that's one hell of an attitude to life!

10. Work Through The Whole Body Of Materials In This Way.
Finish off with a skim through the sections and categories, making sure you can recall the materials being covered.

Further And Better Particulars:
Signs You Passed Words You Didn't Understand…

1. Blankness. You can't remember what you read a few moments before. The failed word or words will always lie just before the blank section, not in the middle of it.

2. Losing interest. You started out well; you have become bored or frustrated with the learning process.

3. Confusion. If you remain confused about the text or lecture, despite re-reading it or re-hearing a recording, then you have misunderstood terms or idioms.

4. Disagreement. You may find yourself rejecting or rebelling against data, because you have not really understood it properly. Ask yourself: is this a reliable source? If you teacher appears to have a good grasp of things beware! It may be your failure at comprehension.

5. Tiredness. Most study fatigue is in fact an accumulation of misunderstandings. Why am I so sure? Because I have seen over and over how a student perks up when forced to get busy with the dictionary.

6. Quitting. The main reason a person gives up study is an inability to grasp the materials. This results in loss of morale and failure. Misunderstood words lie behind this.

Absorbing The New Word:
Practice new words using real sentences. Use the words in sentences of your own construction, until you have made the unfamiliar term your very own. Master that word. Words help create our reality. Man is a verbal-reasoning animal. Therefore to allow failed words in your psyche is to collect loss and failure.

Tip. From the keynote learning scientists of the day, notably Georgi Lozanov, we are told you will learn best in a tranquil environment, with background music playing. Specifically, the music should be slow Baroque (Bach or Handel, etc). Very gentle New Age or soft "mood music" will do almost as well. Lozanov had students learning 1,000 new French words a day, with 98% retention, so you had better take his ideas on board (and before you ask, 2 years later they still retained over 85% of that vocabulary!)

Keith Scott-Mumby

History of this document:
Originally written 1994, revised and re-issued 12 Jul 2012

1. Learning How To Learn!

The Supernoetics™ Embodiment Learning System offers a great deal of advanced self-learning material, which you will encounter on later seminars and courses sponsored by us. What follows is a simplified version of these techniques, which is sufficient for our present needs.

It's a kind of LEARNING PRIMER. Go over these basic principles slowly and conscientiously. Do not be tempted to skip because "I know all that stuff; I was at school anyway". Remember you are developing NEW approaches to living and learning.

If you want to change your life radically for the better, you will need to learn new living strategies. Education in this sense is really no different to study as you learned it at school; merely the syllabus is different.

Forget Everything You Learned at School
One of the very significant reasons why you may not have been getting the outcomes you wanted is that we are educated so very badly right from school years. It might almost be argued that, in terms of self-fulfillment, what you learned at school has had a negative (destructive) effect.

Think about this. Were you taught anything at all about learning to be happy, financially independent, creative, romantic aligned or successful in business during your school years? Of course not. They teach you math, geography, history and biology and expect you to guess for yourself how to meet with people, cultivate zest and integrity, stay out of debt, plan for the future and develop vital interpersonal skills.

The chances are that they didn't even teach you how to study ("must try harder" is about the limit of their understanding of how to get better results in the classroom). Yet study is the key to almost everything. It is the gateway to the magic paradise in which you get what it is that your heart truly desires. It is obvious, therefore that you must learn to become a self-educator. The transformation process begins in the next few sentences and continues throughout this book!

The Hoax That Keeps You Ignorant
Let's kick right off with one the biggest hoaxes in civilized society and the cruellest joke in all education:

"The only reason people fail at study is that they are too stupid to grasp the materials or too lazy to apply themselves properly."

TRUE FACT: the only reason a person gives up study or becomes upset and confused while trying to learn is that they have encountered one or more *Barriers To Learning* and have not been shown how to deal with them.

The whole failing of the existing system is that it blames the student. It assumes that diligence in study is all that is required in order to pass tests and courses. The implication is that if a student is failing, it is only because that student has not gone over the material often enough, has not mastered new vocabulary, does not do his or her homework, does not take proper lecture notes, does not follow a proper study schedule, or does not have other proper study habits.

Certainly, bad habits can cause failure. But advising a student to have good study habits is about as helpful as advising an alcoholic to stop drinking, a smoker to stop smoking, or a drug addict to stop taking drugs. Unless the basic reason they are doing what they are doing is handled, they are unable to follow the advice.

No Such Thing As A Bad Student
Basically, study failures are education failures but teachers, professors and academics are very adept at passing the buck and blaming the "bad student" instead of lousy, or more often absent, teaching methodology.

The whole point of study is to *fully assimilate* the materials. It is not merely to learn facts. Understanding and being able to overcome the obstacles to assimilation is thus one of the most important life-tools you can acquire. It will free you from the limitations imposed by earlier learning failures and enable your efforts towards your goals in life to succeed in a way that never happened before.

A Paradox
Knowledge (knowing HOW) is the doorway to everything you ever wanted. Study is the key that will open the door to a new and successful life. **To learn to succeed you must learn to learn.** Here we encounter a paradox: how can you learn to study if you don't already know how to study effectively?

Well, fortunately it isn't quite as impossible as it might at first seem. It simply requires that you overview the subject of study itself, which you can do quickly using the first study advantage given below. THEN RE-STUDY THE 10-POINT FAST LEARNING FRAMEWORK.

Do not omit this re-study. Remember honest learning and attention to getting results is one of the key requirements you will be needing from now on, especially if you embrace the many brilliant and life-transforming tools of Supernoetics™..

Test Your Data
True learning does not mean to absorb data from others, passively and uncritically. Real study means to explore information, test it against your own experience, integrate it with existing your knowledge and make it part of the way YOU think.

Real learning, education in its fullest sense, means *to make the data your very own*.

You owe it to yourself to adopt new study attitudes and not just let yourself become a mop or sponge to absorb whatever other people throw at you. Be an active, enquiring, critical, even sceptical, learner but above all be involved.

Memory is Not Enough
It is not sufficient just to memorize what is being taught. This is a meaningless and dishonest standard of learning which pervades our schools. So much so that it is generally deemed adequate to study a subject with the sole aim of passing a series of examinations which do not seek to test the student's application of the knowledge. Gaining certificates merely for status then becomes the phoney objective and not learning in the fullest sense in which we use it in Supernoetics™.

Education in this climate of dishonesty serves society and the individual very badly.

Ironically, if you really understand the data and make it your own, you will find you are able to retain it easily. Where memorizing is essential, as with learning a sequence of instructions to be carried out, retention can be aided by repetition. There is no question that several times through the data improves its memorization. BUT ONLY IF COMPREHENSION AND APPLICATION HAVE BEEN ADDRESSED FIRST.

Think WITH your materials
OK, we don't study for status, or just to pass exams or with the intention of bluffing our way through a course. We are focused on attaining

a proper understanding of the materials. This is the key to being able to apply what we have learned.

Knowledge at this level means you can think as one with your subject. You can LIVE it. This is very powerful and you will learn more about this heightened learning in our Embodiment Learning method.

Naturally, we don't start out at this standard. It is something to aim for. You may not have all the data there is to know in a speciality subject. But if you have this extraordinary degree of affinity with it, you will absorb a mass of facts comfortably and easily.

Honesty is What Counts
Speed actually has very little to do with it. Neither has memory. Comprehension and reasoning are what count. A bright student will know when he or she is off track: it won't feel right. You know you aren't getting it.

The honest diligent student will back up and ask, "What has gone wrong?"

The answer probably has to do with one of several barriers to learning that we call *Obstacles To Assimilation*, which now follow:

1. There is Something to Learn
It might seem obvious but no one can learn who doesn't feel there is something to be learned. A know-it-all attitude is commoner than supposed and comes in many guises. Make sure you are not guilty of this one.

The wiser people become, the humbler they get because the more you learn about a subject, the more you realize what there is to know. It takes knowledge and skill to recognize the extent of one's ignorance.

You might catch yourself being a little superior at this point. Perhaps you feel you know all about study; you don't need a primer? Maybe the idea seems childish or embarrassing to you, that you should need to be told how to do something so elementary as study? Be warned: these are insidious obstructive attitudes that could stumble you on your quest for ultimate knowledge.

2. Word failures
DEFINITION: a failed word is one which is not properly understood, an unfamiliar word or a word that you thought you knew but have a wrong meaning for, or a meaning which is misleading in the present context, or a word which has such an unpleasant emotional connotation that makes it hard to think straight with it.

Words define our experience. You don't believe it? Could you have "honesty" without a word structure attached to this concept? No. But beauty is still beauty, you say, even without the word. But that isn't true. What you are looking at may be just a sunset or a picture. The beauty is in the verbal idea, not an inherent characteristic of sunsets or oil paintings!

Still not convinced? Would it sound a problem if someone had creatively rearranged ownership of some object of yours? Probably not, but if the word was stolen you would feel very differently.

Count Alfred Korzybski, in his prodigious book *Science And Sanity*" (1934), was probably the first person to write about the blockage of word meanings as a major obstacle to assimilation. Russian language psychologist Lev Vigotsky (1896-1934) also taught us that words shape our thoughts and that misunderstood words cause addled thinking and confusion.

This has been one of the biggest failures in education. Unless it is clearly understood that words and language are the key to human knowledge, then too little attention is paid to word definitions and mastering the dictionary. The result is that very many people struggle at trying to learn a subject, without realizing that what is obstructing their assimilation of data is not stupidity on their part but a missing or confused definition.

Actually, it isn't only missing definitions that cause confusion. Sometimes the student has the *wrong* definition for a word. As we all know, most of the words in the English language are capable of many different definitions. If you apply the wrong meaning, or you are unaware perhaps that there is an alternative meaning, you will experience the same upset, bafflement or estrangement from study.

In effect they create we call "thought holes". These are blanks in your assimilation of what you are studying. The principle reason a person becomes confused or gives up study is because of this misunderstood word phenomenon.

Major Study Rule
The fact is that if you go past a word you don't understand you will go blank. The data will simply vanish from the page. This is very curious. Unfamiliar words will obviously have this effect but so will words which have been MIS-understood from the past or words which are highly charged with emotional associations.

If you pass a lot of words, you will feel like quitting study. This could happen for some people after skipping as few as 2 or 3 words, especially if these are very crucial terms. It produces a feeling of alienation or cut off from the topic of study.

An important rule of successful study therefore is NEVER PASS BY A WORD YOU DO NOT FULLY UNDERSTAND, IN CONTEXT.

Always study with a comprehensive dictionary to hand. You might also need a specialist glossary for the peculiar words connected with your subject.

Take care: it often isn't the highly complex nomenclature that will stumble you. Big unfamiliar words are easy to detect. The surprising revelation is that IT IS THE SIMPLE ENGLISH OR NATIVE LANGUAGE WORDS THAT CAUSE THE MOST TROUBLE.

Words like "although", "precept", "integrated" or "inexplicable" often stumble or confuse even the adult reader.

If you find you have gone blank or distanced from an assignment or topic, stop and look for the word you didn't understand. Here is an important tip: it usually lies in the part of the text *just before* the manifestation of blank hole turned on. Make sure you get it. You will brighten up somewhat as soon as you spot it and feel fine once more, once you have cleared up its meaning.

Think of this as RECOVERING failed words.

Practise with Real Sentences
In line with the precept that we learn for APPLICATION, make a point of using words that you have just looked up the meaning for in a dictionary. Practise each recovered or newly assimilated word in use in a few made up sentences, until you start to THINK with the new word.

WARNING: Don't substitute a familiar word for the one you didn't understand. This will not clear the hole.

For example, if you find the word GERMANE means relevant, it is no good thinking "relevant" each time the word germane turns up. You must think "Ah yes, germane... (got it)". Practice with sentences is the way to bring this about.

No Dictionary To Hand?
If you can't get access to a dictionary but feel you must go on reading, at least write down the words you didn't understand. But don't forget

there are several online dictionaries and wikis, easily accessed from a smart phone or tablet.

What to Do When You Are in Big Trouble
If the whole subject has gone away from you, recognize you have passed a number of misunderstood words. The trick is to GO BACK TO WHERE YOU WERE LAST DOING WELL. If you read forward from there, you will encounter the first failed word quite soon and can deal with it. Then proceed to the next and so on.

After clearing up a word meaning, probably the section of text will come back into focus even before you re-read it, however, re-study is always advised.

If you find yourself right back at the start of an assignment or course and decide you never felt good with it, there are three main possibilities:

1. You may be suffering from the feeling there is nothing to learn

2. There may be a problem with pace (see below)

3. The basic words heading up the topic or text are misunderstood. It's surprising how often people cannot give the true meaning of words like GEOGRAPHY, METALLURGY and PHYSICS, or general words like SYNOPSIS and THEORY that might be encountered in titles.

Failed Words in Life
Finally, remember this word-failure effect operates in everyday life not just in study. If you are engaged in a conversation or listening to a broadcast, or whatever, and you pass a word you didn't understand or thought you understood but you didn't, it will block your intake of whatever you are reading or hearing. Once you have passed a number of words, you will feel alienated from that subject and the people involved with it.

This is strong medicine. Take heed!

3. Study Without the Reality
This one comes from a famous saying by Alfred Korzybski: "The map is not the territory" or as he sometimes put it, "The word is not the thing". In other words, one's mental concept is not the physical thing.

There are certain physiological symptoms that people sometimes get in study: a sort of washed out, squashed, stretched weird feeling and sometimes a head pressure or stomach pain. This is found to be due to too much significance (meaning or notion) and not enough "stuff" (solidity and action). We call these interactive pairs The Concept and The Concrete, or Matter and Meaning.

Korzybski called these two aspects of language function the EXTENSIONAL meaning (outside of self) and the INTENSIONAL meaning (inside self).

Both are vital. While it's alright to get pumped up with theory for a short time, after a while, unless you get some physical grasp on the objects involved, you begin to feel a bit strange and spaced out.

The answer is simple: get some MASS. Something solid. So if you are studying about combustion engines, go take a look at one. Find the parts you have been reading about and touch them.

If some action is being discussed, try it out: DO IT! Make the theory come to life. Even a good diagram or photograph to illustrate the text is better than nothing. In this way you can extend your understanding of the meaning of what you are trying to assimilate.

Makeshift Valuable Study Aid
In desperation, if the physiological effects switch on, you can lay out paper clips, rubber bands, buttons, coins, old batteries etc. to represent the parts you are studying. In fact the smart student keeps a little stock pile of such bits and pieces to hand. We call it a "Show-Me Kit", for obvious reasons.

Use it for abstract ideas too - like demonstrating the different aspects of a word like "dishonesty"!

But there is no substitute for the real thing. Can you imagine the folly of training a soldier without putting a rifle in his hands and showing him how to load and shoot it? All field craft lectures and strategic theory without a route march or manoeuvres would become oppressive to the mind by stacking up mountains of ideas (thought) and no soothing reality (stuff or matter). In other words, too much concept and not enough concrete!

The two have to balance properly, otherwise this mental weight becomes a considerable obstacle to assimilation.

4. Wrong Pace
Too bad that mainstream educators don't abide by this simple obvious problem in learning. Quite simply, if you go too fast and push too

hard, the student fails to overcome the necessary barriers to comprehension and loses it.

The ruling datum is: **every student has his or her own optimum pace and it should not be violated**.

This is just as valid whether learning to play the piano, training to be a therapist or figuring out the intricacies of the calculus. Nothing can be grasped all at once but has to come by degrees. When there is too much pressure and haste (or a degree of dishonesty creeps in) a student may inadvertently be tempted to skip a valid step.

When this happens, he or she will come unstuck, either immediately *or several steps further along*, which makes it more confusing. The usual manifestation is that the student becomes flustered, loses confidence, feels confused, spinny and overwhelmed. There will usually be a conviction of failure and maybe unworthiness ("I can't...", "I'm no good at this, really...", "this is too much.")

This problem applies most obviously to learning physical skills but it still totally applicable in the domain of intellectual subjects. Thus trying to work out a cube root of a number before you have understood multiplication would be a definite skipped step in mathematics.

The answer, as with failed words, is to go back to before the difficulty started. The student assumes that the problem is the section or technique he or she is on currently, since that is the one which appears difficult. But it will be found that really the trouble lies earlier. He or she hasn't fully mastered a prior step. This is quite surprising.

So, if a piano pupil cannot master the key of E (4 sharps); it is because he or she hasn't fully got to grips with the key of A (3 sharps) or even D (2 sharps).

It's Not The Step You Thought.
Go back to the step before the trouble appeared and work on that some more. After a thorough review, you will improve your handling of this earlier step. You will find that, when you go back to the troublesome step—which you thought was difficult—you will now find it is now easy!

This can be truly astounding when you first see it in action.

Too Slow
By the way, don't forget that pace can be an obstacle in the opposite sense. If a pupil is taken too slowly through the materials, he or she becomes frustrated and bored. It also implies a slight insult in that

he or she will generally feel it is "beneath them", in other words that they are being patronized. This antipathy is just as likely to lead to abandonment of study as being pushed too fast.

As in most aspects of life, there needs to be a sense of challenge to operate as a stimulus and call forth resources.

5. Fixed Opinions

Finally, don't let fixed opinions get in your way. A student who isn't open to new data won't learn much.

This problem is actually a relative of obstacle 1 (feeling there is nothing to be learned). Obviously, the blustering dude who knows all about a subject and has resounding fixed ideas, isn't about to be put off by mere facts. His intake of knowledge will be next to zero, unless he (or she) can be parted from these cherished notions.

Know it all arrogance is the complete antithesis of the humility and willingness that would best serve a true seeker of knowledge.

6. Status

This derives from the previous barrier: this question of fixed opinions usually comes down to a problem of status. He or she is afraid to appear foolish or ignorant. We must blame Western attitudes, and schooling in particular, for instilling this false standard. The person to admire is the one who says he knows little and wants to learn more, not the clod who tries to look good. The latter is really pathetically submitting to others' attitudes and judgments.

Don't allow yourself to be afraid of not knowing. There is a great deal of difference between being stupid and being ignorant. Frequently, usage of the latter word has an unpleasant connotation, meaning something akin to "crude and ill mannered".

Actually, ignorant simply means *without knowledge*. Can you hold a conversation on 8th century Irish illuminated manuscripts? Well, that's ignorance.

But it isn't stupidity!

Without the data you might look stupid but it isn't really the same at all. An ignorant person can always acquire the missing data; someone with fixed opinions, which makes them really stupid, cannot learn.

Hoaxes: The Kiss of Death to True Learning

We now come the one of the most telling and destructive barriers to a happy and fulfilling human life. This applies far beyond the field of study and is, indeed, the ruling failure of all thinking, behavior and emotions.

Hoaxes. Stamp them out! If you learn nothing else with us, learn to identify hoaxes and have the courage and integrity to eliminate them from your thinking wherever you have been able to spot them.

HOAXES are dangerous flaws in knowledge disguised by the supposition that "Everybody knows that's true". Often this uncritical generalization means that nobody has bothered to check and the "fact" in question is untrue and therefore dangerous!

HOAXES as we define them, are really just fixed opinions on the scale of group thinking. A related modern concept is that of a meme (thought virus). But a meme need not necessarily be wrong or destructive. "Love thus neighbor" is a reasonable and positive thought virus, even though few people let themselves become infected by it!

But for now - beware. Hoaxes are a formidable hidden obstacle to true knowledge.

Facts that are not facts are bad enough. But hoaxes start wars, kill people, spread disease, dismay and disaster. People tell you things that are just not true. Even worse, others begin to believe these 'facts' and they get established in everyone's thinking.

Hoaxes abound under the disguise of 'everybody knows that...' And when you come right down to it, they don't know it at all. It's rubbish! A good example from my own career was the hoax that you cannot be allergic to food or made ill by eating everyday substances such as milk, cheese and chocolate. We now know it is true and this opened the door to many recoveries. But until the 'everybody knows that isn't true...' was stripped off the case, it stuck in the road of real medical progress.

The Second Biggest Hoax

Let us complete this swift overview of our radical new study techniques by debunking another major hoax perpetrated by educators on their pupils and tell instead the truth behind the absurdity.

HOAX: Remembering data comes from effort in "learning" and repetition.

THE TRUTH: If you seek to fully understand your data and assimilate it, remembering it becomes automatic and without effort.

In fact international language educator Michel Thomas goes further and states plainly that attempting to "remember" is stressful to the student and is counter-productive.

Work only on comprehension of your studies and you will find that it becomes easier and easier as you do so. Cease trying to cram "data" for examinations and—as if by magic—you will enjoy your subject and know it without effort (let's say *almost* without effort!) You will remember things you never thought you would, because it is YOUR knowledge and not someone else's that has been stuffed into your head.

We are now ready to move forward and start to learn some of the real secrets of wealth, power, fame, happiness and achievement. Don't forget to apply the principles you have hopefully just assimilated!

2. The Power Of Knowledge

"I believe all suffering is caused by ignorance." HH The Dalai Lama

What is it about people who hold great wealth, power and prestige that makes them different? All through history, human society has been dominated by individuals who stand apart from the herd; for whom the ordinary human rules of mediocrity, failure and oblivion don't seem to apply.

These are the Rothschilds, the Fords, the Carnegies, and the Trumps, or even the Schweitzers and Schwarzeneggers of our planet.

Are they a special breed, persons with unique abilities that are simply exclusive to them - so that only certain people can manifest this coveted stature?

Or is it that they know something we don't? In which case, surely, if we can learn what it is they know, we can do it for ourselves and learn how to overcome our self-limiting conditions and gain freedom for ourselves and our loved ones.

Supernoetics™ will help you find the answers. Because it is a fundamental precept of any philosophy based on ultimate truths that the mechanics of the universe and how it operates are inviolate, enduring and permeate everything. There can be no such thing as esoteric or cryptic knowledge.

There is only hidden data. But once you unearth it, it ceases to be unknown. It becomes useful knowledge - practical and life enhancing. You can apply it as you wish, share it, amplify it or modify it according to experience.

If the knowledge is valuable in any degree, it means it is simple and applies universally. There cannot be a truth that works in Cleveland, Ohio, or on the moon, but does not work in Manchester, England or the Kremlin. It sounds silly to say it; yet there are people who treat specialist knowledge as if it were such a strange hybrid of reason and fallacy.

You Are The Celebrity In Your Own Life

What is certain is that to be more, do more and have more, you have to grow. Success does not fall from the sky. It has to be built and if you build it for yourself, you have gained something that no-one else can give you: the power of knowledge.

But fundamental knowledge, any philosophy, is only as valuable as the use to which it is put. How you apply it—and to what aspect of your life—is entirely up to you. What we provide is the raw materials. You must design the ultimate outcome. You are the celebrity in your own life, the star, the teacher, the student, the philosopher. Only you know what's needed to make your life move forwards as you would wish.

But we can help you with that too. Most people need some guidance in defining what it is they really want. If you don't know already, the chances are you will uncover a trigger to help find what you are looking for, somewhere in these materials.

Study them well and remember - safeguard and respect the knowledge you are gaining - it will change your life forever, if you let it.

Supernoetics™ has strategies that will help you grind away limitations until your mind-edge is keen as a razor. You will find yourself achieving things you never imagined yourself doing. It won't happen overnight—you will need patience, courage, focus and above all determination.

But even these are not enough to guarantee success. No matter what you read in motivational hype books or hear at self-belief seminars, mere inspiration is not enough. You need know-how. That's where our life enhancement tips, tricks, techniques and teachings course come in...

You don't have to grope blindly, learning by trial and error. You can benefit directly from scores of key hacks and change techniques that have already been test driven for you. They work; they work well. All you have to do is step inside and turn the ignition key.

Look out for workshops where you can practice the techniques learned here, until they change your world view.

Leverage

Yes, knowledge is power. These days we might say knowledge is leverage. From the beginning of time, the successful creatures of God's earth have been those that knew how to exploit resources more skillfully than others. That's what evolution is all about.

One thing that biological science teaches us is that survival is not a static phenomenon, based on tradition. It is constantly and rapidly changing and interpreting events. As new food supplies or new territory opens up, those who get to do best are those creatures with the aptitude to learn fast. It all comes back to knowledge.

When territories become hostile – like the events that wiped out the dinosaurs – the ones that survive were those which adapted their knowledge to new conditions.

It's the same with human evolution.

3. Living In The "Age Of Anxiety"

The labeling of our times has run the gamut from the 'Space Age' to the 'Age of Aquarius' to the age of 'Sexual Revolution'. However, the one epithet that probably fits more accurately than all the rest is the 'Age of Anxiety'.

Anxiety is the one negative force that cuts through all levels of society affecting the rich and poor, young and old alike. Anxieties and tensions are insidious forces which exist below the surface of your awareness, smoldering and building up, until you reach a 'breaking point' and explode in a fit of anger or a violent argument, or some other unreasoned behavior.

It also manifests in over-indulgence in food, alcohol, cigarettes, sex or work, "pumping up" (gym), in headaches, fatigue, impotence, clumsiness, sleepless nights, or any number of physical ailments.

Conscious worry and fear also enter the picture to compound the feeling of frustration already being experienced because you are not able to identify the source of the unconscious anxiety and thus eliminate it.

Consequently, if you are like most people, you will gulp down a handful of pills to alleviate that dull aching feeling, or your 'escape' will be in the form of the after-work booze-up. Or you'll change your job, or get a divorce, or move to another town, or some psychologist will tell you to 'adjust' to your problems.

Or you will grin and bear it because your religious leader piously proclaims that sorrow is this life's just reward, and so on.

But you find that you receive nothing but temporary relief and that you carry your problems with you wherever you go and whatever you do.

To add to this state of tension, is the sense of 'alienation' that modern society produces. A sense of isolation, separation, loneliness, powerlessness, apathy, non-involvement, pessimism, meaninglessness, rootlessness, and lack of authentic values.

Alienation may be described as that state in which the individual feels dislocated from himself, from others, from the world in general. With mechanization, specialization and automation increasing every day, man has become lost in the giant machinery he once controlled and created, and thereupon he has become a mere 'cog in the machine' - mechanized, reutilized, depersonalized, apathetic, insignificant, an object to be manipulated.

With the threat of nuclear annihilation on the one side, and on the other promises of a super-abundant age of leisure from the resources of high technology, man has become confused, uncertain and schizoid because he cannot relate to or solve problems of such magnitude.

With the instant communications systems of mass media, informing Western man of the struggles for freedom of men throughout the world, he feels helpless in his inability to do anything about the situation.

Learning about constant crime, the world seems a dangerous place. And stuck in urban dwellings, he becomes increasingly isolated from Nature with all of its beauty, peace and refreshing naturalness.

And while the population of the world is exploding at a fantastic rate, he finds increasing difficulty just communicating with his neighbor.

Thus it is that man drifts aimlessly through a world seemingly without meaning or purpose - a world he created but over which he no longer exercises conscious control or power.

Man today has lost his identity and his purpose for existing. He has lost his sense of the Game of Life. He is an unknowing and unwilling games player. Never before has man been so much of a problem to himself.

Why does man, with all his intelligence, allow this situation to exist? Is there a practical answer? Man does not know himself.

The task now before you is to begin to know yourself. To possess self-knowledge you must first become free of illusions about yourself, the people around you, and the Universe. Until you begin to understand your illusions you will never be free to see the truth about yourself or anything else. That is, as knowingness, not 'knowing about'.

Illusions consist of all sorts of mistaken ideas you hold about yourself, false assumptions as to your abilities, erroneous concepts about your place and purpose in the world, and so forth. It is difficult to break-up these illusions because they are deeply engrained habit patterns.

To be able to change, which is the only way to gain self-knowledge and freedom, you must do things you have never done before, and recognize that viewpoints that you were determined must be right, may possibly be wrong.

The greatest barrier to consciousness is the belief that one is already conscious. Just considering the matter, one for an instant wakes-up, then returns to slumber in the illusion that, yes, he is conscious.

The truth of the matter is that 99% of the time, man is behaving mechanically - he is determined by external influences.

Nearly all of man's thoughts, ideas, emotions, aspirations, words and moods are triggered by external influences. We are, as we say, "other-determined". Events, circumstances and trains of thought trigger this reactive mind automatically, according to his previous conditioning, upbringing, education and experiences, and his innate human nature, instincts and drives.

The application of free will is only possible if vision is unblinkered by preconceived fixed ideas or reverence to singular ideologies and cultural norms; this requires relative freedom from such reactive clutter and automaticities.

The subconscious and unconscious minds play the major role in controlling your life and behavior, when you are not fully awake and self-aware in the present moment. In the normal human person it is responsible for over 90% of everyday thoughts, feelings, motivations, desires, prejudices, anxieties, tensions, illnesses, illusions, personality problems, and everyday behavior.

We tell you more about what to do about that in the *Transformational Mind Dynamics*™ of Supernoetics™.

4. Happiness Is The Journey But Where To?

There's a great saying by the Dalai Lama: happiness is the journey, not the destination. It rightly emphasizes that happiness can never be postponed; you don't wait for something to happen, in order to become happy.

In fact people who think only: "I'll be happy if she changes her ways," or "I'll be happy once I'm rich," are never going to be happy. Fact.

Relying on outside sources to be happy is a sure way to postpone happiness forever!

Real happiness, real contentment, is enjoying your journey towards some desired goal.

I love riding steam trains (it's a thing I've had since I was a kid, OK?) But I couldn't care less where we are going to! I love the sound of the engine, the smell of steam and hot oil, the rumble of the trucks and carriages... It's the journey that inspires me! That's my idea of steam happiness.

But of course, the train has to be going somewhere. So the destination comes into it somewhat. It's the same in life.

Happiness is the journey: but where to? The train ride to a prison camp sure wouldn't be. So the destination is also critical. We can restate Old Giggly's maxim into: *happiness is the journey towards a desired goal.*

In fact I would edit this carefully, as follows:

Happiness is the overcoming of not insurmountable obstacles in pursuit of a worthy and dearly held goal, with the reasonable expectation of success.

If all obstacles were impossible to overcome, you wouldn't be happy. But if you can surmount them, you'll feel good about it.

If the goal is silly and not fulfilling, you won't get much enjoyment out of that.

Finally, there has to be some chance of success, otherwise you will not be happy striving and making sacrifices!

Now in my writings, I point out a very important difference between a goal and a purpose. Purpose is a far higher creation. A goal is what you need to fulfill your purpose. But I'm not going to do all that stuff just here: it's in my "Success On Your Own terms" course.

Let's keep it simple and say that a purpose is where you want to be, what you want to do; not so much of the what you want to have. The goal is the outward expression of your purpose.

We can have several purposes at one time, though usually one is the dominant purpose in life.

Kids form their purposes early on. Kids are not as immature as some adults like to think. I remember my early purposes. I wanted to be the king (that one hasn't left me, by the way)! But very early on I formed the purpose of being a writer. I didn't think to myself in terms of a writer; that's an adult concept. But I wanted to write! I got great marks in school essays and stuff.

Hey: as an adult, it's my number #1 purpose. It's my life purpose. And that's true for a lot of kids; their early purposes remain valid often, right into adult life.

Of course the pressure of "sensible" adult advice often steers a kid away from what they want to do. So they are dismally unhappy for the rest of their days (or unless they can break free and do what they really chose to do in life).

All Else Is Waiting

So we can conjure up a couple of terms for higher living: on-purpose and off-purpose. They seem pretty self-explanatory. To be on-purpose, or living and fulfilling your dream, is to be truly alive and happy. There is no other kinds of happiness that counts.

After the disaster which wiped out three of the "Flying Wallendas", Karl Wallenda was asked if that meant he would give up his high wire act, which was famous for performing death-defying stunts without a safety net. His answer was a classic response for a man living his purpose: "I will never give up. Life is being on the wire; everything else is just waiting."

Karl himself was killed just 38 days after the comeback. He was trying a walk between the two towers of a ten-story building, 120 feet above the ground. A high wind blew him off. But you can bet he died happy. He was 75 years old and most folks at that age are having trouble moving around. They are just waiting, for death...

As a happy footnote, just a few weeks ago on June 4, 2011, his descendant Nik completed the high-wire crossing that killed his great-grandfather, citing Karl Wallenda as his "biggest hero in life"

As the Victorian poet Robert Browning said:

"Ah but a man's reach should exceed his grasp, or what's a heaven for?"

There is no heaven unless you are stretching yourself to do more, become more and create more.

All this relates to mastery, by the way. Mastery is also about getting there and the importance of the journey. Arriving at the destination is rather inconvenient, because it interrupts the flow (in fact those in search of mastery will always says that a lifetime is not long enough: you never actually arrive on your journey to mastery).

5. The Three Questions

Magic Vs. Science //

Psychologist and philosopher Wendell Johnson, a follower of Alfred Korzybski (whose name you will meet a lot in Supernoetics™, points to "magic" as the opposite of scientific method. He defines this as "no process" (in other words, it just happens). Whereas I concur in this, it is important to point out that much of what was considered magic once upon a time became scientific, once the mechanism was known.

An event is only supernatural (beyond nature) if it is not understood.

To a primitive tribesman, radio and television would appear magical. But even the least educated person in Western society understands that radio waves travel through the atmosphere, even if he or she cannot be said to fully understand how broadcasting works. It isn't magical; just rather awesome.

In the same way, with a few deft moves with Supernoetics™ *Transformational Psychology* we can clear a troublesome illness that defied treatment; we can take a drunk and render him pretty sober in minutes; or clear up basic confusions in a study topic, using alphabet clearing and our Enhanced Reading study method, to find the child's IQ begins to soar and even overtakes his or her peers.

It would only appear magic when the real mechanics of the procedure were not understood.

The Rigidity Of Magic And Tradition //

Not that Johnson himself falls into this trap of considering magic as mere mystery. He further categorizes the magical orientation as the "...rigidity, the high valuation of tradition and Authority with a capital A, the Authority of age and precedence...", which he downgrades as a kind of immaturity.

You get this with so-called "channelings" and dependence on so-called psychic "laws" that other people tell you are out there.

"In this kind of immaturity there is a tendency not to explore one's own world, not to develop one's own potential for original thinking, not to see or evaluate what there is to be seen" (*Living With Change: the Semantics of Coping*, Harper Row, 1972).

The opposite to this passive view, we encourage freely here, is as Johnson says:

> "To explore the world all around him, to engage himself with his environment, to trust his own nervous system, to look with his own eyes, to hear with his own ears, to have his own thoughts, to speak as he hears and sees, to become adaptable, to be concerned with process, to be highly attracted to the authority of [one's own]* evaluated experience".

> "So a person doesn't ask others, "What should I believe? What should I think?" He does his own believing and thinking on the basis of observations of the so-called reality around him."

*Wendell Johnson, essay "Living more Sanely". Addition in brackets by me.

Three Questions As Tools

Before we leave General Semantics, it is valuable to consider three questions which Wendell Johnson gave us with which to examine and further understand experience.

Even these questions could be seen as powerful Tools Of Living. They are so simple and yet so profound:

1. (for clarity) "What do you mean?"

2. (for validity) "How do you know?"

3. (for disciplined generalization) "What then?"

As Johnson says, a child sharpens his sense of reality and his capacity to tell a fact from a phoney by asking often enough and with due courtesy, *What to do you mean?* The child will persist until curiosity is satisfied.

The second question revolved around Korzybski's dictum that "the map is not the territory". Our mental representation of something is not the thing. Knowledge and experience is not an abstract thing, a kind of mental baggage, as we are taught in schools.

Knowledge is meaningless unless you apply it to something in life.

The third question, "What then?" leads directly back to the theme of a practical philosophy. In other words, what should one do as a result of the information gained from the prior questions?

It matters not only what you know but what you do with that knowledge.

My Three Questions

With due respect to Johnson's ideas, we can broaden his three questions into a valuable trio that is the property of Supernoetics™:

1. "What exactly do I observe?"

2. "What general rule can I draw from this, if any?"

3. "What use is that?"

Step 1, surprisingly, is the hardest. Most people do not observe what is before them. We tend to see what we want to see; or more exactly what we expect to see. Our mental patterns lead us to see the world in terms of the framework we have already constructed in our inner space.

Obviously, if this framework is deficient, there are limits to how we look at the world. This is back to the important mechanics of perception and recognition, referred to at the start of this issue.

One of the most valuable things that Supernoetics™, and especially the workshops, can do for the individual is to change his or her appreciation of what is actually out there in what we loosely term reality.

From there we can seek out general laws and applications, much as a scientist would do. Note that Korzybski was very particular that one could never make any meaningful generalizations from a specific case.

Logically, strictly, this may be true. But we have added one important additional criterion, which makes all the difference: "Does this set of observations form a rule that has any practical value?" (never mind how "true" it is).

If we can deduce something that clearly improves our lives and increases the percentage of successful outcomes, this is truly meaningful and valuable knowledge, no matter how much the boffins may try to argue that "logically" we are on uncertain ground.

Thus we are back to strategies and the main theme of this little book: tools for living!

6. A Gentleperson's Guide To Good Behavior

A Gentleperson's Guide To Good Behavior

Key Principle: Good manners cost nothing, show mutual respect and make life much more agreeable.

Centuries ago, in Britain, to be a gentleman (or gentlewoman) went far beyond the simple gender statement it makes today. It was a recognition of important social status. More than that, it was accepted that upper class people, the toffs, were somehow more easygoing in their manners and interactions than rough, ordinary folk. They followed an elaborate code of etiquette which meant (supposedly) that they didn't rub each other up the wrong way and cause unnecessary friction. All the 'best people' behaved well and were kind, at least on the surface.

In other words, they were by disposition gentle with each other!

Most of this elaborate code of behavior is lost to us now; it was mostly phony ritual anyway. But it is worth re-visiting the idea of being a gentleperson. Nothing wrong in that. So what kind of code of manners and decent behavior can we compile, by thinking things through intelligently?

We could start with three long-standing favorites, which cover a lot of territory:

1) Do not kill or harm others

2) Do not steal or take what is not yours

3) Conduct yourself honorably in all that you do and say

Most civilized people would take each of these as a given. Of course 2 and 3 are pretty dispensable, according to many corporate and low-life elements (let's throw in the bankers too; they are serious criminal fraudsters that are right now threatening the very fabric of civilization).

Fortunately, most of us "get it" and see the need for these simple basics.

Manners

But what about manners? I see manners as agreed styles of speaking and acting towards other people. It doesn't really matter what you think, or what's in your heart. These are simple rules for not hurting other people.

It isn't phoney to cover up your negative opinion of someone. It's not even a courtesy: it's downright logic. YOU might be the screwball, buddy! So tone your language down and act respectfully.

Refer to my chapter On Rightness (#21) and remind yourself that we are all in this together and—no matter how stupidly or wickedly people behave—they choose their actions in the same way that you do: because they think it's the right thing to do.

People commit murder, for example, because they think it's the right thing to do! Sounds crazy but a moment's reflection will tell you it's true... Yes, they may know they shouldn't... but something just happened to make it "right" to sidestep the normal rules. Of course he or she is always sorry afterwards and acts contritely but in my experience that's just to try and soften the punishment, not because he or she thought the act really was wrong.

I'm not trying to justify crime or bad behavior; I'm merely trying to point out that, fundamentally, the deep and dark criminal is operating on the exactly same algorithm as you and me: do what you think it best in a given situation.

So it's a leveler. You are not really superior; just smarter, because you can see the consequences of your actions right through to the end. A murderer or bank robber can't.

The Golden Rule and The Platinum Rule

Everyone (I hope) understands the so-called "Golden Rule". It appears in all the world's religions and philosophies. It is simplest stated as: "Treat other people as you would want them to treat you." It's brilliant and simple in its logic. Why should you get special treatment if you are not willing to accord it to other people?

Even kings, queens and presidents have to acknowledge this one. Bloody and heartless rulers only last a certain time and then they are busted. And their first reaction when carried off to the dungeons is usually screaming for the mercy that they would not show to others.

Another way of looking at the Golden Rule might be: treat others how they want to be treated, rather than how you want to be treated!

But there is a better twist to the Golden Rule, which Tal Ben-Shahar has christened "The Platinum Rule": treat yourself the way you'd like others to treat you. The Platinum Rule may be far more important than the way that you treat others, because inevitably the way that you treat yourself determines the way that you treat others. Be kind to yourself, honor yourself, and you'll find you do it automatically with others.

In the converse, individuals who are hard on themselves, bitter and self-critical, rarely make good travelling companions in life. They carry their self-hate poison deep inside but inevitably it spills all over the highway!

The Two Most Basic Needs
Back in 1965 psychiatrist William Glasser MD pinpointed what seem to me to be among the most fundamental of all human needs. These must be honored. These are the basis of Glasser's "Reality Therapy":

1. The need to love and be loved.

2. The need to feel that we are worthwhile, to ourselves and to others.

I think these should always be borne in mind and others helped to become secure in these needs or be helped in adopting them.

As Glasser pointed out, although the two needs are separate, a person who loves and is loved will usually feel that he or she is a worthwhile person and one who is worthwhile is usually someone who is loved and who can give love in return.

But there is an important caveat, with which I agree wholeheartedly: to be worthwhile, we must maintain a satisfactory standard of behavior. That's what my Gentle Person's Guide To Good Behavior is about...

1. Honor A Person's Being. Acknowledge their presence if nothing else. Nod or smile or otherwise let others know you see them, as they see you. The slightest head nod is often sufficient. Try to be warm, even with strangers. Remember the lovely greeting among the Navi people in the movie Avatar: "I see you!" It acknowledges a person's being and it is one of the finest gestures you can make. It honors YOU too.

2. Be A Good Listener. Allow the other person to speak in equal share and listen to what they have to say. Listen sufficiently before you try to talk. Being in any kind of relationship with people (business, family, love etc.) affords them the right to reasonable communication.

This right includes the entitlement to be listened to, so walking off in a huff is actually a violation of Rule 1. Only when communication has become toxic are you required to shut it down, to avoid further hurt.

3. Never Tell A Person What Or She Is Thinking. You will always be wrong and it's conceited. You know the kind of thing: "Your problem is you can't deal with women" or "Your trouble is you just want to play the victim." There are millions of these put downs and they serve no useful purpose. Trashy, inadequate therapists do it, to try and make themselves seem clever or important. You must not. In Supernoetics™ you are instead required to open the topic with a questioning approach: use the Socrates' method! "Tell me how you feel about women…" or "What did that look you gave me mean?"

4. Be Observant Of The Effect You Have On Others. Recognize when your communication is painful to another person and STOP! Say something else. Despite the widespread acceptance that it's OK to be nasty just because YOU are feeling upset, it achieves nothing; solves nothing. Nobody has any right to splash around hurtful or negative emotions. However everyone has a right to refuse to listen to bad communication loaded with unpleasant emotions.

5. Never Say Or Imply To A Person 'You Are Wrong'. Say, 'I don't agree with you there' or 'I see it differently' (it might be YOU who is wrong!) Avoid insulting words and phrases, like "Stupid bitch," and "Douchebag". They are demeaning to the speaker, as well as the target. Why not make yourself a list of "reasonable" insults? Write the down and learn them… Not ninny and nincompoop but more like "You need to shepherd your facts more carefully," or "I don't think you are thinking quickly enough for this conversation." Or even more edgy: "Your lack of knowledge is encyclopedic". Seriously though, don't take insults seriously! They are degraded currency.

6. Gossip Is A No No. Never discuss a person in pejorative terms if they are not there to defend themselves. Never pass on critical remarks about another, unless you know it to be absolutely true from first hand experience. Even then, limit it only to those who need the facts for their own safety. Passing on destructive gossip or inflammatory judgments on another, especially when these turn out to be untrue, is a species of evil and recognized as such in all decent codes of behavior. You wouldn't want others to do it to you, therefore it is a violation of The Golden Rule.

7. Don't try to deal with important matters with persons who are tired, ill, hungry or otherwise distressed. Wait for a better moment. Especially never try to take advantage of someone in such a condition. When we are near shut-down in biological terms, we cannot do our best work as spirit beings, nor easily seek the most advantageous outcomes. Wisdom and caring are our duty. We need to be refreshed and alert to do our best in these key endeavors.

8. Don't Use Sex To Punish Someone Or Gain Favors. Never use your position over a person to gain sexual advantage. Don't use sex, or the withdrawal of sex, to punish or hurt someone in a relationship. Also, don't use sex to solve problems. Honestly repair the break and then enjoy intimate loving sex afterwards.

9. Be Open, Honest and Fair With People. Do not use lies under any pretext, including little white lies. Figure out what you are scared of and deal with it; then tell the truth. If others make a mistake in your favor, give it back. If something you have done is not satisfactory, replace it, repair it or refund in full immediately.

10. Hold To Your Undertakings, Once Made. Complete what you begin. Deliver what you promise. Do not let people down; you don't know to what extent they are relying on you and to not perform might be a disaster for them. Your reputation will soon stink if you are known as not reliable or untrustworthy.

11. Don't Respond To Bad Emotions With More Bad Emotions. If you find someone is upset or disturbed, you may choose to help. Just remember not to share in the disorderly emotions. Be kind, efficient and effective. That is far more use than sympathy.

12. Similarly, Don't React To Bad Behavior With Bad Behavior. It's very impolitic to do what other people are doing around you, especially when you know it to be wrong. Better to stand out from the crowd and keep your own space.

13. Tolerance. Respect a person's religious beliefs and never attack their spiritual path, no matter how strange. Just NEVER. Is that clear?

14. Don't Use Or Advocate Violence. It has a nasty habit of escalating. World War I cost millions of lives and started with just a single shot in the town of Sarajevo. Do not even advocate violence, except in defense of property or life. According to Confucius, 'He who strikes the first blow admits to losing the argument'.

15. Don't Try To Beat Someone Else Down. Just don't rush to pass others, get to the head of the line, grab the nearest parking space or otherwise seek to disadvantage others by being aggressive and selfish. Remember, what you give out you get back! Show courtesy and allow others first place, even if not every time. The warm satisfaction is a pleasant thing to enjoy.

16. Win-Win. Make sure all transactions benefit all participants in some way, so there are no losers and no winners. Give added value, where possible, without jeopardizing yourself. Play the biggest games you can, in which the maximum number of people stand to benefit. Now that's courage!

17. Never Make Another Person The Butt Of Humor. It can be mortifying to an individual to be laughed at by a group. This applies even if the person is not present; word may get back to him or her. It isn't kind to get laughs at the expense of others. Humor is a fine and valuable thing but when used to attack or discredit people, it can be cruel.

18. Be Careful About Touching Others. Touch is a tricky subject. I've labelled it The King Of All Communications but it very easily misunderstood. Don't shun touch (because it is magical), just be sure you understand where the other persons sits in respect of being touched. If there is any doubt, touch only the hand and lower arms. Shoulders and back are possible but be careful indeed.

The Right To Courtesy And Fair Treatment
To all of the above, you might also add these points, suggested by my colleague Peter Shepherd of Trans4mind.com:

Without Being Discourteous, Each One of Us Has the Right to...

* Say no to a request.

* Not give other people reasons for every action we take.

* Stop others from making excessive demands on us.

* Ask other people to listen to our point of view when we speak to them.

* Ask other people to correct errors they made which affect us.

* Change our minds.

* Ask other people to compromise rather than get only what they want.

* Ask other people to do things for us.

* Persist in making a request if people won't respond the first time.

* Be alone if we wish.

- Maintain our dignity in relationships.
- Evaluate our own behaviors and not just listen to evaluations that others offer.
- Make mistakes and accept responsibility for them.
- Avoid manipulation by other people.
- Pick our own friends without consulting our parents, peers, or anyone else.
- Let other people know how we are feeling.

When Criticizing Others...
- Make your comments specific.
- Attempt to provide the person with some valuable information.
- Help them to understand exactly what needs to change.
- Be sure the criticized behavior can be changed.
- If the person can do nothing about the problem, you will probably just make things worse by being critical of it.
- Use firm and business-like communication.
- Speak calmly and try not to let your emotions dictate the conversation.
- Try not to shame, humiliate, or blame the person.
- Give the person a reason to change.
- Inform them of any benefits which might come out of acting on your suggestions.
- Avoid criticizing someone in public.
- Time your criticisms well. Wait until the person is in a reasonably good mood.
- View constructive criticism as helpful feedback not punishment.
- Positive change should be your goal.

I think you will agree that the world will be a delightful place and meeting our fellow men and women would be much "gentler", if we all respected each other in these several ways. It's very important to inculcate these manners into your children and get them to incorporate this improved design of living as part of their psyche.

Take Action

For the next seven days, make a really big effort to respond to others only within these guidelines. Judge the result. You'll find it to be very healing; others around you too, will be happier.

If it suits you (it should if you did it right) make a resolve to live that way for the rest of your time on Earth! Be a gentle person, an aristocrat of good manners and breeding... Build it into your emotional genes!

History of this document:

Originally proposed by the late Robert Ross, who shared it with me.

I re-wrote it and published my own version in Dec 1994.

This much-extended version was published as an Ex-Press Apr 2014

7. Slices Of Eternity

The Anatomy Of Events And Process
This is one of the simplest yet most profound elements of philosophy.
It is so obvious you would miss it. However without applying this
knowledge, either inadvertently or by design, nothing in life or living
will work satisfactorily. Your outcomes will be limited, confused or
zilch.

Axiom: The fact is that every event, occasion, activity, transformation, circumstance or time-bite has a beginning - a middle (the process) - and an end.

Call it the "anatomy of an event" if you like. Our Supernoetics™ term
is a process loop. Everyone today is familiar with the concept of loops;
threads or strands that come around, loop around and need closure
(completing).

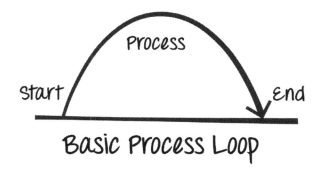

Famous British philosopher Alfred North Whitehead (1861 – 1947)
invented the concept he called process reality. His 1929 book *Process
and Reality* is difficult and diffuse but this is its core concept: that
reality progresses in loops or cycles. That transformation, or becoming, is a process which breaks down to a beginning, a change, and an
end, or the result.

This sounds too simple to be of any value, you might think. You would
be wrong! I have transformed this into something vigorous, practical
and of immense worth. Let's follow Whitehead and see where it leads
us.

Process: a state of being in progress or carried on; a course; a series of actions or events; a sequence of operations or changes undergone; progression; proceeding (The Chambers Dictionary 1994).

Websters Seventh New Collegiate Dictionary gives - something going on; a natural phenomenon marked by gradual changes that lead towards a particular result (as for example the process of growth).

This tells us that the keynote of process is change. No change means no process – nothing is happening!

Everything we do, every step, every action, is about change. No change... nothing happened! Think about it.

So we have invented the concept of an action loop; a doingness. Each action has a start, a change process and an end. There must be an end, or a conclusion, otherwise nothing is ever resolved (anything like your life? Or someone you know?)

Efficiency
Our Ability Express life foundation course is about personal efficiency. We now have a technical definition of efficiency, which is the ability to complete each event—to close the loops—rapidly and satisfactorily. The more events you can undertake and complete in a unit of time, the more efficient you are. To be truly efficient and competent, each event or task must be completed once and for all. Open-ended loops are distracting and hold your attention.

Badly done assignments and incomplete jobs will come around to haunt and taunt you in a manner which is most draining of your energies.

There is now a technical term for this: the *Zeigarnik Effect*, named after Russian psychologist Bluma Zeigarnik (1901-1988). It started when she was out to lunch and noticed that waiters could always remember the details of an open order but as soon as it was closed (paid) and done with, everything would vanish from their minds.

Zeigarnik started to ask herself whether the fact that there was no completion caused things to stick in mind. She did some tests and proved her point. Unfinished jobs, open loops, clutter up the mind inefficiently.

The first rule of efficiency then is: complete each task quickly and completely.

Rule: Competence is being able to finish actions terminatedly.

Rule: Efficiency dictates the number of actions completed in a given time. (low completions = low efficiency and competence, no matter how much activity).

Rule: Real success requires the termination of each step of process to completion.

If you think about this for a moment, it is not difficult to understand the mechanism: time is measured by cycles of change. These small sub-units I have jokingly christened "slices of eternity" for that reason.

You can see from the following schematic that closed loops even appear like time is racing past. Whereas the loops which hang give the opposite effect: it looks like time is "hung" and not rolling along.

That's exactly how it feels.

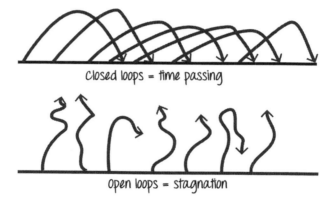

Closed loops = time passing

Open loops = stagnation

Attention Units
We have only so many mental "attention units". When those are all used up, you have nothing with which to concentrate on the task in hand. You would be inefficient and likely to make mistakes.

Incomplete events snarl up attention units, which become stuck to the incompleteness. It sort of hangs up time. It certainly lowers your efficiency.

It also saps energy in a big way. They say "procrastination is the thief of time". Well, it does more than that; leaving too many open loops gradually erodes your energy supply. If you are all tired and spent from life (executive "burn-out", for example), you will find that completing all the open loops will free up your mind and release a great deal of energy for the present, instead of having it hung up on the past. (see mental hygiene below).

It's really refreshing!

Physical Objects
The cycle of an "event" or process is quite evident in relation to physical objects (creations). A motor car, for example, will be manufactured (start), run through its useful life (process) and then decay and be broken up for scrap (end).

Physicists tell us that matter cannot be created or destroyed. But its form can be altered or lost, which is what is obviously what is referred to here. The molecules of the car may still exist but, since you can't drive them around, the actuality of a motor car, once broken up and re-cycled, has certainly ceased.

Everything has its span and then disappears. Daily newspapers don't last very long. Sub-atomic particles are being created today by research workers which exist for only billionths of a second and then are gone forever.

Mountains last quite a while but over the aeons gradually disappear. The physical universe may eventually run its course and vanish. That hasn't been settled for sure, since in this we are bumping up against the actual nature of Time. Our *Propositions Of Being* state clearly that time is an illusion. Modern physics has come to the same conclusion.

But you can take something pretty vast and permanent like a star and it will certainly eventually disappear, after billions of years.

In other words, the anatomy of an event applies to everything there is in existence. Everything is drawn into these fundamental process loops!

Obviously, human experience is based on far smaller units of time. We are talking here about small slices of eternity! If you think about this for a moment, that's something very powerful and profound. Small wonder that it has powerful impact. This is especially true now we are living in a far more complex and confusing world. If we don't chop it up into manageable bites, it becomes too much for our hearts and minds.

So time is cut down and made manageable by this concept of process loops. Time (or at least the impression of time) is change; change is transformation, so let's finish with a depiction of a transformational loop...

There is a very important lesson here and I want you to learn it well. It is that everything comes in bites and chunks. Get used to clearly identifying each section of the whole, each piece of the puzzle: and then do that and complete it, if possible before going on to the next thing.

It's a simple kind of organization actually; we are organizing time, to bring it under our control. We are learning to exert personal power.

Some Thoughts About Control
Another key tool you will be needing in the pursuit of success is control and an understanding of its anatomy. Control is the outer face of mastery. Without control you will not only fail to get the outcomes you want, you will certainly get many outcomes you DON'T want! Not least will be frustration, stress and unhappiness, but possibly, danger.

Integrated rational thinking relies on the efficacy of control mechanisms. It is no use having the power to deduce successful strategies to nourish your dream if you are unable to exert sufficient mastery to enact them in the real world.

Unfortunately, control has got itself something of a bad name. It tends to be associated with all the DOs and DON'Ts of school, Church, parental authority and other domineering and unwanted regulatory systems. The arbitraries and widespread absurdities inherent in the legal system also tend to reinforce this belief that control is something negative, to be avoided. Control has come to mean STOP or don't!

What happens is that we become so confused with oppressive control that we tend to fight against it. A person may even invert the flow and try to obsessively control others, because of these earlier bad experiences. Such people (who are quite common) want to give out control but are in bad shape when it comes to being controlled. They are stuck on one-way control. We use the term "control freaks".

It is just as bad to keep initiating things which we then cannot seem to be able to finish. You probably know someone like that. Maybe you are this type of individual?

Or do you keep changing things, restless, never finishing, unable to complete an action and see it through to the end?

Starting things and obsessive change alone are equally irrational and represent a lack of control, an inability to grasp hold of events and make them do what you want. In other words, failing to manage our action loops.

Unfortunately, there are a number of negatives to poor control or lack of it.

For one thing, the environment becomes chaotic and random. The less control, the more unpredictability or confusion.

This leads to fatigue. Random events and particles keep bouncing up to hit us. Motion becomes opposition.

Lack of control and confusion are two facets of the same state of existence. You had better align it with failures in your life. Because this is where they are coming from!

Set aside these negative impressions of control. Control is essential for the mastery of success you are seeking.

Anatomy Of Control
There are three key elements to control:

1. Causation. Things will happen when you want them to happen, because you cause it to come about. This implies the element of WILL. What you want is an implied part of control. So knowing what you want is also part of good control, as I have been teaching all along.

This applies to small desires, such as making a cup of coffee. Or very large desires, such as creating a million dollars or more.

2. Prevention. Things will not happen if you don't want them to, you don't allow it. You can STOP things.

3. Initiatory change. The outcomes (changes) that you get will be the ones you desired.

If all these are in place, you are fully integrated and in control of your life, your business, your relationships or whatever.

The reverse is that you cannot start, stop or change any aspect of what you are doing. In that case you are not in control, whatever the apparency. It doesn't matter what position you hold, no matter how senior your status, no matter how vast your business empire, if you cannot bring about these three elements, then you are not in control.

An elementary example would be driving a vehicle. If you are in charge of a vehicle and you cannot make it move; even worse you cannot make it stop; or the steering is so faulty is won't turn as you require, then you are not in control of that vehicle. In fact, you would be very likely to have a serious crash.

In the world of entrepreneurship, you are in control of a situation only when you can make things happen the way you want them, dismantle them when you want and that you can guide your goal so that it comes out the way you wanted.

Personal Power
Now, if we take the anatomy of an event and now add the matter of WILL (intention or desire), we have all the defining elements of control. It also qualifies POWER!

Will defines power.

Alasteir Crowley (a rather bad man who wrote a lot about "Magick", which he defines as the materialization of will), claimed, "Every intentional act is a magical act." There is nothing really magical about control. Manifestly, if the process that takes place isn't the one you want, then you are not in control. It has to go from where you are to where you want to be, in order for you to be effectively in control. Power is simply the ability to get what one wants, when one wants, as often as one wants.

Crowley gives two further guiding parameters:

1. The first requisite for causing any change is thorough qualitative and quantitative understanding of the conditions lead-

ing up to the change. I see nothing magical in this; just hard logic.

2.   The second requisite of causing any change is the practical ability to set in right motion the necessary forces. Again, that's elementary.

You can tell real power from the fact that individual does not have to exert it. There is no effort. It's WILL, not sweat. Merely knowing that it is present is sufficient to create calm, confidence and authority. As soon as one resorts to exerting coercion, real control is lost.

The hardest thing you will have to learn, but the most rewarding, is to be able to make your thoughts dictate to the universe what you want. However, and this is a big caveat: it won't happen for you unless you are where you should be, doing what you should be doing, with the right people. This also defines love, incidentally. Love will propel you on your quest; it will not help you much if you are not on a quest or on the wrong one!

The most important prerequisite for this ability is to recognize you have already got it and stop counter-creating it. These counter-creations are very invasive and subtle. One tends to make them instantly, right after once has made the key decision. "I'm gonna get rich!!" then, "But I don't see how". Or "Everybody loves me!" followed by "At least they do at first..."

In this way we are constantly opposing ourselves. We prefer to blame others or fate. But it's our own self-inflicted wounding. This reflex is pervasive and ruins most dreams. In Supernoetics™ it is known as the reverse vector mechanism.

Let me quote a simple case of what happens without the negative cut-back: in the 1970s Demis Roussos left his native Greece to come to the UK as a singer. When he first arrived he was interviewed for a newspaper. He dodged from door to door and was insistent that if people spotted him he would be mobbed with adoring fans. The journalist took great delight in a sniggering account of this obsession and how, in reality, nobody had ever heard of Roussos and not one single Londoner appeared to notice this enormous fat man in their midst.

Yet within 5 years Roussos was known and mobbed by fans wherever he went. The journalist's name I have forgotten and he or she has vanished into oblivion! Roussos wasn't a great singer. But he was a great spirit and totally believed in his ultimate triumph.

He won!

7a. ACTION!

Do It For Yourself
Time out: do this key exercise. It's one of the most powerful I have ever used. It will help you spot and overcome that tendency to counter-create what you want!

Go to a private place where you are not inhibited from talking out loud. Say loudly and clearly:

I am successful

The write down the first thought that came into your mind, tear it up and throw it away symbolically. It will probably be something like, "Well, I wasn't when I bought the grocery store".

Say it again out loud and write down the next thought to intrude; something like "Actually, I usually screw up, let's be realistic..."

Keep going and going until you exhaust all the negative ideas you can attach to this power statement. Notice how you feel more innervated.

Next work on other empowering phrases and clean them of reverse vector counter-creations. Try:
> *I am lucky*
> *I am serenely happy*
> *I feel full of love*

You can extend this exercise by picking a key goal or dream and cleaning it up:

> *I will go to California next year!* Or whatever your dream is.

Get the counter-creations and dump them. Pull them all off. There may be dozens. Just be careful not to empower the counter-creations with solidity as you do this. They are mental junk, nothing more substantial than that.

What Then?
If you want to attain anything in life, you are going to have to master the elements of control and thus manifest personal power. There are countless individuals who start on the road to their dreams. They never get there.

They have not established control over events and life's fortunes. Awaiting the dictates of fate is not effecting control; it's being deeply passive and ineffectual.

Winners—those who can enhance their own life potential to the full –are people who can control things. They snap off action bites and chew them to completion. Then take another, then another and so on.

You force reality to its knees in front of you. Your WILL ensures this is so. It's the only way.

Leverage

Finally, let me talk a little about leverage. It is very pertinent to the subject of control. It's one thing to be able to create a process loop. That's control. But what if you could create dozens or hundreds of action bites, all at the same time or all with the same small investment in effort? That's what we mean by leverage.

It's rather like breaking the laws of physics and get out more than you put in. The Second Law of Thermodynamics says you can't do that; you can't create energy, so it says. Power uses up energy but doesn't give it back.

But I'm talking here about a different phenomenon- the power of the mind. And there is a whole school of philosophy that thinks that living things, most especially the human mind, is capable of overcoming the 2nd Law of Thermodynamics. We do that with *information*.

We get out more than we put in because we add the magic ingredient of information, or knowledge. There is a little model called Maxwell's Demon which shows us how it works. I also teach this fits with Einstein's famous equation. Probably the most famous equation in physics is $e=mc^2$. That says energy is proportional to mass times the speed of light squared. Huh? You can't square the speed of light! Not with a light beam, anyways! That's a pure informational concept, a mathematical expression.

In other words, it's just information. The mind at work.

So we really can get more out than we put in, if we do it the right way, and that's what I mean with leverage.

Now in this day and age there is a mechanism of sure leverage that we all have access to and which is one of the most powerful informational highways that ever existed. I'm talking about the Internet.

Not only is the Internet changing our habits and the way we do business, the Internet I predict will soon change the way that humans think about things. It's already started to do just that.

The great thing about the Internet is you can leverage just about any dream. No matter how bizarre or obscure your interests, somebody out there will replicate your desires and want to communicate with you, maybe even buy your product, if you have one.

It's the perfect leverage because one person can reach millions of others. You can write a message or article and have it replicated thousands or even millions of times. That's powerful. Ask Mary Appelhof! In 1982 she wrote a cute little book entitled *Earthworms Eat My Garbage*. Not a best-selling book topic, you might think. But in no time at all, thanks to the Internet, Mary had sold over 50,000 copies. That's enough to make a book a best-seller in a small country like Great Britain!

Her success continues and you can find this book on Amazon.com. Sales when I last checked had topped 100,000. Mary really has proved that you can sell almost anything on the World Wide Web.

So, there we have it, a look at the subject of control, power and efficiency. Once again you will see that this Ability Express program is not like any other. We can take a basic philosophic truth and turn it into a powerful weapon of success. Far from being boring, logical philosophy can materialize our dreams, far more efficiently than just wishing for something.

7b. Completing Loops To Decompress

Take Control Of Your Life Now! //
One of the greatest mental "refreshers" you can give yourself is to clear out incomplete tasks and activities. These are areas where control has failed (remember, anything which is not complete is an open loop—an incomplete process and no STOP factor). Therefore we feel less than good about it but also it is disempowering, because of the message of personal inadequacy and loss.

But there is another, more subtle, reason why tasks hanging around in our psychic space are so damaging. As I have already indicated, undone or unfinished actions snap up attention units and cause dispersal of thinking. Mind power is locked up in these past failed actions and made unavailable to us in present time. Obviously we are not at our most efficient with only half our mental equipment in operation.

To find out for yourself, try this 7 to 10 day program of mental "cleansing". You are guaranteed a good result, if you do it conscientiously. In fact you will notice the benefits within hours. That's how powerful it is.

1. Make a list of incomplete actions in any aspect of your life. You can target a specific area, rather than trying to look at life as a whole.

If you are tired and increasingly apathetic about work, for instance, choose that area to clean up. If you've had countless failed projects in the past, better look at them.

Go through your correspondence and assemble a large pile of unhandled letters etc. If you are feeling lazy and unwilling to confront tasks around the home, maybe choose those.

What about those car repairs? A study assignment or thesis?

2. Whatever your target area, put every incomplete attention-snapping activity on the list.

Don't try to rationalize or make excuses to yourself for not completing the tasks. Especially do not allow your failure to confront unfinished tasks persuade you to omit them from the list, just because they are hard to face.

This won't work unless you get a comprehensive list.

3. Look over the list and visualize in your mind's eye having most or all of these tasks done. Finished completely. You will probably feel better just with this thought alone.

4. Now choose the easiest task to complete. Deal with that and get it out of the way. Now you feel a little more confident.

Choose another one and do that.

It is vital not to make the obvious mistake of picking the biggest problem and trying to tackle that first.

Pick your stuck actions in reverse order of difficulty, starting with the easiest, unless a great many incomplete enterprises depend on one big action that has been stalling everything.

5. If this is the case, take the major task that is holding everything up and list the parts of that difficulty as incomplete activities.

Start with the simplest of these subdivisions and do it! Then the next, then the next and so on.

This way, you can chunk down a daunting problem which has been holding you back. With that out of the way, you can cruise more easily through your remaining list.

6. Do each task conscientiously, so that it will not recur and come back to haunt you. Time is not of the essence in this handling.

Complete termination of the unfinished task is the proper target.

7. Notice how you feel fresher, brighter, more energetic and, yes, younger, as you crash out those un finished attention-snappers.

Repeat this any time you feel bogged down and crowded in by an area of work or activity.

You are re-asserting control. That's why it feels so good. Isn't it also a bit like the stuff the *Feng-Sui* boys and girls teach? I call this the *Feng-Sui* of mind spaces!

8. The Constellation Of Accord

The children of Adam are limbs of one body
Having been created of one essence.
When the calamity of time afflicts one limb
The other limbs cannot remain at rest.
If you have no sympathy for the troubles of others
You are not worthy to be called by the name of "Man."

Abu Muslih bin Abdallah Shirazi (1184 – 1283/1291),
Persian poet, better known by his pen-name as Sa'di.

Probably nothing in our lives has as much potential to bring happiness to our lives or cause such withering pain as the relationships we share. Whether it be family, friends, work colleagues or romantic sexual love partners, those with whom we share our lives are at the same time our greatest asset and our biggest problem.

Let's turn our attention in that direction and see if we can shed some light, and, of course, create happiness! Equally importantly, what can it teach us about creating and managing relationships in a competent, rational, non-destructive fashion?

Have you ever thought about the components of a successful relationship or what we really need and want from family and friends? I don't suppose many people have. If you start to take it apart, there are some very useful and pleasant surprises.

Since our "anatomy lesson" is also our definition, let's get straight into the mechanics, which I find most compelling. After more than a quarter of a century, I can honestly say that whenever I apply this data, the results are incredible. Conversely, whenever I "forget" or overlook applying it, the consequences are invariably humbling.

The Constellation
Human relationships at whatever level are comprised of several important identifiable elements: liking (of course), maybe as strong as affection; agreements (including values); propinquity, which is just a snarly word for closeness; and communication (or interaction). Plus there is a subtle energy dynamic, which few writers seem to acknowledge, yet we in Supernoetics™ think is crucial (*atunement*).

This constellation of elements are core to our Supernoetics™ private ontology (ontology: a complete set of axioms and propositions, governing Being and existence). A constellation means a "cluster of stars". These are indeed stars in our firmament.

We define ourselves and how we relate to all of existence in these mechanical elements. It is the quality and nature of the interface between our own awareness and the physical universe and between our own universe and that of others.

Liking, agreement, propinquity, communication and dynamic attunement are the giant "viewscreen" or gestalt, through which we perceive everything. This is a startling and bold statement. But let us follow it through and you will surely agree.

Time Out:
Before we proceed, write down here:

Someone you like a lot

A person or subject you like very little

An important upset which you experienced in your life (don't dwell on it, though!).

A genuine misunderstanding

You will be asked to return to this list at the end of this section.

Next, take a look at this schematic:

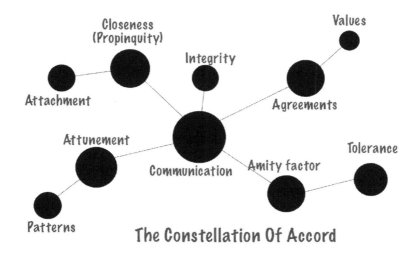

The Constellation Of Accord

Agreements

Let's kick off with this one.

"Peoples cannot love one another unless they love the same ideas."
—George Santayana, Spanish philosopher (born Jorge Agustín Nicolás Ruiz de Santayana y Borrás, 1863- 1952)

Agreements, in which we include shared values, are the very essence of our relationships. We tend to be attracted to people who share our values. We agree with them. Those who do not share our values tend to alienate us; this is no basis for a satisfactory and trouble free relationship.

People become friends and feel they understand each other because they have common interests, such as gardening, opera, sports, walking, poetry, or whatever.

Conversely, it is less than pleasant to spend time with people who do not share our values. It may even be a source of irritation or conflict. Lack of values detracts from a relationship, as the sharing and adding of mutual values is one of the fundamental building blocks of living together.

I would go further and say that love and caring is a matter of seeking to add values to another person's life (as opposed to your own).

Without common agreement, derived from profitable, attractive and mutually shared values, there is the strong likelihood that strangers and aliens will remain so. They won't be able to fully understand us, because the feeling of warmth and companionship is missing. There is little chance of successful communication or affection without proper agreed values, as you will see.

Worse than that: communication of conflicting values is definitely stressful and most dangerous to harmony and friendship. This is where opposed countries get started on endless and stupid wars which achieve nothing. Each is so detached and estranged from what the other side are saying and thinking that quite ridiculous thought processes get started.

So this principle has wide application. But let's keep focused down at the person to person level. Even there, for harmony's sake, we need to have plenty of common shared values with those we interact with.

And before you ask, no it isn't necessary to share entirely the same values with another to get along with them! Just plenty of overlap.

A Good Rule:

Allowing other people to enjoy their own values, unchallenged, is one of the golden rules for harmonious living. Make a point of honouring the views of others. You will be amazed how the empathy and liking improves.

Education

Values are critical in the field of education. Values are what set the standard.

Learning and knowledge can operate quite freely under the same guise as agreement. To incorporate knowledge into your own mind set—what we call embodiment learning—you must be able to agree with it. It must fit your personal values. You cannot incorporate into Self what you don't agree to. At best, you are only aware of the datum, but that isn't knowledge in the deepest sense. Knowledge, real knowledge, means integrated values.

The problem with much of modern education is that it relies on forcing data into minds that don't necessarily want it and certainly do not value it or agree with what is being imposed. You could take this as a definition of teaching at its worst. It's indoctrination, not education and certainly not learning in the sense we use the term. The enforcement of data in this fashion violates the principle of self determinism.

One of the big complaints with globalization today is that education worldwide is being subsumed to Western values. Those in turn are subsumed to a materialistic, consumer-oriented life, which is definitely not appropriate for the majority of Earth's peoples (indeed, is it even appropriate for the education of our own kids? Many think not).

Embodiment learning, our highest standard of education, is a very important theme and is visited in considerable depth in our powerful learning system, which you will come to eventually.

Culture

Culture is basically an agreement phenomenon; cultures rely on embracing a unique set of values. Ethnic groups, such as the North American Indians, Australian aborigines or African Zulus, each have a clearly defined social order which everyone belonging to the culture agrees to. It is based upon various assumptions about Man and the environment which interpret the world according to principles we would recognize as religious beliefs.

This group order is their shared values—it comes as a social package, complete with rules, categories, dictums and derived meanings.

The same holds true for other cultures, such as Judaism, which is a very ancient social order, as well as a religious creed. Indeed the late Dr. David Freed, a personal friend and a Jewish doctor, once told me that, being objective, the social codes were probably more important to the continuing existence of Judaism than the religious content. It is an enduring and viable set of values that has survived through good and bad times remarkably intact.

The rest of us don't have to agree with those values. Indeed, we can strongly disagree; but that's what holds Judaism together, through thick and thin.

There are many subcultures within the overall umbrella of any society. The youth generation drug movement is an example. Quite aside from the question of whether drugs are harmful in the long term, the kids are bonded together by shared values that include mannerisms, special language and dress code, coupled with rejection of authority and an almost reckless desire to experiment.

Exercise: Take a few moments to jot down examples of your own. I'm sure you can think of 2 or 3 different cultures or subcultures. Try to pinpoint some of their principal agreements or values.

Trust
Part of maintaining values or agreement with people is being trustworthy. It's an obligation. If you tell lies, you pervert communication and that breaks down trust. Agreement is a mutual truth. Others may not share it but any two or more people who do have a common value: it is agreed.

Thus there can be no real affinity and trust where lies are approved, no matter how much people pretend. We all know it from experience, yet sadly, some members of the populace still try to override this key rule of social harmony.

It's just a myth that lies work in your favor. People know when a falsehood is being aired; but it is often less painful to let it pass than embarrass the group or the perpetrator by challenging it. Nothing is said and the liar then tends to believe that they have succeeded in hoodwinking others.

Lies, cheating and dishonesty don't work. Don't kid yourself on this.

Forget about the Hollywood version of a crook, who commands great affection and respect from his fellow gangsters. It's a myth. They are all a pretty sorry bunch, anyone of whom would kill or cheat their "friends", if only they had a chance or perceived need. These people will never know the true warmth of affection and friendship.

Don't be fooled by the pretence of a good boxoffice story. It is a story, nothing more.

Belief in this sort of nonsense is just another way that phoney media breaks down our community values and integrity.

Keep Your Word
Another aspect of the same problem, judged less harshly, is failing to keep your word. You will not be liked by people if you cannot be relied upon to do what you say you will do. Letting people down, especially if they depend on you, is a pretty sure way to break down mutual values and damage affection.

Stick to your undertakings, even if it means some loss or pain for yourself. The greater pain will be to find you are lonely because noone likes you. That's exactly what will happen, if you can't be trusted or depended on.

Values mean just that: they are valuable, so people cherish them. Break values and you lose, heavily.

The Social Contract
All societies are really aspects of fundamental values being agreed and shared by a group of individuals. The Constitution of the United States of America is an example of a set of very firm and wonderful values on which a whole country was modelled. The fact that successive politicians have deliberately trashed the meaning of that Constitution doesn't alter the subject matter or the spirit of its wording.

In the UK we have a much more shadowy set of agreements. It is often said that the British Constitution, which is an unwritten one, is really a set of rules for social order designed for the benefit of just a few powerful families (the Establishment). You could say we live by their values.

But the fact remains, it is an agreement. We live by it and, when all is said and done, the British way of life is more supportive and tolerant than almost any other on Earth.

Thomas Hobbes, philosopher (1588-1679), painted a bleak picture of a world in which there were no shared values, no agreements and

60

thus no industry and commerce, no arts, no co-operation—and so no buildings, no navigation, no knowledge of the face of the earth, no account of time, no society... Thus no restraints on behaviour and constant fear of violence and sudden death. The life of Man would be, to use his now famous words: "solitary, poor, nasty, brutish and short".

That's how important agreed social values are.

The Amity Factor

Now let us turn to look at the second element of relationships, which we might describe as "positive connectedness". Affinity, affection and love are aspects of this element. Let's go ahead and call it the "amity factor" for the time being.

Definition: amity (from the Latin, *amo, amare*, to like, to love. Dictionary.com gives it as: friendship; peaceful harmony; mutual understanding

Considered further, this amity factor is an attitude or state of mind which implies a state of toleration, a mutual accord, saying that—in effect—communication, agreements and the exchange of ideas can take place. Philosophically-speaking, liking and toleration are one: a willingness and ability to allow other viewpoints and welcome them.

At its fullest expression, the amity factor may rate the label "love", with cooler and cooler degrees of it we might say, admiration, friendliness, harmony, acquaintance, and so on...

The important thing here is not to mix up "love", meaning romantic sexual desire, and love, meaning positive accord and affection. These are quite separate and were identified millennia ago by the Greeks who labelled these two feelings *eros* (sexual) and *agape* (platonic love).

For this book I specifically set aside erotic attraction. Not that it isn't important; it is. But because it comes from our creature life and not the life of soul or spirit (theta). Both can exist together, of course. But when erotic love has run its course, it disappears and may be replaced by non-erotic love, or by separation.

In it fullest sense, non-erotic love can be unconditional. Romantic sexual love always has conditions; that's it very nature.

In Supernoetics™ we have a comprehensive *Scale Of Loving And Connectedness*, which is the subject of another essay entirely. What it tells us, briefly, is that as more and more space, and thus matter and energy, come between the consciousness and the object or person in contemplation, so gradually this quality of love and accord, or connected-ness diminishes, until eventually there is none of it left.

This gradation model has added immensely to my appreciation of love and affection; I hope it does for yours.

Closeness (Propinquity)

Propinquity is a snarly word but one that all psychologists use! All it means is closeness (Latin: *propinquitas*, closeness, physical proximity, nearby). We can also use the term togetherness, which is common.

However, the first thing to clear up is that in relationships we do not necessarily mean closeness to be understood as distance, measured in feet, furlongs or miles! It can mean metaphorical closeness, or lack of it.

We have many cue words in the language, telling us that people find this concept very familiar: "there are close", "he behaved very distantly", "they were as one" or somebody is "aloof", or "attached," or they are "separated".

A very interesting series of experiments was done some years ago, by a team from Harvard. They created some Venn diagrams, showing circles (representing "self" gradually overlapping each other). These charts were then shown to couples in a relationship and each was asked to point out which representation matched closest to their relationship with their "significant other." Here is my own series of schemas to correspond to that chart:

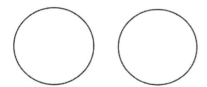

Strangers: never met.

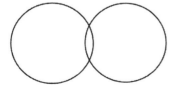

Almost never connect and never very deeply or for long.
More of their lives separate than together.

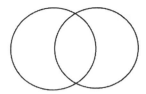

Connect some but there is a limit to how deep and how often.

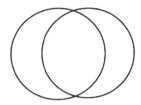

Connect deeply and regularly, sometimes for long periods.
Equal share of time together and apart.

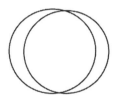

Connect deeply with most kinds of closeness.
Share more of their lives together than apart.

Connect closely as a way of life.
We might say they co-exist "as one".

You can try showing these diagrams to your friends; see which they choose for their crucial relationship!

You will readily appreciate that a couple could be very "close" (in love) and yet thousands of miles apart. Or they could live in the same house but be very, very "distant" with each other.

Only occasionally is distance the problem. For example the house-wife who has an affair while her husband is away fighting in a war; it might seem that physical distance has driven them apart. But likely as not, the relationship was never that close, before the husband was called up.

Three Degrees of Influence
You may have heard of this theory, proposed by Nicholas A. Christakis and James H. Fowler. The pair found that social networks have great influence on individuals' behavior. But social influence does not end with the people to whom a person is directly tied. We influence our friends who in their turn influence their friends, meaning that our actions can influence people we have never met.

Christakis and Fowler proposed that, "everything we do or say tends to ripple through our network, having an impact on our friends (one degree), our friends' friends (two degrees), and even our friends' friends' friends (three degrees). Our influence gradually dissipates and ceases to have a noticeable effect on people beyond the social frontier that lies at three degrees of separation".

This argument is basically that peer effects need not stop at one degree, and that, if we can affect our friends, then we can (in many cases) affect our friends' friends, and so on. However, across a broad set of empirical settings, the effect seems to no longer be meaningful at a social horizon of three degrees. Christakis and Fowler have examined phenomena from various domains, such as gaining weight, happiness, and politics.

Interestingly, in relation to happiness for example, nearby neighbors may have more effect on our outlook the actual friends and acquaintances.

Attachment Model
For humans—and probably many other species—there is a curious need for closeness and touch. In 1951 British psychologist and psychiatrist John Bowlby published a seminal report, commissioned by the WHO, which became the basis for what was soon dubbed "attachment theory". This is the first crucial appearance of propinquity in modern psychology.

Bowlby had been asked to study the outcomes for thousands of babies left orphans after World War Two. Due to staffing shortages, the babies were denied real connection with their carers; nobody touched tenderly or held them; there was no language contact of any note. The result? The children grew up retarded and had a marked tendency to die—no obvious signs of disease; they simply faded away and died. That's remarkable. It tells us a great deal about what it means to be human.

Interactions with other humans or "strokes" appear to be vital to growing up normally. We read of "imprinting" of baby geese—that remarkable adoption by newly hatched goslings of the first moving creature they see as "mother"—and we find it cute and amusing. Yet no-one until this time suggested that such a phenomenon could be important to humans. Why should it come as a surprise?

New research is now undermining old and wretched "scientific" notions, like the no-touch rule for premature babies. Gentle massage of preemies in their incubator has been found to reduce mortality and help them grow along normal weight and height parameters and eventually merge with society in a balanced and functional way.

The most important tenet of attachment theory is that an infant needs to develop a relationship with at least one primary caregiver for the child's successful social and emotional development, and in particular for learning how to effectively regulate their feelings. It doesn't have to be the biologic al mother. Fathers or any other nearby individual can find they have become a principal attachment figure, by providing the necessary physical contact. The presence of a sensitive and responsive caregiver will give the infant a "safe base" from which to explore.

There is a great deal to be learned from the theory of attachment and how it applies to us all, not just babies.

The Most-Beloved Computation

In Supernoetics™ we recognize an attachment phenomenon not much described in academia and conventional psychology; we call it the "most-beloved" computation. It arises directly from attachment theory.

A "most-beloved" is a person close to the individual, not necessarily a parent (indeed, usually not a parent), who had some extraordinary helping aspect during the formative years. This person was a strong ally or helper, someone who nurtured, sheltered or protected the individual, when he or she felt in danger or pain.

A classic example would be Grandma, who was there nursing the child through measles encephalitis, while parents continued to work. Grandma, with her soft voice, slices of cake and bowls of tasty broth, feeding the youngster by hand, would be seen as a very valuable ally.

With measles encephalitis (I had it) there may be terrifying nightmares, that could haunt the child for many years afterwards.

But Grandma was there, to keep the person safe and less fearful. She would be deeply loved and valued. For grandma, read: neighbor, uncle, sister, priest, nurse on the wards, or whatever person the individual elects as a "most-beloved".

So when that person dies, there is an exceptional sense of loss. The client in piloting is distraught and once again feels threatened and unsafe, because the ally has deserted their station! These are heavy secondary memonemes to run out but very important on a case, as you will readily see.

It's a fact that loss of a most-beloved will often occasion more grief than the loss of a parent.

Communication

Now we come to the big one! Communication is without doubt the cement which holds together relationships; it's the glue that bonds fellowships. Communication is the means by which we exchange our views, share values and express our positive regard. It's also the thing which stumbles us the most and leads often to misunderstandings, quarrels and breaks in affection. Beware!

In the previous section I pointed to key scientific research which makes it clear that infants do not thrive without adequate attention and interactive "strokes". The child never really becomes functionally human, in the absence of meaningful communication.

Reading the accounts of individuals who have spent long periods in solitary confinement also make it clear that humans begin to wither and fade very quickly, once out of touch with fellow creatures; that's why it is such a cruel punishment. Hermits and recluses who shun human contact at least have a choice and probably get along by talking with animals, plants and other living things.

In an even more extraordinary instance of this finding, British explorer Felicity Ashton recounts how, on her memorable solo Antarctic crossing, where there were not even any animals to connect with, she began to crumble mentally. She talked to the Sun, had hallucinations, and "I felt very uprooted from any kind of reality," Felicity was quote as saying (Marie Claire, Oct 2014, p. 284)

Instances such as this illustrate just how core to our Being the faculty of communication is. Always keep at the top of your mind an awareness of the wonder of this gift, its glory and the duties it entails. If you waste it, you are a fool and nobody wants to behave stupidly.

To make this Constellation Of Accord work, people have to agree to a far higher standard of communication than is customary. Gone is the supposed entitlement or "right" to angry, nasty words, just because we are experiencing a discrepancy between what we wanted and what we got.

This very immature attitude is based on the untenable belief that the other person's viewpoint is unimportant and can be discounted. It also presupposes the absurd idea that we did not contribute in any way to our own discomposure. Well, that would mean surrendering our power and responsibility, which is abhorrent to anyone who has tasted the freedom, truth and power of Supernoetics™.

It is simply not acceptable to claim that another or others "caused" us to be upset. Contrary and disempowering emotions are purely our own choice. Whatever he/she (or they) did, the hurt and reaction are entirely our own creation and therefore entitle us to nothing. Indeed, the expression of irrational anger, verbal attacks, *ad hominems* or cursing is to remove ourselves from the pool of accord and therefore dis-entitles us to anything but scorn.

Definition: *ad hominem* (Latin: at or to the man) marked by or being an attack on an opponent's character rather than by an answer to the contentions made; appealing to feelings or prejudices rather than intellect.

Perhaps our loyal and loving friends will excuse us and patiently wait until we recover our composure? If not, we must apologize and make amends, not spread insults and dismay.

What You Can Do
Immediately add much more warmth and kindness to all your communication outflow, whether by touch, spoken word or writing. Reach out with love and include the person you are talking to in your own space.

Smile (you don't need a reason to smile; there are reasons NOT to smile, but those are pretty invalid anyway).

Take the other person's eye and be willing and friendly about it (no threatening military "eye-balling"). If you feel nervous about this, remember he or she probably does too. So, no need to feel embarrassed or in any way inferior.

Just assume the lead.

Do not talk at, or even to, him or her. Just share what you want to say. Speak clearly and gently but in modest bites. Then shut up and let the other have a turn while you listen.

Learn what we call "respectful" silence. It's a skill to practice but basically it means (and shows) you are listening, even though you are not responding. Your body language tells the speaker you are right there, attentively.

Done right, the "respectful silence" encourages the person to keep talking, openly and willingly.

At each stroke end (back-forth, back-forth), acknowledge that person and his or her views. It could be as simple as a nod, a slight deepening of the smile, or a murmur of approval. Just some way to say that you are listening. Be interested; it oils the process far more than being interesting.

Respect what the other person says, even if it sounds wrong to you. And don't try and climb on top of that person's views with "I know that...." Or "Yes but...."

If you want to try and get something over, be patient. Assume you are putting it badly if it won't go across; do not assume the other is an idiot or rogue.

Finally, if you can't agree, agree to stop! Talk about something else. You will encounter nothing but aggravation and hostility if you fall into the mode of trying to be right at the other's expense. He or she won't have it. Making them see your point of view will never work (trying to see their point of view just might, though).

Gear up to new standards of positive communication. Make this important change in your life. Outflow love, intelligence, rationality and ease in all you say and do for a week. Don't attack or criticize but encourage free expression. Smile whenever you have the chance. Say "Thank you", or similar, far more often than has been customary. Review what happens. You will be amazed at what comes back to you.

Do it especially for a friend or lover. You could mend his or her heart!

Atunement: The Energy Dynamic
You don't see this written up in textbooks but it's real and very important. Hippies first gave us the neologism of a person's "vibes" or vibrations. Still the concept usually raises a snigger or scoff. But you

don't have to be a Californian youngster high on drugs to realize there really is something to "feel" in a relationship, something that goes beyond just the emotional tone. It's a quality or resonance and this dynamic can keep a relationship alive, through many difficulties and misunderstandings; or rapidly kill it stone dead, where there is an awkward mismatch!

The truth is that there are energetic properties to any relationship and, like any balance of energies, there can be coherence and harmony or clashes and lack of sync. Probably the energy dynamic, which is at the core of any relationship, is influenced most by the communications which take place. Quality of communication is as much about it's tone and feel as about the words. This has been stated often (body language concepts).

But the energy dynamic, if healthy, can survive a serious disparity in beliefs and values, if both sides act intelligently and rationally.

The whole structure we call atunement has great importance when it comes to Supernoetics™ piloting. Deeper examination into the question of human relationships soon reveals that we are continuously and heavily interacting with others and this can be oppressive, even destructive.

Over eons of time we have fallen into massive patterns of conflict, which never seem to quite resolve but slowly evolve and escalate into something new but equally destructive. You will learn more about this in the band I call Viewpoint Engineering.

Patterns
On the subject of kinetics, I must bring in a mention of our behavioural patterns, to complete this important constellation. We all have recurring patterns of behaviour, that conform with a formula or sequence of repetitious actions. We are driven energetically by our past and tend to repeat the same moves over and over, looking for satisfaction or resolution. This is often totally subconscious; indeed a person is rarely as aware of his or her behavior patterns as are friends or onlookers.

It's often said, for example, that a woman marries her father and a man marries his mother. This means that he or she will be comfortable with a person who is somewhat like the parent and is attracted to them. The "Oedipus complex" described by Freud is only an extreme (and somewhat silly) display of this kind of behaviour.

What it really means, energetically, is that we are looking for a "fit" or resonance between ourselves, our inner world, and someone or something on the outside.

The trouble is, these patterns can get deadly and without being able to control him or herself, the individual can get locked into patterns of repetitious violence, abuse, confrontation or whatever. Even the victim is not guiltless: the "victim" is subconsciously looking for someone to fulfil their apparent "need" for abuse and can draw in other people to fulfil their patterns, just as surely as abusers do.

In fact "victims" can be very bad news and get a lot of people hurt in their needy dramas. In Supernoetics™ we look down on victims as decidedly as we do upon abusers. Neither is rational. Both are driven by deep, dark energy patterns. There is a better life script for all, that just needs writing and enacting.

Besides, at the end of the day, all patterns are energy baggage we would be better off without. It is a saying I find myself repeating constantly: beware of encountering wild passion. Chances are you two have met before and are dramatizing a pattern which is coming around, again and again, till one of you gets smart enough to spot it and say "Enough!"

Fresh life of the spirit, experienced in the now, is far superior to any been-there-done-that emotional dramas!

Upsets
We can now look at upsets and quarrels in a totally different light.

The Supernoetics™ term for the upsets of life, the moments of sudden unpleasant emotion, the quarrels, the setbacks, those fits of anger and indignation that we all dread and do our best to avoid, is a "crash of accord" (crash from computer terminology: a sudden cessation or failure). You can now understand these mystifying disturbances, simply by grasping the anatomy of what has gone wrong [plural, note is: crashes of accord, not crash of accords!]

When this Constellation Of Accord is disrupted, the amity factor and communication automatically drop. Once communication fails and starts sending bad messages, then the relationship becomes very corrupted and ugly, or even ceases altogether. Values tend to dissipate or even be overturned. I have heard people say crazy things like, "I don't want your love", just in order to win and argument!

Most crashes of accord stem from either bad communication or misunderstood communication. Therefore it is vital that we keep our communication high tone and free flowing.

The other elements of accord can initiate the upset too. If someone says something you find violates your values, you are likely to become upset. At the very least, you will find yourself having to bite your tongue and try damned hard NOT to become upset on occasion. Bite your tongue, by the way, is just a way of saying "blocking communication"!

Opposing values is dangerous ground for discussion if you want to avoid upsets. Remember, you can rarely change another person's mind by head on thrust. What is the point of taking an argumentative line with another person, especially a friend?

A much better plan is to find something within their values you can agree with and, by talking about it, get them to expand it. With enough luck and some skill, they may even come up with something you find acceptable. That means you can get what you want by having them think it was their idea.

Effects

By whatever means it comes about, a crash of accord has clearly identifiable effects. You will feel unwilling to communicate, you suddenly don't like something or somebody and you feel a strong sense of disagreement. Your values have been violated. These are pretty universal feelings.

The lack of communication is quite characteristic, of course. We use the term sulking. People who are upset deliberately shut off communication with hurtful and unpleasant remarks or even explicit comments like yelling "Shut up!" He or she may simply go to a private room and slam the door.

Yet abandoning communication is the very thing to avoid at all costs.

TIME OUT: Now think back to the big upset you wrote down at the start of this article.

Wasn't that an crash of accord? Can you identify the missing elements? Perhaps you can even spot the cause; was it, in the first instance, a break of communication or values?

Is it true that the person you chose who understands you the most shared your values, communicated easily with you and you liked them?

Does the person you felt alienated from share few of your values, isn't easy to talk to and there is a 'distance' or lowering of propinquity?

The misunderstanding you noted down - was that a break in Communication? Values? Propinquity? The amity factor?

8a. Repairing Crashes of Accord

Now we come to the million dollar question: is there any way to fix crashes of accord quickly and simply?

Yes there is.

The key to it is good communication. This is the most productive element of our constellation. You will have read that communication will solve everyone's problems. Well, not if it is bad (hostile) communication, it won't. It could even make matters worse.

To be of much value in a relationship, communication has to be what I call quality communication.

To repair upsets, it takes kind, gentle and persuasive communication, with lots of warmth and concerning only matters which are filled with potential agreement (stick to agreed values). There is no use whatever in going on communicating the hate, the argument, the discord, the hostility. Neither party is ever going to change the other person that way.

Don't start from "There's a big problem here, let's talk about it". Start from "Hey you remember that lovely evening we spent with Jim and Lisa?..."

When the communication starts flowing again in a friendly way, you'll find one of two interesting things will happen:

It's easier to now talk about the upset and get it resolved

You no longer need to talk about the upset; it resolved itself!

Don't Force Your Own Viewpoint
Everyone habitually tries to "solve" disputes the wrong way; by getting the other person to see their own point of view. They try to enforce it, in the belief that "If only they could see what I see, it would all resolve", which is wrong.

You should be trying to duplicate the other person's point of view. Be them. Think like them!

Keep clear of the dispute and cool things down with generalized remarks that will definitely avoid discord. Don't be shy or feel stupid about switching to the weather or something good to eat for lunch when there is a heated argument.

To do so, you are not "ducking out" but applying basic scientific philosophy.

Compromise isn't a comfortable word. It enjoys little repute since it smacks of failure; neither side getting what they want.

To finish, here's an even better idea...

Sondra Ray, in her incisive book *Loving Relationships II*, gives a brilliant technique which she calls 'Highest Spiritual Thought'. It's a game that both parties have to agree to. However, anyone would be crazy not to introduce this game into their role play and relationships.

Instead of the usual ploy of trying to get the other to 'give in' and so triumph over them --- whatever that could possibly mean in terms of making others we love wrong --- both have to try to find the best answer. There are no winners but the two (or more) individuals have to strive to outdo each other in finding a loving and rational thought that makes sense of the situation.

Whoever comes up with the nicest answer wins. But of course both win! It's brilliant.

How much nicer than yelling, "You bitch, you didn't show up, you never keep your promises" to sit down and say "OK, you forgot our dinner date. But you wanted to go to night-school because you want to learn to paint. That's nice".

She replies "But it's your loving inspiration that makes me want to strive to get better educated and impress you".

Then he says "You don't have to impress me. Our love is based on mutual values and I admire you a lot. "

And she says "Tell you what, let's go to dinner tomorrow night instead. We only lose twenty four hours."

And he says "That way we get to share a date and talk and I can treat you to good living and you get to learn to paint!"

He wins! He came up with the highest thought. But do you think she cares a damn? She didn't lose, did she?

My Extra Strategy

It's hard to improve on Sondra Ray's beautiful concept. But I'd like to add a couple of quickie paragraphs:

To solve a dispute, you must try to work together to get into the other person's point of view, rather than trying to make them accept yours.

Recall a couple of instances where you took the wrong line. Work out what you should have said, to get a better outcome. If there is still time, go out and do it. Note the result.

It's Never Too Late

The nice thing about these solutions to crashes of affinity is that you can do them retroactively. You can go to past upsets and undo them, remarkable though that seems.

You can take a relationship which has gone sour and neither party talked to each other for years. Just encourage them to start talking about general issues they both agree on. Forbid any attempt at figuring out, "What went wrong between us?"

The talk only focuses on "What went right between us?"

Pretty soon, you'll see the affinity start to rise.

I have a saying: If love between you ever meant anything, it will always mean something. It doesn't go away! It just gets buried with anger and hurt. The fact there is anger and hurt, as I said, means there is also love. Think about it.

To paraphrase Winston Churchill's famous phrase "Never, never, never give up".

Never, never, never give up on love and affection. It's far too precious to let go...

9. The 12 Channels Of Being

I said peace is sometimes narrowly interpreted; it's the absence of conflict between nations or something. But peace is more inherent, more basic to human life, human beings, what we feel about each other, what we feel about life around us and what we see in our future. —Mohammad Yunus, Nobel Laureate for Peace, founder of banking microloans.

With the advent of Supernoetics™ we have a powerful new grammar of spiritual living. We can redefine old concepts, invent new terms, re-structure our notions of wisdom and enhance appropriate activities.

It allows us to re-visit debates like right and wrong, good and bad, ethics, morals, sanity, values and happiness. One of our powerful and unique thinking tools is the 12 Channels of Being.

With good reason, these were first named R-Zones or zones of responsibility. They could equally well be labeled the 12 Acts of Being. These are a set of core values that are intelligent, workable, healing, radical and in which we can all share. These 12 Channels make us all accountable for our actions on Earth.

Let's take a look...

Channel 1: The Inner World Of Self
The mind, memory, imagination, personality and character.

This is in a very crucial sense our principal Channel Of Being. It is essential for realization of our full potential that we keep our mental mirror clean and bright, so that we truly reflect our environment. It is important to separate our existence as conscious beings from that as biological creatures. These are not the same and running the two together has caused endless confusion in biology, religion, psychology and politics.

As a creature, we have biological drives (which are sometimes hard to resist). These are for the purpose of survival and procreation. But as spiritual beings, pure consciousness, we cannot do anything else but survive. Consciousness does not die, just because the body ceases to function.

Probably the biggest disaster for most people in their Channel 1 is that they allow themselves to slip out of present time and produce efforts and actions that are really inappropriate re-actions to past situations.

Count Alfred Korzybski, to whom Supernoetics™ owes an enormous debt, called this detachment from the true situation un-sanity. There is much written about it elsewhere in Supernoetics™ and its accompanying Transformational Psychology.

Channel 2. The Outer World Of Self

This is an extension of our creature world and our spiritual life. Channel 2 includes the perception and enjoyment of one's own possessions, career, achievements, skills, interests, etc.

As well as the inner environment, one's "self" is represented in one's belongings and immediate surroundings. Happiness and drive come in the form of physical objects which enhance our status, health, good emotions, creativity and ability to attract and live with others. Even your playlists are part of your Channel 2!

Living with beauty and harmony is now recognized by leading doctors as an absolutely vital factor in enriching our lives and diminishing the destructive impact of stress. Look after your Channel 2 and fill it with paintings, fine music, good food and enjoyable recreation.

Remember health plans, exercise and good nutrition are among the many important aspects of Channel 2 survival. Sexuality seems like it should be part of this (overall health) but we have a special Channel for that, which is...

Channel 3. The Romantic Sexual Urge

Procreation, which is of course major survival for all living creatures, can be compartmented into activities with the mate, mostly sex (Channel 3), and activities connected with the genetic line, meaning forbears and progeny (Channel 4).

Humans are a little different to most animals in that a great deal of life, vitality and Beingness is wrapped up with our mate. Romantic love is perhaps uniquely human and of course intensely interconnected with—but not exactly identical to—sexual activity. In fact romantic love is really a kind of sublimation (or substitute) for the sexual act, with stylized intellectual conquest and penetration, rather than the real thing.

It is one of the most powerful of all urges for humans, so much so that life may be set aside for the continuity and survival of one's beloved. Probably because it is so strong a force, sex in humans has become an almost constant presence and no longer seems confined to estrus (or being "in heat" as we say of animals).

When considering the feeling we describe often as "love" it's very important to distinguish it from need and desire. Attraction and cherishment are positive urges; but the mere animal responses (low-level brain responses) of need and desire are not so worthy. These are like the drives of addiction; it's version of craving, not true attraction.

Beware your drives. Beware you are operating on this Channel and not Channel 2—your own selfish animal drives.

I have often warned couples of the intense madness of wild desire, when you first meet someone. It's just a re-encounter—it's not love. Be careful! It basically means you have been circling around each other for countless past lives, battling your way through lust and conflicts, still coming around and around, bent on matters like revenge, reconciliation, strong urges and fulfillment; with rage and revenge often at the top of the list.

You will burst into flame, experience wild frenzy and then it will all turn to tears; trust me!

Court and marry someone you've never met in a past life! It will be far less stormy.

To violate your Channel 3, or experience major loss in it, is a great disaster indeed to one's own Being. Cherish it always. Without it, all the remaining Channels make little sense.

A word of warning: it's virtually an axiom that sexual misalignment at the top will likely crash any organization. If you are engaged in business in any way, shape or form, with your significant other or spouse, take care!

The desire for spite and revenge can loom large and cost you everything you worked for together. You probably know that saying, "Hell hath no fury... etc."

When leaders start to sleep around or flip partners, the general staff often take it as a cue that nobody is serious about work as well as relationships. It can quickly lead to a disaster.

I speak from experience: when my first wife suddenly left in favor of another man, she very soon went to work for one of my erstwhile rivals. She had learned all my medical secrets over the years, so there was nothing I could do. I'm sure she found it very amusing.

Unfortunately, the empire we had built together over the space of some 15 years did not survive and, in the end, after a messy breakup, neither of us came out with any money or kudos. It took me years to gain back my confidence and re-launch myself.

Meanwhile, her new lover did not last. We were both losers.

I have treated of this topic in a piece entitled *Breaking Up Intelligently (If You Must)*. I hold it as a moral truth that it is mandatory on all conscious beings who aspire to be civilized, intelligent and caring, to seek for the means whereby loving values can be preserved and the growth of either party left undamaged by a separation.

We must seek to find ways to leave our ex-partner in a calm and relatively unshaken state of mind in which they can function properly. Failure to do so will sooner or later rebound on those who perpetrate such unconscionable acts, whether motivated by folly, spite or evil intent.

Channel 4. The Genetic or Protoplasm Line
Procreation is a powerful survival urge and the basic procreation unit, the family, is a fundamental and great influence for humans.

With the recent scientific and technological revolutions in Western culture, we have shrugged off the reverence for our ancestors which has typified most human society since the dawn of time. It is a severely disruptive trend. Not only are we cutting ourselves off from a deep and moving influence in our lives but we commit the ultimate folly of failing to understand that we ourselves will one day be "ancestors"! It is a kind of ritual suicide and no-one seems to pay much attention to the lemming craze.

Speaking as a doctor, I am well aware of the profound influences of our forbears on both our constitution, mental make-up and life habits, as well as the more obvious "genetic" inferences (many so-called genetic traits are simply acquired conditions or un-sanity passed on from one generation to the next).

We would do well to pay more attention to the wisdom of those who still revere their ancestors and to aim to be both worthy of such acclaim from our successors and smart enough to teach them the value of this Channel!

Finally, by diminishing the stature of our elders, we lose out on a great deal of acquired knowledge. The youth cult which established itself in the 60s has been synonymous with the displacement and even disparagement of the elderly. Yet they have the collective years of experience which the young do not.

It has been said that the presence in the home of grandparents is a buffer against child abuse. At the very least, it means baby sitters who are close kin, instead of money-earning strangers.

4a. Family Constellations
I can talk here about what I call constellations or "clustering". This is about groups of beings circling round each other and interacting, usually for karmic reasons. It runs through many past lives; these individuals meet up over and over, often switching roles, to try and resolve issues.

It's very important and incredibly powerful as a hidden family dynamic (just as relevant to Channel 3 as Channel 4).

There is often conflict, abuse, criminality, pain and the desire to resolve it all. Parents become children and their own grandchildren; children become parents in subsequent dramatizations.

Lovers from earlier lives, I have found, often keep meeting up intentionally. In fact it's the source of a great deal of incest, rape and other sexually non-optimum behavior. The father sees the child he loved as a sweetheart in an earlier incarnation. The child probably gravitates back to him and may even have chosen the incest vehicle, according to some past life workers (see Robert Schwartz's book, *Your Soul's Gift: The Healing Power of the Life You Planned Before You Were Born*).

The father becomes aroused again and misbehaves. This is also behind the heavy burden of guilt carried by the victim: he or she still carries the dim memories of the earlier time and even the child knows it is part of this constellation. This truth is often the last to surface.

Bert Hellinger wrote of a similar phenomenon when he talked about family constellations. These are a previously unrecognized systemic dynamic that spans multiple generations in a given family and to resolve the deleterious effects of that dynamic by encouraging the subject to accept the factual reality of the past. Such connections are, naturally, Channel 4 connections.

Hellinger practitioners claim that present day problems and difficulties may be influenced by traumas suffered in previous generations of the family, even if those affected now are unaware of the original event in the past.

The theory of ancestral "invisible loyalty", according to Professor Anne Ancelin Schützenberger, recognizes that supposed loyalty owed to previous generations may indeed predispose us to unwittingly re-enact their suffering and unfinished business in our own life events.

My own Supernoetics™ gives great importance to this dynamic we call *atunement* but which is hardly acknowledged in other psychologies. But merely recognizing this effect allows resolution of apparent "family curses and "inherited bad luck".

Recent findings in epigenetics research supports the concept that after-effects of trauma can be passed to subsequent generations

Channel 5. Your Place In The World
Here we have an outward extension of Channels 1 and 2 and of course it bears heavily on Channels 3 and 4 as well. You face outwards to meet the world with the love and strength of your family behind you (or not as the case maybe).

Moving outside the family, you begin to participate in the world at large. This Channel touches on your role in the bigger arena, including your job, your prosperity rating and exchange with the others. In the old days of fiefdom and vassals, you tended flocks and grew whatever food you could. That was about the limit and it was not until after the industrial revolution and the urbanization exodus that it became possible for an individual to claw their way upwards and carve an independent fortune.

Responsibility for one's zone of work and any income earning activity, whether several separate jobs or as part of a larger personally run wealth creation plan are part of this Channel. Responsibility extends to all one's fellow workers and to the organization or business of which one is a part.

There has been a suicidal trend, especially, in post-war Britain for example, for "workers" to attack the administrators and management of their company. Firstly, management are workers too, supported by the company. More importantly, if the company goes down, the "workers" will no longer have anything to do.

That's exactly what happened. Under a mad communist union agitator, Britain was repeatedly brought to its knees economically by the fact that dockers (stevedores) went on strike over and over. Britain could no longer shift its goods internationally and for the first time being an island became a liability, not an asset.

Pretty soon ports closed, workers had no work, they ended up on the dole. But it was worse than that: Britain ended up ruined and her once-renowned manufacturing base never really recovered. All Brits felt the chill wind.

Look after your work group. If you feel you can't, change employers until you can. The attitude of most—simply to get by with a minimum effort short of getting fired is treason to both the company and yourself. This kind of self-degradation may be the norm but it is deadly for morale and self-esteem (see also the section of exchange ethics and the secret of affluence).

Channel 6. Tribes and Communities.
Tribes and tribing are buzzwords today. A tribe is generally agreed to be a group up to about 150 people... just small enough that it is possible to know all members of the tribe by name and sight.

Larger associations, up to and including the size of a whole country, we can call a community. It's a large raft of people with common values, common interests and a mutual dynamic towards survival.

This includes the "extended family" concept or clan (tribe) system. A sense of community and belonging with others is probably one of the most profound human survival longings. When it is thwarted, things start to go seriously wrong for society as a whole.

Loneliness and isolation, especially in old age, seems to be the misfortune of an increasing number of people.

Unfortunately, our tribal communities have tended to break up into job-and-family units. In the 60s and 70s we embraced concept of the so-called "nuclear family" but the sad truth is that it is quite unable to sustain all our needs. This unrealistic expectation has led to such intense pressure on the family and the core relationship (man and wife) that even this unit has started to break down, leading to rafts of isolated and largely unhappy individuals.

Channel 6 would stretch to include our nation or the state to which one belongs, as I remarked, but would not embrace narrow and destructive ideals of so-called "nationalism".

Tribes are dangerous in the political arena, everyone who shares one group of values is likely to want to overthrow (even kill) tribes who do not share their values. (for example, Christians and Muslims; communists and non-communists...)

The Roseto Phenomenon

But tribes are not just divisive; they have a positive quality too. The power of community is seen in the case of the town of Roseto in Pennsylvania, which became known for the extraordinary health and long-lived tendency of its inhabitants. Virtually no-one under the age of 50 died of a heart attack or showed any signs of heart disease. For men over 65, the death rate from heart disease in Roseto was half the national average. The death rate from all causes in Roseto was 30- 35% lower, overall, than the rest of the United States.

When scientists finally figured out the story, they realized that the very close social ties in that community were what kept people happy and healthy. At the start of the twentieth century, Roseto was almost 100% Italian; not just that, but from a specific region of southern Italy; they shared the same dialect. The folks there had a strong sense of group and belonging.

That's how powerful and healthy tribing can be! So it will pay you many times over, to be conscious of your strong tribe connections and it will reward you to foster them in community, whether as a volunteer worker, or just a good neighbor!

Non-Local Tribes and Communities

I introduce this concept, to separate the idea of geographically or ethnically related tribes and associations from that of widely-spread groups with a common interest or fulfillment.

Nowadays, thanks to the Internet and Facebook and other social media, we have tribes such as the dog-lovers tribe; the golf tribe; the antique collectors tribe; the UFO hunters tribe. Then there are smaller but delicious nonetheless tribes, such as fans of Jane Austen's writing or lovers of Early Music.

In these cases, individuals are drawn to each other because of intellectual connectivity, rather than peers, race or locality. Members of associations of this sort may never actually meet each other physically!

The phenomenon remains just as valid, perhaps more relevantly so in our modern world.

The Small Highly Energized Group Of Fighters

Finally, let me end this section by pointing to the enjoyment and merits of being part of a small band of dedicated people who are fighting for something worthwhile. In our case, it's fighting for a better world and deeper insight into the mechanics of consciousness and Being.

It's one of the most inspiring and exciting feelings you can get to: that of sharing in a compelling cause. In wartime Britain, there is no question that a whole dynamic evolved of fighting the common enemy. It really was, as Churchill judged, their "finest hour". Everyone (well, almost everyone) was on the same page; social barriers came down; people who had been bored with civilian life suddenly found themselves heroes at the center of the storm. It was thrilling and very spiritually elevating.

Once you have known this feeling and immersed yourself deeply in it, you'll find yourself going through life looking to repeat the same experience. It's something I hold dear in our Supernoetics™ march to planetary sanity. You'll probably get the same feeling too, as you commit more and more of your time to getting out the word, changing people's lives, healing conditions and working our amazing transformations.

British philosopher Thomas Carlyle introduced the inspiring concept of "A life of hallowed fire"! It is spirit at its best. Carlyle was thinking of a newly formed and expanding group on a spiritual mission with a great purpose, just in the early stages (a new religion, for example).

But we in Supernoetics™ take this concept to our hearts and think that a life, fully aligned by these 12 Channels of Being, with explosive growth and the potential to transform our world into one that is just, sustainable, peaceful, rational, esthetic and pleasant, is indeed a "Life of Hallowed Fire".

It's Channel 6 at its best!

Channel 7. Mankind, the Species
Awareness and responsibility for mankind as a whole, irrespective of race or gender is our seventh major domain of responsibility. We are all the same species biologically and can interbreed for survival; black, white, yellow and red. With the gradual emergence of a "global village" concept we are made more aware of our demographic identity. However the problem which diminishes our mental health in this Channel is that any sense of participation is submerged in the sheer vastness of it.

Moreover, there is increasing unease today that we are being manipulated by hidden power groups, which are managing resources and control mechanisms for their own ends and primarily for the purpose of enslaving the population to their whim.

It is frustrating and dis-empowering to feel we have no way of influencing events on the planetary scale. Or at least we didn't have; until...

Channel 7a! The Internet And Social Networking
In 1979 artist Andy Warhol famously said that every person can be famous for fifteen minutes. He was thinking of TV slots. But that was nearly 40 years ago. Warhol didn't foresee the Internet.

Thanks to the Internet, anyone can have far more than just the 15 minutes of fame that Warhol promised. If you join a reality TV show you can be a celebrity of an obnoxious kind for weeks or even months. But on the Internet ANYONE can become famous, build a following and hold onto their celebrity status for years or decades.

The Internet is its own place; it's a whole new realm of consciousness and I have pinpointed it as a step forward in the evolution of consciousness. I believe something will ultimately come out of it that is bigger and more embracing than anything we can possible imagine from today's perspective. That "something" will be a whole evolved conscious entity that is more than the sum of its parts.

This terrifies politicians, who seek to control the Internet, because while there is a free Internet they cannot enslave a society and force it to live by their lies.

But while this new creation was giving them nightmares, a whole new phenomenon jumped up, right on the back of the Internet. I'm talking about what is called "social networking".

These are worldwide groups of people (see Channel 6, tribes and tribing), linked by the Internet. The first of any note was MySpace (www. MySpace.com), where anybody could create themselves a web presence and publish it within a matter of minutes.

This was soon followed by Facebook, which is now the giant of this field. More people visit Facebook every month than visit Google! Facebook ranked as the sixth most trafficked website in the USA with more than 30 billion page views per month. Facebook's growth is still increasing exponentially. As of 2009, Facebook has over 200 million active members. Over half of the users log in at least once a day, to trade chat with their friends, to preen, boast and swap interesting stories.

Then came Twitter and it too went stratospheric. It's far smaller than the other two networks but is growing faster than all the rest combined. It allows only very short messages (140 key characters) and is very suited to this modern, hectic world of instant thought "bites".

Twitter has become such a powerful social phenomenon worldwide, a means for citizens of all nations to rapidly and freely exchange facts (those very truths that politicians abhor), that the Chinese government was force to shut Twitter down, before the people learned they were slaves and a better world lay beyond China's borders.

More recently (2011) a mass demonstration by the population of Egypt was able to oust an unpopular president, Mubarak. It merged that the revolution had been initially fermented on Facebook, with people swapping messages and getting galvanized into action, even before they took to the streets.

That's how powerful social networking is and why I am giving it such emphasis in a treatise on happiness and harmony.

7a Internet Update

Since first writing about Channel 7a, The Worldwide Web (w3) twenty years ago, things have advanced rapidly. I predicted it would change human consciousness. It has done that and more: it has physically united us all across the globe.

Of course the one-world dominion movement, whoever and wherever they are, will not be happy about people freely communicating; it's the very opposite of slavery!

Governments are constantly threatening to "regulate" the Internet, meaning take away its freedom and make it do what they want. China has already shut down parts of the Internet, to prevent its slave-citizens finding out what the world is like beyond its borders. Ousted president Mubarak of Egypt probably wishes he had!

I predict that the first really major move to shut down the free Internet will come from the United States. There have already been threats. The USA has the attitude it owns the Internet, just because most computer and web-based companies are US in origin (Apple, Google, Microsoft, eBay, Facebook, etc.)

The threat to international freedom and accord when this fascist act finally takes place has worried me for a long time. But this morning a new concept emerged for me; it's the combination of the above ideas and something else I've been teaching for years as a doctor.

Life will find a way!
These are (to me) portentous words from the movie Jurassic Park. Mad Doctor Hammond (Richard Attenborough) is trying to control his population of dinosaurs by breeding them dependent on the amino acid lysine. Since they cannot make their own lysine, they cannot breed—or so thinks the naïve Hammond. But Jeff Blom's character, Dr. Ian Malcolm, warns him that it won't work; life will always grow, change, expand, find its way round blockages. It will evolve. Life cannot be contained; it's too clever, too relentless, too ingenious.

And sure enough, the nightmare starts when they find that some of the raptors have learned to breed and reproduce without the lysine. Life will solve its needs somehow.

I take that to be what will happen if ever there is a threat to control or destroy the Internet. All over this planet there are 7 billion clever life forms called Humankind. Many of them are industrious, card-carrying geeks, who will see control as a personal challenge; something to be worked around or overthrown (rather like hackers do now).

Somehow they will come up with a solution, like the movie dinosaurs did. I don't know how it will be solved but I do know this: Life will find a way.

Channel 8 The Biosphere
Responsibility and care for the survival of all living things, the animal kingdom, plants, other vegetative forms, microbes and our interest in the survival of the entire biosphere is our Channel 8. The problem of sustainable ecology now grips the attention of all thinking individuals and we need to get into gear in this Channel quickly, or we may do irreparable harm.

Since 1969 we have all been treated to the privilege of seeing our planet as it looks from space. Logically it ought to make people aware of how fragile and precious it really is. Sadly, this epochal event has produced little change in mankind's attitude overall.

James Lovelock introduced us to the term Gaia, the ancient Greek mother of life for our Earth Mother spirit. This is our 7th Channel.

But it's more subtle than that. Cleve Backster, in 1968, showed that plants and animals respond to human interaction. Plants can sense people and even identify them. Using a simple wheatstone bridge, testing changes in surface resistance (like a lie detector), Backster was able to show that plants reacted to being damaged, as if they were feeling pain.

But they could also identify the individuals who hurt them. Moreover, plants knew when animals were being killed in another building (brine shrimp dropped at random into boiling water).

Plants and humbler animals are quite clearly conscious and perceive, as we do, even though they don't possess a brain or nervous system. That leads to a key concept in Supernoetics™: *non-sensory perception*—Backster used the term primary perception.

Pierre Paul Sauvin, an electronics expert from New Jersey, showed that plants wired to electronic detectors reacted briskly whenever he experimentally hurt himself. Also, at the precise moment he and his girlfriend were having orgasmic sex, in a forest eighty miles away, the plant reaction sent the needles off the dial!

Such phenomena put a different interpretation altogether on our traditional concept of the living world and our part in it. It carries a great deal of responsibility. We are most definitely intertwined and part of the "matrix" of life.

The implications of all this are vast and startling. We are impacting everywhere in our environment. Our sphere of influence travels outwards an unknown distance. In the same way as a field in physics has no boundaries, maybe our Beingness has no limits: we are as vast as the Cosmos we inhabit.

That's what is emerging in Supernoetics™ research.

Channel 9. Physical Reality
When I first wrote this piece, over 20 years ago, I put "physical universe". That, it transpires, was rather naïve. There are probably an infinite number of physical realities. Indeed, advanced Supernoetics™ finds imprints of these on the core memory of every single individual we have come across. More of that in Supernoetics™ Advanced.

Let's just say responsibility and awareness of the workings of our experiential physical reality (whatever it is and however it came about) contains all our heritage and constitution. If you believe, as many teach, that we are here on Earth to learn, you will be upset at the thought of your blackboard and slate being snatched away! (I suppose now I would express this as having all your software wiped by a power source failure).

The husbanding of non-renewable sources of energy and non-destructive commerce is important to our continued existence here.

This Channel stretches to astronomy, cosmology and the origins of the universe, all of which may have as-yet-unguessed consequences for our survival.

You may think it's a bit daft that we should be "responsible" for stars and galaxies that we cannot even reach, never mind take care of. That may be true for the moment but not for long. Some of you, with Supernoetics™ ascension, will be off to look after other worlds in due course.

And don't forget that, if physical reality is a property of consciousness, we are indeed FULLY responsible for the Cosmos. Without us, it won't be there.

This reminds me of a great science fiction story I read over 50 years ago. It was about a grumpy sullen kid, who kept wishing away bits of the physical universe and he did have the powers. The short story picks up where there is just a few small acres of reality left and beyond that, a void, nothing! The frantic parents were doing everything in their power not to upset him, in case he wished away all that was left. But you knew, they couldn't keep it up for long...

In the quantum world, there are strange manifestations which we can hardly grasp, that are taking us to new levels of understanding and, curiously, seem to be wrapping around to come into contact with the phenomenon of consciousness itself.

There is a whole thought school that our Universe must, by definition, have been created by human consciousness. It's called the "anthropocentric" view (Mankind centered). There is abundant evidence in the form of unlikely mathematical formulas, measurements and constants buried in astronomy and physics that strongly imply that if the universe had been created even slightly differently, there would be no conscious life and therefore no knowable Universe!

Big stuff, indeed!

Adaptive Evolution

What does this have to do with "intelligent design"? Nothing. The same would apply whether the Universe was directed by multiple human consciousnesses or a divinity. We can call it creation by "conscious intent". My term is non-doctrinal and does not imply that evolution cannot have taken place and does not rely on the notion that the world was created ready made in an instant by some overarching power.

Adaptive evolution is a new buzzword, referring to the ability of life to renew itself and conquer restrictions. This even includes over-riding inconvenient genes. It happens, so classic genetics is really dead, as is Darwinian evolution.

What this model allows for is that the life force, including consciousness, can design the hereditary future it wants, in response to the environment. The cranky idea of life as just a series of "lucky mutations" is dead forever. It just requires the scientific establishment to catch up with the evidence they have been wrong.

Life—consciousness—controls the world, not math and random events. In just a few words: we created the reality we experience.

Channel 10. Thought Forms and Abstraction
This refers to everything to do with conscious thought and creation. It means the non-material world. It includes abstract ideas, like "history" and "future". Whereas simple animal life is clearly able to make predictions about the future (estimations) based on past experience (memory), it is one of the glories of our conscious Being that we can step outside our experience and see ourselves being ourselves.

We can also think about thinking. We can experience having an experience. Gurdieff and others have noted this and called it witnessing, observing or mindfulness. It is impossible to give too much importance to this ability.

The contents of an encyclopedia are Channel 10.

Continuity and preservation of all forms of thoughts, concepts, art, spirituality and the mystical dimensions is a valid and important channel of being. Shakespeare and Beethoven, for example, certainly survive in some conceptual form today.

That's not to say you have to be a Tolstoy, Michelangelo or Beethoven to have a valid place on the 10th Channel. Far from it. The fact of being a worshipper of the arts more than qualifies you to expression on this channel. Not all football fans need to play football, to justify their interest. Indeed, it is the fan's contribution which keeps the players on the pitch.

Similarly, it is the patrons of art galleries, concerts, rock festivals and such like that pay the artists to go on creating.

The awareness that this is, indeed, a valid channel of being, even by proxy, is a major arousal of interests for many people.

What To Do With All This Knowledge?
From earlier centuries, where the problem was the preservation and
handing on of knowledge to subsequent generations (at least before
printing came along), we have now reached a much greater predic-
ament in the so-called "information over-load" and that so much
knowledge is now accessible that it becomes self-defeating and disruptive to thought continuity and mental health.

Currently, the combined Wikipedias have a total of more than 8 billion words in 19 million articles in approximately 270 languages.
The English Wikipedia alone has over 2 billion words, over 50 times
as many as the next largest English-language encyclopedia, *Ency-
clopædia Britannica*, and more than the enormous 119-volume Span-
ish-language Enciclopedia universal ilustrada europeo-americana.

There are also many online databases which combine several encyclopedias and encyclopedic dictionaries and allow users to search all
of the works simultaneously. For example, the Oxford Reference Online — a combined database of 221 encyclopedias and encyclopedic
dictionaries, offering a total of 1.4 million articles as of 2011, with
expansions planned for the future.

But the largest paper book encyclopedia ever produced is possibly
the *Yongle Encyclopedia*, completed in China in 1407. It consists of
11,095 books, 370 million Chinese characters. That's twelve times
the size of the 20 million word French *Encyclopédie*, the next nearest
rival.

That's a whole lot of consciousness, in just a few channels! People
worry about information overload today but, really, it's been beyond
grasping for many centuries.

Yet all that knowledge comes from one source. The alphabet. 26 squig-
gly symbols we learn as kids.

History, too, belongs in Channel 10. History is a mystical, semi-di-
vine subject for some people, whether that's just Earth history, Cosmic evolution or the Akashik Records. There is a lot to say about this
level but no room here in this introductory piece.

Channel 11. Spirits, Transcendence and Other Realities
Awareness of the possibility and diverse implications of the soul, or
spirit forms, such as are endowed with energies to visit and impact
on us here, both as carnate and discarnate "entities", is part of our
11th Channel. We ourselves, of course, are embodied spiritual enti-

ties. As Teilhard de Chardin wrote, "We are spirits having a human experience and not humans having a spiritual experience."

Here we enter the theatre of shamanism, ghosts and other realities (so-called).

We recognize entities and consciousness particles, which are not necessarily independent beings but certainly "think" and are aware. Torrents of papers and books attest to this phenomenon, even if you are unfamiliar with it.

Unless you come from the Planet Zod (a made up place, so remote that nobody there knows what's going on!), you will be aware we have started thinking of other realities and the spirit world as something very real.

According to physicist Russell Targ, there is no longer the possibility of any reasonable doubt, that phenomena such as ESP exists [*The Reality of ESP. A Physicist's Proof of Psychic Abilities*, Quest Books, Wheaton IL, 2012, p. 12].

Science itself is predicting, instead of contradicting, the possibility of multiple universes, our own doppelganger in other realties and the validity of conscious intention in changing physical reality. What was a concept, a dream, from former times is no longer a metaphysical construct but it's in the world of advanced physics.

Where we are unfamiliar with the mechanism, there is a tendency to regard certain effects as "magic" and be dismissive. However it is sobering to reflect that, to an uneducated tribesman, the workings of a radio set would be "magical".

In our Extreme Mysticism™, and higher advanced Supernoetics™ techniques, you will come face to face with the startling fact that we are all made up of multiple consciousness particles. There is no true "I", just the Being in charge!

It's a world which we feel omnipresent and yet have little direct experience of. That's because it is constantly being drummed into us, from being small children, that it's all nonsense; there are no "ghosts", or fairies, or magicians and romancers.

Those who can reach out to this world are in a decisively stronger position to act out responsible control in this Universe than those who want to pretend there is "nothing out there"!

Channel 11a. The Cosmic Web.
One of the most basic beliefs of shamanism is the belief in the web of power that runs through all things. Shamans believe that everything is alive and is connected in a mutually supportive way to everything else in the world. It is this web of power that brings sense to the world. The web has an unlimited amount of potential and power to send to the physical world.

Today, advanced physics recognizes this semi-mystical phenomenon too. With a grasp of non-locality comes the idea that space is an illusion. What we call "space" is something which unites everything, not something which separates, as considered in classical physics.

The Cosmic Web becomes something that unites all of reality and everything in it. The web is the stuff between the stuff; it's in the gap.

Movie buffs might call it The Force. It certainly contains prodigious power. American physicist the late Richard Feynmen used to say that one cubic metre of this "nothing" contained enough energy to boil all the oceans of the world!

Whatever we are, think or experience depends on everything else in the Cosmos. This is not simply dysfunction, with co-dependence phenomenon. It means All That Is is not an aggregate of parts but a whole from which it is impossible to meaningfully separate any parts. Even if we manage to separate a chunk, studying it will teach nothing of meaning, until we put it back into the whole and study the whole.

That's where modern reductionist science is at fault. Conventional science can never connect with matters spiritual: they have broken the model and then pronounce it non-existent!

However, even cosmologists have now started using the term Cosmic Web. The most widely accepted cosmological theories predict that matter clumps on a larger scale in the so-called "cosmic web," in which galaxies, embedded in filaments stretching between voids, create gigantic wispy structures.

So perhaps physics and metaphysics are eventually going to land on the same page, after all.

Meantime, be a little bit wary of the stock-in-trade guru babble that talks about the "great oneness". In most mouths and texts, I find it to be meaningless, insincere pap. It's the easiest job description in the world: put on an orange robe and start talking about "one-ness"! You'll soon be surrounded by believers and, if you get lucky, you'll be given dozens of Rolls-Royces and billions of dollars (like conjurer and pedophile Sai Baba).

Channel 12. Highest Spiritual Abstraction
Energies directed to connection with the Creator of the Universe or Supreme Being are never wasted! It doesn't matter what you call this Channel (providing you leave others alone and let them call it whatever they want). In Supernoetics™ we make no quasi-religious pronouncements—the 12th Channel, and arguably the most important Channel, is an entirely personal matter.

In fact the best expression for what we are dealing with here—avoiding provocative religious words and intellectual strangle markers—is "highest spiritual abstraction". That sums it up nicely for me and I would ask you to start sharing this frame of reference, rather than get into religious territory with discussions involving Supernoetics™.

Those who claim monopoly of knowledge at this level are not merely psychic monsters of the most stupid kind; they are fools beyond measure!

Speaking of folly, the idea that you can condense down the essentials of Channel 12 to a few statues or "holy" images and a ritualized frozen text from the past is unspeakably nonsensical; yet that is the basis of all religions.

If there were such a "person" as God, he'd laugh his head off at the actions and attitudes perpetrated in "his" name.

If you want to use the word God, I think it best said that God is a state of Being, not an animated, grumpy, vindictive busybody in the sky.

Of course these short cuts are the imaginings of imperfect people who want an easy solution to what is quite a tricky problem; face it: what do we have left when we speak of something beyond all, out of reach of time and space, with infinite knowing and infinite potential?

It's hard for a mere human mind to grasp (though some, I believe, have glimpsed it).

To the Brahmin, all manifestations we call reality and consciousness come out of an underlying ground source which is itself conscious and creative but which we cannot see by looking up at it "from below", so to speak. Knowledge of it comes only from immediate absorption into its state, which is a kind of divine enlightenment

The Christian message confuses things rather by assuming that Man is somehow of lower material or metal than the Creator. The one phrase to rescue from the muddle is that "God created Man in his own image". It doesn't mean he looked like us (which is how it is usually backwards-interpreted). I think it means we are God.

Those who have had near death experiences (NDEs) and returned have reported a state of wonderful, sublime and all-embracing love, into which we are absorbed after death. It's like going home.

Probably we surrender our separateness and identity. I'll let you know, if I go there and figure out a way back! In the meantime, read Anita Moorjani's amazing and insightful book *Dying To Be Me*, in which she described God as a state of being, not a being.

Notice I have repeatedly used the word responsibility. That's because all of these Channels belong to us and we have to look after them. Being uncaring and ignoring them does not make them go away. Trying not to do gardening, you will end up with a jungle plot full of weeds. Nobody is magically going to come and cut your lawn or prune the vegetation if you don't look to it yourself. At least hire a gardener!

Time Out:

Think of an idea or belief you hold. That lies in your first Channel.

Think of something you own, that is personal to you. It belongs in your 2nd Channel of Being.

Have you a sex partner? He or she lies in your third Channel. His or her ability to charm you is a gift from your 3rd Channel!

Think of someone in your family, either offspring or parents, for example. He or she is in your 4th Channel.

Think of a group you belong to, or if there isn't one, consider the country you belong to and its people. That is part of your fifth Channel, and so on...

How Many Channels Is Enough?

Remember, you can add to or subdivide these Channels or self-fulfilment zones as much as you want. However there is little point in complicating matters too much. If you dreamed up fifty channels (present day friends, past boyfriends, former lovers, former bosses, primary school, college frat, and so on...) would hardly have any workable merit either. I think these divisions are about right but you are free to add or take away, providing you can come up with something more empowering (and... please... don't try to force it on me!)

Only extend or reduce the scope of each if it actually benefits you in some way and brings things more clearly into focus while working through things.

Hierarchy or Circles?
These Channels can be looked at in various ways. For example, some people might think of an ascending order hierarchy, a stack, starting with the First Channel and building up from there.

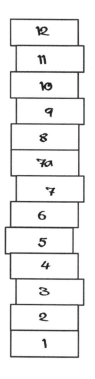

Thus the Second is above the First, the Third over-rides the Second - and so on, with the Twelfth at the top and giving purpose and meaning to it all.

This is a schematic only but from it can be inferred that, taking Life as the overall issue, one's self is not as important as the family and future generations; these in turn are not as important as the group, or the species; which in turn is not as important as all life forms; and so on. There is quite a persuasive logic to this.

Outward From The Centre
Not everyone would see it that way, however. An alternative view is to see the domains as concentric circles. The First is contained within the Second, the Second within the Third, the Third within the Fourth, and so on.

It does seem to portray the idea of growth inherent within these Channels. This also accords very well with the Buddhist set of values concerning Life, whereas the hierarchical view, which is nearer to the Judaeo-Christian attitude, puts the individual down somewhat (though not when followed to the full, as you will see here).

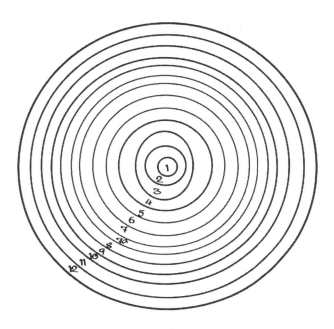

A Wheel or Clock

Perhaps the best insight can be gained from using the model of a wheel, rather like a clock face. The First gives effect to the Second, the Second gives to the Third and soon, round and round the wheel, the Twelfth leading back to the First.

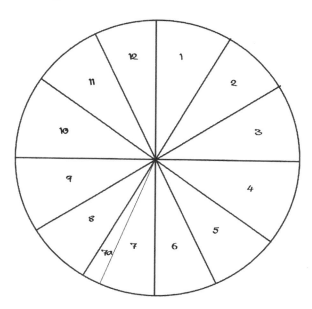

This is the best way I can think of to remind ourselves that the 12th Channel is really the source of our self; our view of the 1st is derived from whatever meaning we ascribe to the 12th and from this flows all others. That's about all there is to religion, really!

Thus everything stems from the 12th Channel - or the 1st - depending on the line of reasoning you use. The 12th Channel is really an image of the 1st and vice versa.

The circular argument itself is a rather nice and tidy logic. As if there was no beginning or end. But the sequence of movement and growth is what it is all about.

Some Concepts Redefined

Right away, this model gives us some novel insights into vexed old questions. Let's take a look:

Sanity

Using the concept of these mental zones or energy channels, it is possible to flood much more light on the definition of optimum behavior and it gives us a clean new definition of sanity. This could be redefined as positive action on all 12 Channels, with no damage or destruction, either through faulty acts or through neglect.

It is obvious that an individual capable of exerting such control over his or her life would be supremely happy. Happiness or Integrated Happy Living, is defined for the first time by these Channels, and it is just about the highest principle of good to which any human being could aspire.

That puts good behavior and happiness in the same place!

Rationality

Supremely rational behavior is defined as someone who is balanced and attaining control, awareness and responsibility in as many Channels as possible. Note again, as I keep saying throughout this work, that happiness, rationality, good behavior, sanity are all different words for the same basic concept: intelligent reasoning.

Right-Wrong

A new way of looking at right and wrong. An act is basically right to the degree as preserves and enhances all Channels and is "wrong" to the degree it damages one or more Channels.

Morality and Ethics
Activity is moral and ethical to the degree it does no damage to these 12 Channels, nor interferes with the balanced functioning of anyone else's 12 Channels.

Since this is cutting edge work in terms of isolation and definition of phenomena, we need now to extend our glossary with two words to cover misdeeds (bad acts). Notice we are not being judgmental by using terms such as "wrong", merely being scientific and calculating the general overall effect of certain types of behavior.

This is a far more precise and less pejorative view of the vexed question of morality.

Transgression
We can now redefine this old biblical word in terms of an individual's Channels. Basically, a transgression is an act of commission or omission that causes harm broadly across the Channels. In other words more Channels are harmed than are enhanced.

Infringement
This is a more subtle degree of incursion and harm towards an individual, family unit or tribe. An infringement means taking over and altering or controlling time, space, objects and energy that are strictly speaking not ours to manipulate in this way. Infringement means taking something away from somebody else. Technical extension: it is almost impossible to even conceive of an act that brought no good in any Channel whatsoever. Good conduct is guided by the computation of the number of Channels helped or harmed and to what degree.

Acts Of Omission Are Just As Deadly
Remember that we are not just talking about committing acts of folly or destructiveness. There are times (many times) when to fail to act is a severe transgression against one or more persons or Channels.

Many people overlook this vital point and fondly believe that if they do nothing at all they are being ethical. But to fail to intervene if you see someone being harmed would be an irrational act. This is what the story of the good Samaritan is all about. To leave someone to suffer a reversal whom you could help is despicable and operates mentally as a transgression, producing the same negative effects as those discussed below.

There are many workaday situations where the same principle of harm by inaction applies. You can probably think up several, though some require debate.

Responsibility In All Domains
Obviously it is important that each and every one of us learns to advance our behavior to the point of optimum rationality, otherwise we may all end up fried by nuclear war, that is, no 7th (or probably 8th) Channel, which would be the greatest conceivable folly and loss of survival.

Those who wish to build such bombs and promote the necessity of nuclear war, you may be sure, have no concept of Channel 7: Mankind. They are thus by my definition here insane, so don't rely on them to realize that if the 7th Channel perishes they'll be gone too.

Terrorists are scary because they don't seem to care if they die or their family is wiped out. There is no concept of good or survival for them; and yet they could bring us all down.

Fight stupidity as hard as you would fight evil... or harder! It's the same thing!

Taking Full Control
Development of awareness and personal growth brings with it a recognition of the need to take responsibility even at government and executive level. It is thus a heavy burden.

I like to quote Plato, who said wryly: One of the penalties for refusing to participate in politics is that you end up being governed by your inferiors.

However we don't start by solving the world's problems at the political level. While we are still personally inept in these matters, we might end up with insane destructive solutions, much as terrorists do.

So we begin where help is much easier.... Channels 1 and 2: self. Don't be apologetic about this. If someone asks you what you are going to do about the world's crisis, you can now tell them that you are going to improve your IQ and ability; sort out your own behaviors and find something better; bring love, wisdom, truth and beauty back into your life and do the same for family and friends and anyone else who wants to join in.

New Age psychology research, backed up by particular scientific studies such as the Japanese monkey miracle, is quite clear that if enough people unite in this way, there will be an almost universal shift in thinking and living.

Now that is morality in its highest, most enjoyable and gratifying sense! That is also, by the way, supremely rational thinking.

Supreme Definition Of Intelligence

Finally, then, we can come to a brilliant and comprehensive definition of the term "intelligence". It has nothing to do with the stupid
fashion of believing that quick mental tests can measure innate com-
putational ability. Intelligence has more to do with problem solving in
life than on an examination sheet.

In Supernoetics™ then, intelligence is a life of full and rational integration of all twelve Channels, with maximum positive performance
and best outcomes on each. I repeat: you do not need to spend 1/12th
of your time on each Channel to be "balanced". Indeed, you should be
24/7 on Channels 1 and 12!

For certain reproductive years, you should ride hard on 3 and 4 and
then slack off for the Third Age of life!

9a. The 12 Channels Hacks

Definition: hack (current high-level slang); a clever solution to a tricky problem; to hack is to modify or change something in an extraordinary and useful way.

A hack, an ingenious series of steps or manouvers, designed to bring about a beneficial change, whether in learning, mind control, health etc. for example, a practise exercise, a trick or shortcut. It is a positive and helpful short-range technique or strategy.

[This use is not connected with hacking (computer intrusion and piracy); or horse riding; or a corny writer].

1. Be able to name faultlessly from memory each Channel number and name.

2. Write up in your own words what abundance on each Channel would look like.

3. Write yourself a short essay (500 words minimum): Explain how plant life would fit on the 12 Channels. Do they have a 1st, 2nd, 9th etc.?

4. Pick 3 – 4 people you know well and measure them against Channel: how is he or she doing on each?

5. When you are ready, find a willing stranger to do this with (NOT a family member or friends, there is too much chance of being judgmental). Sit down with them and explain the 12 Channels, emphasizing as much as you can remember about the benefits of such a thought structure.

6. Finally, estimate yourself against all 12 Channels, as honestly as you can. Pinpoint one aspect of one weak Channel you could strengthen... and DO it!

10. The King Of All Communications

Ask anyone what is the most powerful mode of communication and many would come up with telepathy: it's redolent with magic and spiritual dimensions. Maybe others would opt for music; that certainly moves us, heart and soul; it's powerful stuff all right. But actually, humble everyday *touch* is the unequalled king of all communications!

The sense of touch is visceral, immediate, and memorable. When you touch someone or something, you have a direct physical connection between yourself and the person or thing - impossible with written words, images or video. What's more, it's fast - you can transfer a lot of information in just a few seconds, which you can't by talking about yourself or your feelings!

For all our reticence about touching, especially with strangers, touch can enable us to communicate our feelings with an astonishing accuracy. Whereas visually the only really reliable emotion that can be identified is joy or delight, participants in a 2009 scientific trial run by psychologist Matthew Hertenstein of DePauw University were able to communicate eight distinct emotions - anger, fear, disgust, love, gratitude, sympathy, happiness, and sadness - with accuracy rates as high as 78 percent, using touch.

Touch and Accord
Touch is rightly important in our Supernoetics™ Constellation of Accord (chapter 8). This powerful intellectual property of ours brings together, in a dazzling formation of stars, all the workable elements of accord between people.

Touch would indeed be a key form of communication. But students of advanced knowledge and understanding will quickly see that it also nestles rather nicely alongside the attachment theory and is part of what we call togetherness, closeness or - to give it its technical term - propinquity.

Touch is for greeting, touch is for harmony, touch is for love and touch is very much for healing. This powerful communication modality is so important that many peoples consider it an important act of devotion to merely touch an advanced spiritual being. Indeed, merely touching the hem of his or her robe is considered sufficient to pass on a blessing and distribute some healing force.

I hope some day members of our Supernoetics™ tribe will evolve a simple but elegant form of touch greeting, by which we can share our values of love, wisdom, strength and giving care to others. In the meantime, a well-meant hug communicates volumes of compassion and connectedness.

Spiritual Powers

Touch may seem a very down to earth, humble, mechanical means of interchange between individuals. But it does have very powerful spiritual dimensions too. Touch is sacred and should be cherished as such.

Stories of divine miracles often rely on touch. Christian healing stories of this genre, such as Jesus reviving the dead, are well-known in the West. However there are many other similar tales of magical touch in other cultures and religions.

The context may not even require religious overtones, just intense love. The revival of dead baby Ogg is well documented. Jamie Ogg was born premature at 27 weeks in 2010, pronounced dead, but then revived simply by his mother's touch. As mother Kate Ogg bid her son a sad goodbye, she hugged and soothed him, telling him his twin sister Emily was fine and that she loved him.

Five minutes later, the couple noticed their son gasping for air. He revived in full and grew to a normal life. This is an example of what today is called "kangaroo care" of premature babies; a reflection of the marsupial nurturing pouch of the mother.

New research is undermining old and wretched "scientific" notions, like the no-touch rule for premature babies. Gentle massage of preemies in their incubator has been found to reduce mortality and help them grow normally and develop along balanced functional lines.

Mother's Touch

Touch is our first language.

We begin receiving tactile signals even before birth, as the vibration of our mother's heartbeat is amplified by amniotic fluid. Her voice is the first human communications we hear, even though we don't understand the language as yet. It's just a reverberation in the waters.

Mother has many other body sensations too which transmit to the fetus, from breaking wind to sexual arousal. The developing fetus gets it all!

This symphony of maternal sounds becomes part of our Eigen resonance field, our own personal store of energies and vibrations. The Eigen field defines our physical self and what we experience.

After birth, a mother's touch enhances attachment between mother and child; it can signify security ("You're safe; I'm here") and, depending on the type of touch, it can generate positive or negative emotions. Positive touch interactions can include games; negative might mean a warning or alert signaled by mother's firm touch.

Everyone knows that mother's touch is soothing and healing, when in pain or sick.

University of Miami School of Medicine's Tiffany Field, director of the Touch Research Institute, has linked mother's touch to a slew of benefits, including better sleep, reduced irritability, and increased sociability among infants - as well as improved growth of preemies.

Of course there are recognized benefits from father's touch too.

One of the key physiological phenomena behind gentle touch is the release of the "cuddle hormone", oxytocin. It's a two-way traffic; the one touching receives a similar hormone "dose" to the one being touched. Studies have shown that a person giving a hug gets just as much benefit as a person being hugged.

Touch Against Fear and Anxiety
In a series of classic experiments, Jim Coan, a neuroscientist at Virginia University, ran brain scans of married women subjected to strong pain. The women were stressed, of course, even though this was a voluntary experience. But as soon as the women touched the hands of their husbands, there was an instant drop in activity in the areas of the brain involved in fear, danger, and threat. The women reported feeling calmer and less stressed, as soon as they felt a familiar touch.

There was a similar, but smaller, effect triggered by the touch of strangers. But help from strangers can be very striking indeed. Ayana Byrd, writing in *Good Housekeeping* magazine, tells a great story:

Though her passport is full of stamps, Ayana describes herself as the coward of all fliers. For years, every trip involved her taking herbal sedatives, followed by half a sleeping pill as soon as she boarded, followed by a drink of wine to nudge things along. The worst flight of her life was a 90-minute ride in a rickety, about-to-fall-out-of-the-sky plane in South Africa.

As she sat in her turbulence-rattled seat and wept, sure that everyone onboard was going to die, a stranger saw her, went over, and said she could hold her hand until she (Ayana) felt better. The stranger probably didn't think that would be for the entire flight, but it was! Ayana couldn't let go. The stranger's soft skin and firm grip left her feeling more at ease than she'd ever been on a plane.

Here's the good part: now, amazingly, all it takes to keep Ayana calm on flights is remembering that stranger's touch. No more sleeping pills.

http://www.goodhousekeeping.com/author/3919/ayana-byrd/

Touch is a key component of very many traditional healing arts, from Reiki to acupressure; massage to reflexology; and is being increasingly studied in mainstream medicine. Clinical trials show symptom benefits in a number of areas, from asthma and high blood pressure to migraine and childhood diabetes. Other research findings hint that not only does touch lower stress levels, but that it can boost the immune system and halt or slow the progress of disease.

Professor Edzard Ernst, former professor of complementary medicine at the University of Exeter, revealed his widespread ignorance and foolishness when he claimed that the power of touch is all down to the placebo effect. It is very much mind over matter, he has claimed. It has nothing to with the sensation of being touched; it is the expectation and the context of the intervention, rather than the specific effect of that intervention. Yet he produces absolutely NO evidence, data or figures for his ridiculous claim, which flies in the face of current scientific discovery.

But then, windbag Ernst has always put his own narrow-minded opinions in front of valid science. Still, you will sometimes see the old duffer quoted in this.

Social Codes
It seems remarkable, given its powers to connect, that touch is bordering on a social taboo. We are allowed to shake hands with strangers; that's a way of relaxing the touch codes. We are given limited permission to put our arms around someone, slap them on the back or touch their hand or cheek. After that, you may face accusations of

harassment or even molestation. Be careful. Most so-called harassment cases are based upon touch that was not welcomed.

The proverbial handshake is actually a good opener. It's one of the few situations in which it's OK to make prolonged contact with a stranger. Therefore it is an important opportunity for sending and receiving signals. A limp handshake signifies uncertainty, low enthusiasm or introversion. On the other hand, a vice-like grip is not a good alternative; it might signal you are trying to dominate, or that you are crudely unaware of other's discomfort, neither of which are welcome roles to play.

A firm but relaxed grasp is the aim, showing you are a person of natural warmth, not over the top, or holding back. Touching anywhere from the shoulder down to the hands is OK, as for example holding the elbow with the opposite hand while you shake.

Two adults holding hands is a singular gesture, but it takes its meaning from context. We are accustomed to it as a sign of intimacy in a couple, beyond mere friendship. But if you have spent time in Arab countries, like I have, you will soon be aware that adult men holding hands is a normal and very common gesture of friendship. They walk along lost in conversation, while engaged in this particular act of touch. What tends to make us squirm is, to them, perfectly accepted behavior that does not usually imply sexual closeness.

Of course, if you add prolonged gaze or certain other signals, then touch can transform to being sexual very quickly.

Let me next give an escalating code of touch in pursuit of intimacy between lovers.

12 Degrees of Intimate Touch Contact
These come from British zoologist and best-selling author Desmond Morris, published in his 1971 book *Intimate Behavior: A Zoologist's Classic Study of Human Intimacy*. Note that after the first 3 stages, all further steps towards intimacy are based on touch.

1. Eye to body.
One visually sizes up a potential mate.

2. Eye to eye.
The couple attempt to make eye contact. If the other averts their gaze, that's pulling away. The attempts may be repeated but eventually will lead to sundering.

3. Voice to voice.
The next step is to strike up a conversation. If that goes well, sooner or later it moves to...

4. Hand to hand (or arm).
The very first step in physical contact is usually simple and not socially challenging. Allowing someone to touch is a measure of trust.

5. Arm to shoulder.
Putting an arm around the other's shoulder is more significant. It implies possession or bonding; it's a "mine" gesture to others.

6. Arm to waist, or back.
This is not so much a signal for others as a signal to the desired. The active partner is saying, "I want you." Arms around the waist show a growing familiarity and comfort in the relationship.

7. Mouth to mouth.
Kissing. This is the big milestone in deepening a relationship. Mixing body fluids, as they call it, is immediately more intimate. Note that for some races, rubbing noses is considered every bit as intimate.

8. Hand to head.
Either partner can take the lead. Allowing someone to touch one's head shows a deepening trust. The head is perceived as "me" and is an intimate object, second only to the sexual areas.

9. Hand to body.
This step moves the couple into the beginnings of foreplay. It soon takes on erotic overtones, even without touching sexual areas. For some women, for example, to be stroked on the shoulder or nuzzled on the ear lobe is a very powerful turn on; more so than having the breasts fondled.

10. Mouth to breast.
No mistaking this stage. It's sexual. It's still possible for the woman to pull back, although this is another step along the foreplay route.

11. Hand to genitals.
This is probably the point of no turning back. The commitment has been made. If the woman does change her mind, it will be very frustrating for the male. It's also likely to label the woman as a "tease", if she allows it and then withdraws the privilege.

12. Genitals to genitals.

Bang. - All the way. This is the sex act. We all know it has a wonderful sensual touch quality that arouses special sensations that are powerful, yet attractive.

Let me repeat: 4 – 12 are all about degrees of touch. Touch is the music, our bodies the instrument.

Touch Accord

When I was living in Spain, back in the 1990s, I developed a system of healing that I called "Touch-Harmony". Today, I'm sure I would have named it Touch-Accord, in line with the Supernoetics™ Constellation of Accord. I'd like to share some of those thoughts with you here, which seem to me as fresh and appropriate as when I wrote them:

We all touch too little. Some people don't like to touch at all. Contact with their fellow beings has become so remote and uncomfortable that it is no longer welcome.

Yet, if we are touched, we access such a strong bond, a feeling of love and belonging that it becomes automatically safe to talk, to open up, and share.

It is a wonder to me, as a busy working physician, that my colleagues - especially those in the field of psychiatry - have not tumbled to this wonderful simple truth of human interchange. How many patients would not feel calmed and soothed if the physician in charge took their hand and held it a while, gazing warmly into the patient's eyes?

It's so obvious; kids know it! Yet, as adults, we get too sophisticated, too hedged around with complicated social rules, that we forget who we are. We drift out of touch.

You see, we even have an expression "out of touch", meaning to be no longer mutually aware of each other's existence. We have another expression "touching", which means that something has tugged at the heartstrings.

So you see the idea of physical contact is central to issues such as love, emotion and sharing experience.

Some Curious Science

Touch is a means of generating energy. It takes two poles, like a battery, to create a current and so it is with the magic of rapport between two people. Take one individual and there is potential; add another and there is an effect. Energy begins to flow when there are two poles; one is not enough.

Now sexuality is also, it happens, bipolar.

There is a peculiar kind of energy between men and women. The basic flow is not - need not be - sexual. But it has definite positive and negative qualities; male and female; yin and yang in Chinese philosophy. It could be said that each aspect of this inter-relationship is incomplete without the other, the complementary half. Put another way, yin makes yang; feminine makes masculine (and vice versa).

What I found with Touch-Harmony is that we can utilize this gift of bipolarity from Nature with great effect. The Touch-Harmony conversations, because they cross the gender gap, have a power and a depth that would not otherwise come about. As a simple illustration of this point, think of a woman who wants to complain about her husband's faults. Now suppose she grumbles to other women: well, it doesn't change her feelings much, because this woman-to-woman grumbling has been going on since the dawn of time and manifestly achieves little. Indeed, it can often reinforce the problems, since other the women are having a bad experience too. They will tend to solidify each others' complaints.

But if that woman talks to a man, particularly one who listens sensitively, everything changes. He isn't the same energy and psychological mold as her. In fact he's the opposite or complementary type.

This concept of complementary is important... It's polarity at work.

The uniting of the strengths of men and women is one of the key features of this method that makes it so successful. The man can joke, or talk back and this often leads to a liberating shift of perspective. This change in viewpoint can be decisive. Any problem viewed from a different angle will seem less menacing and daunting.

In fact, if you can see things in an altogether new light, you'll probably laugh yourself at the absurdity of some of your fears and hates.

It so happens that the vast majority of patients who sought the unique benefits of Touch-Harmony were women. That is not (necessarily) because they suffer more. It really reflects the fact that women tend to look at personal issues more frankly and honestly; whereas men try to avoid things by shutting them out and pretending nothing is wrong.

The fact is that any man who wants to come to terms with his "Inner Male" and is willing to talk openly and freely, will benefit just as much from Touch-Harmony. All the above remarks about gender complementarity apply in full.

But for a woman, there was something special in this: she could make a friend in a warm and relaxing touch relationship with a man who has learned to shut up and listen to her, without interrupting and without targeting her sexually in any way!

All practitioners are vetted and medically supervised. A therapy couch is used and a light state of undress is required, to facilitate adequate skin contact. But there is nothing suggestive or compromising; nothing is done that wouldn't be done in front a group of friends (apart from the sacrifice of privacy).

This technique is not massage as such. It is pretty much what is says: touch to open up the mental pathways and gradually, over the weeks, to create a new sense of well-being, harmony and freedom.

Touch Healing

Touch probably comes into to its own in the field of healing. Nothing is quite so restorative as the touch of another beloved person or a person who is physically well and carries prosperous energies.

Heck, even animals can heal with their touch. It's become big business today; doctors and practitioners will even prescribe the companionship of a cat or dog; even a cheerful parrot has something to offer (reptiles and fish don't quite cut it!)

In Supernoetics™ we take this healing aspect of touch far beyond normal boundaries and discover some almost magical techniques for healing and restoration.

In the 1970s I was an examiner for The St John Ambulance Brigade in Manchester, UK. I would give the first-aiders their final test; most were very good indeed. Invariably, I took the opportunity to hand out an info card, detailing each of the following remedies. First aiders are uniquely placed to use them to bring almost instant calming and relief.

Each is about touch as a form of solid communication.

Feel My Hands

As everyone knows, holding an injured part is comforting. If a special person holds it for you, that's even better!

We can adapt this simple property to get remarkable results. If a person is hurt or injured, and in pain, you can put your hand(s) in contact with his or her body and ask them to "feel" your hand(s).

Get all the first aid stuff out of the way first: removal from danger, sitting or lying safely, stop the bleeding, a Band-Aid, splints or bandages and so forth. Call an ambulance if you have to. Oh, and get rid of waste-of-space bystanders. Then do Feel My Hands.

Take control and with a reassuring, calm voice, touch the patient's body with one or both hands (both is better) and say, "Feel my hand(s)." Get a reply that tells you the patient is cooperating and acknowledge. Then move your hands to another position and repeat the command, "Feel my hand(s)," etc.

Work around but not directly on the injured part; avoid any touch which would intensify the pain. If the person is apprehensive because of this, you can begin on a distant part of the body, and then gradually work towards the injured area. Let him or her gain assurance that the soothing of pain is the aim, not provocation of the injury.

Really, the target is not the injured limb or zone, so don't get obsessed with that. The real target is the neurological system and connective tissues of the whole body. You are re-establishing the patient's communication with their own body, using touch as a cue. It's actually reconnecting the person's sensorium.

You see, when a part is injured, the body tends to shut it off. Witness, for example, the fact that a broken or shattered limb is, at first, quite numb. All nerve messages are closed down; the patient feels little or nothing. Blood vessels are sealed, to prevent blood loss. Only gradually are the nerve conduction and circulation pathways re-opened. The full pain may not come on for several hours, after a severe injury.

To stimulate this re-opening of communication pathways, make a point of placing your hands distal (further from the head) than the injured part. That way the body is coaxed into "looking" beyond the injury and so opening up the networks.

Another important point is to work on both sides of the body equally. It is wrong to think pain affects only the injured part: pain rides as a shockwave throughout the entire body, including crossing over to the other side in a sort of mirror effect. Moreover it resonates backwards and forwards, several times, like a swinging gate, before it settles down. Pain is technically called a standing wave.

Sometimes you may not even be able to get at the injured part; it could be covered in bandages, a splint or a cast. In which case work diligently on the site of the injury but on the opposite side of the body. You be amazed how well this works.

God forbid; if someone has lost a limb or part, you can still heal and reduce the pain, by working on the identical limb or part on the opposite side.

Stay in communication with the person. Listen to his or her responses and acknowledge them - don't ignore what he or she is saying, even if it sounds silly.

Finally, the really skilled Supernoetics™ trained person will take up each squirm, gasp or groan as if it was a verbal communication and ask, "What's happening?"

You can stop when he or she reports being more comfortable. 30 – 60 minutes is about right. Stop if he or she starts laughing it off; the pain has probably all but gone!

Applications: sprains, fractures, cuts and tears, blows, dental work, falls, scuffs and puncture wounds. Remember your usual head injury warnings.

Hands Sweeping Remedy
This is one I developed during experiments with my first wife Pauline, who was a very fine nurse. Working together, we found that using our hands to sweep over a person's body can make him or her feel better, calmer and more harmonious. It can even "sweep away" pain.

We theorized that it was about aligning turbulent energies around the person's body. The general rule in health and healing is that turbulence is bad, alignment is good.

Have him or her lie on a bed, sofa or therapists couch. No degree of undress is required. Tell him or her to shut their eyes and relax.

Start with the person prone (face down) and work on the shoulders, back, buttocks and legs. Take both your hands and sweep along the body. Try to imagine they are covered in mud or jello and you are trying to wipe it away. That will give you the right sort of motion.

It is a sort of cleansing motion and it's a cleansing effect we are trying for.

Note this is a whole body technique. Don't just concentrate on a part. Turn him or her to the supine position (on their back) and repeat the whole process.

This one is quick: 10 – 15 minutes produces fast change; then it fades away. Not much to be gained by going on and on at it.

Applications: fatigue, upset, confusion, ailments, malaise, fever, tooth and jaw pain, earache, emotional storms, sickly part and discomfort short of pain. It's also good for bellyache but you must remember the dangers of the "acute abdomen" (severe bellyache can denote serious, even life-threatening complaints).

Touch The Spot

Again this healing is based directly on the effect of touch. There is an old, old philosophical principle in healing, which is to return to the exact spot where you were hurt and re-enact the injury.

Be sensible, of course, and if the part that hurt a person was a hot stove or object, make sure it is cooled before he or she re-contacts it. If it is basically soiled or unhygienic, clean it up first!

Otherwise this touch remedy is very simple. Have the person adopt the exact position they were in when the physical universe struck them. Get them to make the exact movement they were doing at the time, though much slower, so they don't smack themselves against the hard object a second time!

Very gently, he or she searches for the exact spot they were touched when they were hurt and the exact spot that touched them. Meaning: the exact spot on their person is placed against the exact spot in the physical universe. He or she will always know, because a sharp pain will appear and then fly off.

It's gone; it won't come back. That's it; end of remedy. It sometimes takes just a few seconds. Stop when the pain makes its appearance and then disappears. To keep doing it serves no further benefit. This is a quick remedy.

Again, it relies on the powerful properties of touch.

Applications: blows, injuries, burns, accidentally hitting one's self with an object (like a hammer), anything impact (like whacking your head on a door or beam), electric shocks (with the current turned OFF, obviously).

Miscellany

That concludes my review of touch and touch therapies. You will readily see why I bill it as The King Of All Communications. Nothing is quite like touch.

A person can fool you with words or gestures. But this knocks so-called "body language" into a cocked hat. Touch is real, present and can't be dissembled. It is, in truth, the only way you are really going to know what a person is thinking.

It's powerful and positive. If you hold someone's hand while you talk to them, you can stoke up the meaning and level of rapport quite easily.

I recommend, if you are dealing with a crash of accord (an upset or quarrel), that you take the other person's hand while you talk. Don't resist the gesture, if you are asked to do this.

Touch appears over and over in our lives as something enriching, educational, soothing and purposive. Women will report the especially pleasant feelings of having their hair brushed or mussed, of having fingernails polished and toenails clipped.

Men don't get enough of this sort of rapport and we need more. Something is lacking in just the touch of a fishing rod, carpenter's tools, wood or metal! It's sensualist but not really about accord.

There is no question: if you want to make someone feel good, love you more and stay in rich harmony, then you should include plenty of touching.

My wife Vivien heals me in bed virtually every night, prior to sleep, and I can extol its powerful virtues. By "healing" I mean she gets into communication with Higher Power and passes this rapture into my tired body, by means of stroking and loving touch. I'd like to think my medical wisdom has something to do with my Peter Pan days but I'm sure that this nightly ritual, too, adds to my years of pleasure and vigor on this Earth.

Thank you, Beloved.

11. The Scale Of Emotional Health

Here's a brilliant piece by my colleague Jon Whale. It's from his wonderful book *Naked Spirit: The Supernatural Odyssey* (Clear Lotus Publishing, Long Beach, CA, 2008).

The idea of arranging emotions in a hierarchy is not new. But this easy-reading shorthand gives you a good spectrum of degrees, from people in pretty bad shape, all the way up to those in sacred bliss.

Where do you fit, generally? Ah, that's a BIG question! Wherever it is, just remember Supernoetics™ can move you upwards pretty quickly...

The scale is based on the Supernoetics™ *Emotional Ladder* but this quick short hand is a great way to be introduced to this very important concept. Emotions are crucial to our lives and thinking. Emotions are a kind of marker; a way of thinking about things. Once an emotional response is attached to a particular person or concept and gets settled onto the body-mind system, these emotional reactions seem to work all on their own.

Often we don't know why a particular emotion arises within us. That makes emotions tricky to manage and, in fact, quite damaging and dangerous.

Individuals who inhabit the upper positive levels of emotional health can employ or drop into any level including the negative levels if required to do so. They will only stay there just as long as they need to achieve a solution. The negative levels can be chronic, i.e. long-standing. Anyone who habituates to any of them may find it arduous to find authentic help or techniques to rise to the higher, positive levels. They are often trapped in the chronic negative levels for the duration of their life.

Nevertheless, using this map, many of you will be able to pinpoint your location and that of family, friends and acquaintances. Read it carefully and try to decide where you are, mostly, and where certain of your friends and family sit!

It starts at the bottom, with the lowest level of emotional health, shown here overleaf to the far left at -5 (apathy, despondency, mis-

Supernoetics™ Scale of Emotional Health

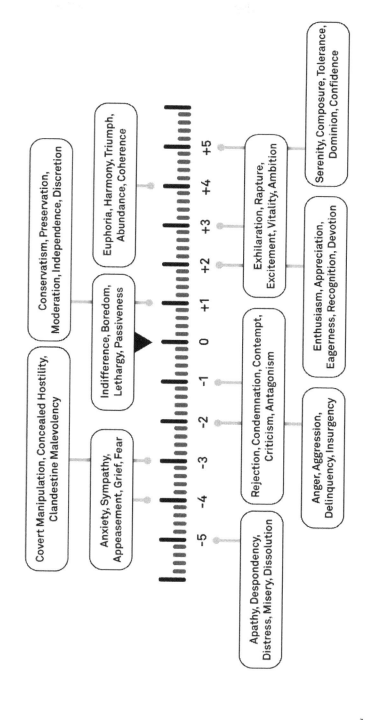

Covert Manipulation, Concealed Hostility, Clandestine Malevolency

Conservatism, Preservation, Moderation, Independence, Discretion

Euphoria, Harmony, Triumph, Abundance, Coherence

Anxiety, Sympathy, Appeasement, Grief, Fear

Indifference, Boredom, Lethargy, Passiveness

Exhilaration, Rapture, Excitement, Vitality, Ambition

Serenity, Composure, Tolerance, Dominion, Confidence

Rejection, Condemnation, Contempt, Criticism, Antagonism

Enthusiasm, Appreciation, Eagerness, Recognition, Devotion

Apathy, Despondency, Distress, Misery, Dissolution

Anger, Aggression, Delinquency, Insurgency

-5 -4 -3 -2 -1 0 +1 +2 +3 +4 +5

Created for Supernoetics™ by Jon Whale, Seaton, Devon, UK. Copyright © 2015

117

ery, etc.) and goes all the way to +5 on the right (serenity, composure, confidence, etc.) The main characteristics of a person at each level are listed.

Negative Minus 5. Apathy, Despondency, Distress, Misery, Dissolution

This is the lowest level of emotional health.

All emotions are turned off or chemically attenuated (drugs, etc.)

The core of antisocial behavior.

Many are drug addicts, alcoholics, compulsive gamblers, suicidal psychotics, vagrants, petty drug dealers and lawbreakers, failures, bankrupts, social dependents, institutionalized inmates, the minimalist, or apathetic intellectuals.

They see no point in owning anything, run up debts, which are seldom paid

Allow property and possessions to decay.

Feel helpless and unable to care for themselves.

Slowly self-destruct, bringing down everyone around them.

Rely on handouts and charity.

Never improve, keep making the same mistakes.

Are often actively supported and subsidized by individuals low on the scale at Negative Minus 4.

They are fed up with life, the world and society, which are to them superficial and no longer interesting.

Negative Minus 4. Anxiety, Sympathy, Appeasement, Grief, Fear

In deep fear.

Here individuals and groups smother creativity and enthusiasm by using pseudo-kindness, leniency, sympathy and generosity.

This creates, and fosters in others, the lowest negative

They collect and help losers, the sick, down and outs or good causes for the purpose of using them to demonstrate their merciful and compassionate generosity and good intentions.

These self-righteous strategies are used to induce feelings of guilt and shame in people of higher positive emotional levels.

They have an overwhelming fear of hurting others and they never turn their back on anyone they deem is in need.

They provide infinite justifications for failure, they presume nobody is all bad and always give the benefit of the doubt.

Pampering everyone, waiting on them, doing favors for them, refusing to accept anything in return, they prevent unfortunate individuals from regaining self reliance, self worth and dignity.

Their children are treated in exactly the same way. This results in those children wanting continual sympathetic attention and so they are always crying, screaming, fighting, or throwing tantrums to get it, never learning to entertain nor educate themselves.

They cling to sentimentality, grief and pain to protect themselves and attract pity, sympathy and empathy.

They constantly worry about health, accidents, crime and disasters.

Paranoid and suspicious, nearly everything is threatening: germs, disease and criminals are just around every corner waiting to strike.

So they never take chances and are too careful as they never know what might happen.

Life has treated them terribly, they whine, are melancholic, dwell in the past, feel betrayed.

Everything is painful. No money, no job and nobody loves them.

They are afraid of hurting others and are caught in indecision.

Show blind loyalty and compulsive agreement.

Negative Minus 3. Covert Manipulation, Concealed Hostility, Sneaky, Sly
Hidden malevolency.

This is probably the most populated chronic emotional level in these turbulent times.

Problem: difficult to immediately assess that they are in this category; only time reveals this to individuals higher on the scale as their game strategy unfolds.

Those in chronic grief and apathy (Negative Minus 3 and 4), never comprehend their strategies.

Always present a cheerful facade, often with a nervous laugh and constant smile.

Appear calm, pleasant and resourceful.

Seem to be sympathetically or morally concerned in politely asking probing personal questions about you, your work, your relationships, your sex life, your politics or your religion.

Their anger remains invisible, yet they are petrified of anyone in anger.

Jealous and extremely dangerous.

Cruel cowards.

Manipulative, they engage in gossip readily but have no qualm in covertly twisting facts around, to knife into the back whenever, wherever and to whomever they can.

When confronted, they change the subject to move away from the point and are always rewriting history or changing the truth about past events to suit their current position. They will do and say anything to avoid exposure.

Through their appearance, words, propaganda or advertising they present themselves, their services or products as being 'so nice, so charming, so condescending and so helpful'.

For objectives that they are too lazy or fearful to undertake themselves, they covertly manipulate and subjugate individuals above and below them on the scale to do their bidding and dirty work.

Their targets are any individual, family, tribe, company or nation that they consider high on the scale and therefore a threat (e.g. +3s, +4s etc.), attempting to bring them down to chronic appeasement, grief and apathy (Minus 4 and Minus 5)

They have little time for children unless they can use them as an introduction or a weapon for manipulation towards their strategy of introverting others down to Negative Minus 3 and Minus 4. They would like everyone on the planet at this level, so they can feel power.

Their unstated aim is to cause ruin, discredit achievements and split up relationships.

At this they can be very successful and gloat when their victims go down into the lower chronic levels of Negative Minus 4 and 5.

Males at this level subconsciously know their fearful limitations. They can be slothful, but have a need to control and suppress women down to the -4 and -5 levels so that they can feel secure in their sexuality, (as also happens in males at -1 and -2).

Males at this level occupying influential or powerful offices can instigate acts of terrorism and war.

You could never trust anyone at this level with your health, your money, your reputation, your safety, your husband, your wife, your children, your business, your company, your country, or this planet.

Negative Minus 2. Anger, Aggression, Delinquency, Insurgency
Individuals at this chronic level are consumed with animosity towards others and are furious.

They dominate and intimidate others into submission and obedience.

They blame everyone else for their problems.

They collect grudges to justify their anger and dump them on anyone or anything that passes their way.

They destroy property, social conveniences and lives.

Everyone they meet is wrong or obstructing their ambitions.

Expressing no kindness, no consideration, being blatantly dishonest and disloyal, they lie, use intimidation and ambiguity to destroy creativity and satisfaction

They cause sabotage by deliberately instigating situations or circumstances where others will fail; afterwards they accept no blame, excuse or explanation.

They handle children by tyranny, sometimes with brutal punishment to force them, by means of pain, into what they want.

Not being interested in any viewpoints unless it reinforces their position, they do not listen and continually interrupt others' discussions.

Negative Minus 1. Rejection, Condemnation, Contempt, Criticism, Antagonism

Interacting with a person that habituates this level can be amusing for a short time, any longer and it can become boring or enraging.

They enjoy, even laugh at, the misfortune of others and never play for the pleasure.

They want to dominate every activity involving others.

Being resentful and mocking, their subsistence depends on finding and engaging a contestant.

Children are there for them to torment and provoke.

They are insensitive, undiplomatic and unsporting.

They love to argue and dispute everything and get a kick out of reducing others to acute anger and lower.

They never listen, continually interrupt, never permitting the other person to establish their point.

They twist facts to defend and satisfy their own reality, doing their utmost to sabotage the position of others.

They do not listen and continually interrupt others' discussions.

Neutral 0.0 Indifference, Boredom, Ambivalence, Lethargy, Passiveness

They are observers being indifferent, mildly pleasant, inoffensive, purposeless and unconcerned about any issue.

Everything is too much trouble.

With poor concentration and no ambition, they never achieve any outstanding feat.

Not having any purpose, being lazy and careless, neither content nor discontent, they are not particularly helpful and never intimidating.

Like all of the lower negative levels, they want more affluence but cannot consent to own much.

Largely unnoticed, they amble along stuck at some routine job never upsetting anyone and are accepted by most people.

Positive Plus 1. Cautious Approval, Preservation, Moderation, Discretion

The conformist, reticent individual who considers everything with careful deliberation.

They demand proof before believing or acting.

They invariably take the soft, safe option to maintain contentment and rely on the authorities to protect them and do their prosecuting.

They resist change and discourage exploration and innovation.

They are not very tolerant of others in the chronic negative levels, insisting that laws should be made to contain them.

Positive Plus 2. Enthusiasm, Appreciation, Eagerness, Recognition, Devotion

The genuinely helpful and constructive active person with good personal conviction.

They have a quiet sense of wellbeing and look forward to the day's activities and work.

They can express a wide range of emotions when called for.

Although not yet a leader, not wanting to take sides, they are active people who inspire others to action.

Are always willing to accept more responsibility towards a larger horizon.

They like a good standard of living.

They can spend time with the low emotional levels of people without getting depressed, compulsively sympathetic or exhausted.

Positive Plus 3. Exhilaration, Rapture, Excitement, Vitality, Ambition

Charismatic personality.

Attract people without effort.

Loved by almost everyone.

Can maintain a strong, sustained interest in their subjects.

Preoccupied with involvement and creativity, they never start something and give in easily.

They are not grasping nor greedy, but are not afraid of possessions.

Not able to tolerate gossip or defamation.

They expect honest facts and, if not forthcoming, they cease communication.

They dislike generalities, insinuations and assumptions.

Have broad spectrum and novel interests.

They can conceive influential plans and ideas that thrust toward a better future for themselves and others.

For them making a fortune is easy and can normally embrace abundant ambitions for survival.

Positive Plus 4. Euphoria, Harmony, Triumph, Abundance, Coherence

These individuals believe and respect the rights of others.

Honesty, affection, ethics, trustworthy, diplomatic, confidential, discrete, discriminating, communicative, are some of the credits of this level.

They do not interfere with or damage others' lives, business or personal affairs, being more concerned about the survival and future of society and the environment.

Always striving for higher standards for people at lower levels on the scale, they listen to others and understand them easily and can help low level people upwards, without being critical or derogatory.

Enjoying and encouraging children to express themselves, they care for their mental and physical well being.

Positive Plus 5. Serenity, Composure, Tolerance, Dominion Confidence

This is and beyod the highest emotional level.

The benevolent hero and champion.

Individuals at this level are rare and priceless.

They can look at new ideas, change viewpoints, being intuitively spontaneous, light-hearted and humorous.

Neither modest nor egotistical, avoiding snooping and investigation.

They know their abilities and what they are worth.

They like themselves and do not care what others think.

They can follow orders but under no circumstances will they compromise their ethics, but if forced to do so will fight with determination.

Should they decide to do something it will be done and should anyone try to stop them, they do so at their own peril.

They never hold grudges and stay on good terms with most people by reserving a magnanimous and light-hearted nature.

They excel, having no need to control or dominate people to satisfy their own ego.

Their enthusiasm and confidence inspires others to reach higher levels and do things for themselves.

They possess tremendous personal power to calm worried or troubled people and find resolutions to the world's problems.

What Comes Above and Below?

I feel inclined to add a couple of levels to Jon's lovely schematic.

At the bottom, even below apathy, despondency and distress, we have a Being who has sunk to the level of death. Sounds strange as an emotion, but deathfulness is something you will encounter, especially in a deeply shocked or dying person. But also we have people who are so numb, they almost might as well be dead. Such a person does not respond, may be catatonic and is as much "out of it" as a living breathing person can be (not to be confused with unconsciousness or coma, of course).

Right at the top, we have the state of supreme spiritual ascension that is bliss. We might call it Sublime Radiance or Serenity of Being. It is recognized in numerous accounts of religious raptures and in what Abram Maslow called "peak experiences" (moments of highest happiness and fulfillment). People who encounter this state tend to use the same words to decribe it: rare, exciting, oceanic, deeply moving, exhilarating, elevating experiences that generate an advanced form of perceiving reality, and are even mystic and magical in their effect upon the individual. [Maslow, A. H. (1962). *Toward A Psychology Of Being*. Princeton, NJ: Van Nostrand]

These outliers states appear in my own *Emotional Ladder*, which is published elsewhere.

11a. Using The Scale Of Emotional Health

Here's a Useful Working Hack
It is a simple matter to integrate the eleven emotional levels of health into your life. Make a list of people that you have known or know well. They can be relations, neighbors, colleagues, politicians, prime ministers, presidents, historical characters, TV and other media personalities, news reporters and commentators; in fact anyone that you know, living or dead. For example, many television soap operas comprise characters acting in the chronic low levels of emotional health on the scale; while the script writers of situation comedies often use characters acting in the higher levels of emotional health.

When you have made the list, compare each person's behavior to the eleven levels of emotional health to determine their chronic or long-standing emotional level.

`Jon Whale tells me when he first tried this exercise, he made a list of all of the people past and present who directly and indirectly participated or affected his life. It was very disheartening to discover that over seventy percent of those on his list were categorized in the chronic negative levels.

You may find the same thing. It is a rare to find anyone who has not been exposed to our Transformational Mind Dynamics™ much higher than 'chronic conservatism' on this scale (Plus 1). The reason for many a person's melancholy is due to a belief which forms, that people high on the scale of emotional health are in short supply, while those low on the scale seem to be very common.

However, you will be disappointed to discover that love and peace is not the solution. Extending these sentiments, showing others the 'pink light' only provides an invitation for individuals low on the scale, (-Minus 3, 4 and 5), to gain access and manipulate your inherent good nature. Before long you will find yourself in the same negative states as them.

One of the biggest mistakes you can make is to believe, uncritically, that others are kind, reaffirming and rational. That path will lead you to fritter away many years of your life in the company of, and under the influence of, intensely negative people.

The Answer

First know this *Scale Of Emotional Health.* Then choose your friends carefully, according to their real position on it. Those who sit below Plus 3 should be dumped unceremoniously. If you can't do so, because it's family or work colleagues, strictly minimize your contact and do not socialize with the toxic lower types.

Secondly, get yourself fixed up with **Transformational Mind Dynamics™** (see appendix), with a competent pilot. You'll never be the same again. It's the only really profound way to release emotional charges form the past and find your freedom in the present, shedding old and destructive patterns, beliefs and feelings.

Moreover, you can easily learn to do it for others and, for many, this has become a deeply fulfilling career or second career. It can be quite lucrative.

12. Private Soliloquy

Talking To Yourself Is Not Madness!
It's a powerful self-growth technique! It's called private soliloquy.

The word soliloquy means simply: talking out loud to self. It's a common device used in drama. Shakespeare, for example, had much of his best poetry in the mouths of a character who was soliloquizing, rather than talking to someone else (Hamlet: "To be, or not to be..." for example).

It's something all of us do from time to time. But here's the thing...

It has emerged as a fantastically powerful self-help tool. You really can learn skills rapidly and "talk yourself up" into a position of wisdom and power! I'm not just saying this: there is real science on the topic and it's pretty exciting.

A review of studies and surveys in *Perspectives Of Psychological Science*, for example, has deduced that self-talk works when you focus on achieving and enacting a goal. [Perspectives on Psychological Science, July 2011 vol. 6 no. 4 348-356]

It then becomes "instructional self-talk" and is something wildly powerful.

Talking Out Loud
The important thing to grasp is that all I am going to say about the positives is based on the mechanics of spoken utterance or speaking OUT LOUD to yourself. This is not the same as inner mind chatter; it's not "thinking" in words or the verbal stream of consciousness, though it may be related. It's a different modality of speech, with a different result.

I have used it with powerful effect in my Theater Of Being, that workshop in which we elect different and valuable identities and then act them out: posturing the way that identity would posture, speaking as it would speak and creating ideas that it would create.

But soliloquizing does not need a workshop environment. You can do it alone—it means doing it alone—and maybe with the help of a mirror. So there is no reason to be reticent, tongue-tied, shy or hold back; it's just between you and Higher Power!

The only thing that comes close to talking to yourself, for yourself, is listening to guided imagery. It works. But that's always someone else doing the talking and discovery for you. This is you doing it for yourself.

But, you say, how will I know what to tell myself to do and think. The full answer is a very long and deep one. Suffice it to say here that you know pretty well almost everything; you just choose not to know certain things, so that life is a game!

You can tell yourself, "I know, deep down, what to do and say," because it's true. You do. Go for it.

What Does Science Say?

The scientific literature on self-talk has provided strong indications that private speech is an effective strategy for supporting learning and enhancing performance.

Through a study from Greece we learn that self-talk interventions were more effective for tasks involving relatively fine muscle movements, compared with relatively gross actions, and that it works best for developing new skills, as compared with improving well-learned tasks.

What's more, instructional self-talk was more useful and effective than motivational self-talk (completely the opposite of that the seminar gurus teach you!) Telling yourself what to do is more useful than telling yourself why you need to do it!

Finally, interventions including self-talk training were more effective than those not including self-talk training. The results of this study establish the effectiveness of self-talk in sport, encourage the use of self-talk as a strategy to facilitate learning and enhance performance, and provide new research directions.

By instructing yourself aloud, your attention is enhanced and you can focus without getting distracted, therefore helping you to steady yourself and carry out your task as calmly as you can.

Another paper published in the *Quarterly Journal of Experimental Psychology* even suggests that talking to yourself can help you locate something you lost. This might be something to try instead of the old, "Strike up affinity with that object" method.

One last point: scientific findings may also indicate a pronounced need for self-encouragement in the face of unappreciative or mostly ignorant surroundings. Thus, positive inner speech might be one of the sensible coping strategies in getting through difficult situations.

I don't know how this applies to other broadcasters and public speakers but, for myself, I find it helpful before any public talk to simply rehearse out loud, including one or two flippant or "spontaneous" off-the-cuff remarks. Not exactly an hostile environment, I know, but tension before acting and public speaking is proverbial. They say it adds to the performance.

So How Do We Cash In?
What use is this information? How does it help?

Step one: get yourself a sizeable mirror you can talk to. Look at yourself in it. Smile to yourself and see yourself smile back.

Examine all details of what you see reflected (don't confuse yourself with the fact that moles and markings will appear reversed, ie. what looks like the right cheek of the reflection is your left cheek really!) Make yourself see yourself in a new light and notice things you never noticed before.

Get used to that persona in the mirror; it's a strange thing but it's YOU and yet it's not you. It is remarkably easy to see that reflected image as a "someone else" phantom.

That's good because it means when that person talks to you, you listen. THIS IS NOT COMBING YOUR HAIR, CHECKING YOUR MAKE UP OR SHAVING IN THE MIRROR!

Step two: now work on really smiling at yourself. Laugh as much as you can.

Nod, get appreciation from the individual in the mirror. Notice how when the reflection smiles, you feel warmth and goodness coming at you. It's remarkable really. How long? Do this until there is no further change but you can keep coming back to it, over and over.

Step three: start talking to yourself. I mean really talk TO yourself, talk to the reflection as if it was somebody else; a person that hardly knows you. That way the reflection will talk to YOU, the real person, almost as someone else!

Get used to it. It might seem strange at first. Say anything you like; just get used to the self-talk vehicle. Watch yourself talking, notice your posture and mannerisms. You can repeat what you say from different postures and notice the difference.

Step four: say flattering things to yourself in the mirror. Smile a lot and really complement yourself—anything you can think of.

You know your best points; tell yourself, emphasize them. But TALK OUT LOUD!

It's great to hear nice things about yourself. How strange it is to hear them from yourself. But the mirror is just enough of a shift that it sounds like real flattery. It works as flattery, which is all that counts.

This is where you learn something good, which is that although you can think satisfied thoughts inside your head, telling yourself you are a good guy or a beautiful gal, it's far more powerful when it comes out as the spoken word. Now you are into soliloquizing.

Step five: describe to yourself what qualities you most need in life. This is not so much flattery for what you have got as to emphasize repeatedly what you need to develop.

This is beyond the flattery part; we are starting in on education—learning. Say to yourself strong skills, like: this is you talking boldly, without reticence, skillfully and with a profound knowledge of your topic. You ARE the queen of bee keeping... (or whatever it is you want). Keep repeating the phrases until they do come out with boldness and confidence!

Start to believe what you are hearing. Yes, nobody knows more about bee keeping than you; you are the TOP expert. Time to go out and teach others...

Step six: tell yourself what you need to do today. Emphasize your amazing abilities, powers and skills. But also don't hold back on introducing things you find difficult: I will make ten sales calls; I will be firm and non-hesitant; I will lay out my offer attractively and the client will listen with interest; I will command his or her attention... (whether or not the client buys anything).

You can plan: today it is crucial that I finish up chapter seven. I will work on it till done; I will keep my lunch break to a minimum; today I will not go to the pub; I will sit home until I meet my target.

I can do this. I know when I set the quotas it was achievable. You will not let yourself fail at this important assignment...

Or self-discipline. This is your seventh week without alcohol. You are doing great. Make sure none of the bottles are in view, so that you see one by accident. Only one more week to go and you can resume social drinking. But you will never fall back to drinking alone, just for the sake of making yourself numb....

In truth, there is no end to the applications of this technique. The important point is that instruction works better than just a pep talk.

Theater Of Being

I mentioned this is the exact same technique I invented for my Theater Of Being years ago. We choose an identity that is powerful and would be helpful to us to occupy (leader, lover, expert, writer, whatever).

After the preliminary stages, where we learn to relax, just be, become present and non-introverted, then we start (effectively) acting out the Beingness. It's a sort of role play, on steroids.

We adopt the persona and speak and act exactly as that sort of identity would. It can be great fun, shouting, ranting and dramatizing some outrageous character that we would hardly dare be in real life. But you know what? Just portraying such characters can be deeply inspiring and helpful.

But it's not about acting it's about being somebody else; adopting a new mantle and identity.

I have seen shy, self-effacing individuals become monarchs, demons and movie stars! I've seen people suddenly discover their long-hidden sexual prowess, in a matter of hours.

You can be Ruler Of The Universe if you choose. How would that influence your confidence?

You'll be amazed at the identities within. Get to know yourself.

This phenomenon of identity-switch can be observed among actors and actresses; many famous and brilliant performers are pathologically shy when they are not in a role. Yet once he or she adopts the character they are playing, they become someone completely different; someone so real that it takes fantastic role play; yet he or she, supposedly shy, portrays the character with all its vileness or glory, just as the script calls for. They literally become the character and no longer themselves.

Then, immediately off the set, the "real" persona returns and the actor or actress loses their power. It's a strange paradox.

Elton John, Audrey Hepburn, Rex Harrison and Johnny Depp come to mind. Even Madonna is like that, according to her brother, though it's somewhat hard to believe!

13. Showing Up

How many times have you heard the saying that "showing up is 90% of success"? You have to show up and you have to be willing to work hard and stick at it, to get what you want.

Another reason these crummy personal development programs are a fraud is that they imply it all happens so easily. They kid you that the "Cosmos" or some divine force is on your side, so nothing will ever go wrong. It all happens by magic; one day you look out of your window and there is a shiny new car sitting on the drive. You "manifested it"

That sets you up for a disaster when something goes badly wrong and you encounter a setback. You think "Maybe God isn't going to help me" or whatever. It's very disempowering.

Listen, whatever divine or mystical powers are out there that may or may not be ready to help you get what you want, for sure they are not going to violate the laws of physics and the laws of life, just to make sure you have it easy. If you mail the wrong sales letter and it's a dog, luck or fate isn't going to step in and make it all better. Wake up! Life isn't a Walt Disney feel-good movie! If you screw up you'll lose money, you'll feel bad and have to start over. If you're smart you'll learn the lesson and move on. If you're not smart, then you'll quit or change and change the formula or even worse, change your destination.

You know that Abe Lincoln failed and went bankrupt several times before he became the most powerful and influential man in US history. Did you know that Walt Disney also went bankrupt more than once, before he created his financial juggernaut?

What I want to teach you is that it's up to you. There is nothing whatever to stop you dusting yourself off and star`ting over—except your own state of mind. So in that sense, your attitude of mind is critical. It's the fuel to drive the beautiful machine along the road that you so carefully mapped earlier on.

To get everything you want, you need to be the best you can be. That's really the theme of this section. We're all different but none of us, I believe, are living our full potential. Some are nowhere near. But of all the parts of the success plan you're working, this one is probably the easiest to control. It really is UP TO YOU!

Showing Up

So let's start with showing up. Stephen Pressfield wrote a great little book called *The War Of Art*. It's a catch-take on the famous *Art Of War* by Sun Tzu. He's writing about the labors of being a successful writer or other artists but the principles he outlines can be applied to any endeavor, anywhere.

Before becoming a full-time writer, Pressfield worked as a copy writer, taxi driver, bartender, tractor-trailer driver, fruit picker, and worked on oil rigs. He then moved to California and began writing screenplays. In 2000, his debut novel, *The Legend of Bagger Vance*, was made into a movie starring Matt Damon and Will Smith.

The hardest part, says Pressfield, is just showing up. He doesn't just mean going to the J-O-B on time. Even if you work for yourself and you drag yourself to the desk every morning to start writing, that still doesn't mean you'd "showed up". You can be there doing stuff and still not really showed up.

The enemy in this particular war is what Pressfield calls *resistance*. You may have heard of it under other guises, like *plausible distractions* or *creative avoidance*; things to do that are "important" and so prevent you from doing what really matters. The irony of course is that doing these creative avoidance tasks can be just as demanding and hard work as getting on with the job! It doesn't make sense (but then emotional issues rarely do!).

But for every positive thing we want to do, there is a part of us that doesn't want to. This is considered a stalling tactic. 'Tomorrow, I will work on it, or next week when I have some free time, or when somebody else does something first, or whatever the excuse happens to be. In my mind I really want to work on it, but I keep coming up with reasons why I can't get started."

It is odd that someone would rather mow the grass than work on their dream. But that's how it happens.

I think there are in each of us 2 opposing desires. One part of us dreams. The other part is trying to protect us from the unknown. It's easy to be afraid of change. While there can be a whole variety of reasons, it doesn't matter – it's still a problem. We are not talking about laziness, but inertia. You want to get the results you imagined, but you just can't find the emotional strength to put your plan into motion.

Does that sound familiar? That's resistance at work. It's invisible, like fear!

Resistance cannot be seen, touched, heard, or smelled. But it can be felt. We experience it as an energy field radiating from a work-in-potential. It's a repelling force. It's negative. Its aim is to shove us away, distract us, prevent us from doing what we know we have to do to succeed.

The important point is that resistance comes from inside but AP-PEARS to come from outside ourselves. We blame spouses, jobs, bosses, kids. These are what Pat Riley used to call "Peripheral opponents," when he coached the Los Angeles Lakers.

But resistance is not a peripheral opponent. Resistance arises from within. It is self-generated and self-perpetuated. Resistance is the enemy within.

Resistance will tell you anything to keep you from doing your work. It will perjure, fabricate, falsify; seduce, bully, cajole, says Pressfield. Resistance is protean. It will assume any form, if that's what it takes to deceive you. It will reason with you like a lawyer or jam a nine-millimeter in your face like a stickup man.

Resistance has no conscience. It will pledge anything to get a deal, then double-cross you as soon as you give up on what you needed to do. If you take Resistance at its word, you deserve everything you get, meaning failure.

Fear
Most resistance is supposed to be based on fear. But I have already told you that fear is not the enemy; fear is your friend. Fear tells you the way to go. The more you fear it, the more you MUST do it. It's for your own growth and majesty of spirit. But also, literally, what you fear will bring you the most rewards. Why?

If it's easy you've probably already done it. So have lots of people. No success there. You need to step into places where few people dare go, if you really mean to succeed.

Fear must never stop you. Even an ever-present fear. Just don't let it stop you.

Henry Fonda was still throwing up before each stage performance, even when he was seventy-five. In other words, fear doesn't go away. The warrior and the artist live by the same code of necessity, which dictates that the battle must be fought anew every day.

Fear is good. Like self-doubt, fear is an indicator. Fear tells us what we have to do.

Remember our rule of thumb: The more scared we are of a work or calling, the more sure we can be that we have to do it. Eleanor Roosevelt is worth quoting; she got it:

> You gain strength, courage and confidence by every experience in which you really stop to look fear in the face... You must do the thing you think you cannot do." —from, *You Learn by Living: Eleven Keys for a More Fulfilling Life*

Resistance is experienced as fear; the degree of fear is proportional to the amount of Resistance. Therefore the more fear we feel about a specific enterprise, the more certain we can be that that enterprise is important to us and to the growth of our soul. That's why we feel so much Resistance. If it meant nothing to us, there'd be no Resistance.

This is the true face of the saying you've heard about people being afraid of success as much as they are afraid of failure. When it's right for you and will bring you everything you ever dreamed of, it will seem terrifying to many people. Just recognize what this gift of life really means.

Courage

Go out and embrace the fear. It's the *best* thing that could happen to you!

So one of the qualities of mind that we need to succeed is courage. It's a kind of positive thinking, if you want to look at it that way.

The man or woman with courage has persistence. He or she states a target and then moves relentlessly towards it. The courageous individual has confidence. He or she will draw in the mental and moral quantities needed to create the world of success.

But the person who lacks courage will equally draw all the qualities of a weak person: vacillation, doubt, hesitancy, and unsteadiness of purpose. You can therefore see the value of concentration on courage. It is a most vital element of success. Lack of courage destroys your confidence in yourself. It destroys that forceful, determined attitude so important to success.

If you lack courage you will encounter endless financial worries, as well as mental and moral conflicts. When a new problem comes, instead of looking upon it as something to be overcome, the man or woman without courage uses it as a reason why things cannot be done and failure is the almost inevitable result.

He or she then blames bad luck.

You know what? Lack of courage, fear, skulking in lowly misery is actually pitiable and weakening. You will draw in to yourself all that is contemptible, demoralizing and destructive. It means you will suffer more than fear itself. Fear seems very powerful but it evaporates like mist the moment you display your courage and step into the sunlight. Whereas giving up through cowardice is with you always, the self-doubt, the shame, the regret, never ever goes away.

So of the two I would choose fear. It's short and painful, not like the long slow death of cowardice. What's best is that when you beat fear once, it gets easier and easier to beat it every time. Whereas if you choose cowardice, it gets harder and harder to face the world every time.

To be the best you can be then, start out today with the idea that there is no reason why you should not be courageous. If you feel fear, say Hello friend. But you are not going to bring me down today. I'm too good for that.

Remember, you are master of your own mind—or you'd better learn to be. Control your thoughts and tell yourself: "I am courageous and I deserve to win through. Fear will not conquer me. It's only a lousy emotion, after all!"

Procrastination

Procrastination is the most common manifestation of Resistance because it's the easiest to rationalize. We don't tell ourselves, "I'm never going to write my symphony." Instead we say, "I am going to write my symphony; I'm just going to start tomorrow."

Someone once asked Somerset Maugham if he wrote on a schedule or only when struck by inspiration. "I write only when inspiration strikes," he replied. "Fortunately it strikes every morning at nine o'clock sharp."

That's the attitude of a successful professional.

That doesn't mean Maugham never felt resistance. It just means he never gave in to it. He sat down at his desk anyway and, sure enough, the inspiration showed up. Probably all artists feel resistance. But they just ignore it, as if it was a pimple on the end of the nose.

If resistance couldn't be beaten, there would be no Beethoven Fifth Symphony, no Shakespeare plays, no Mona Lisa and no Golden Gate Bridge. As Steven Pressfield says, defeating resistance is like giving birth. It seems absolutely impossible until you remember that women have been pulling it off successfully, with and without support, for fifty million years.

Don't be an amateur, be a professional. The word amateur comes from the Latin root meaning "to love" (amo). The conventional interpretation is that the amateur pursues his calling out of love, while the pro does it for money. That's not the way Pressfield sees it. In his view, the amateur does not love the game enough. If he did, he would not pursue it as a sideline, distinct from his "real" vocation.

The professional loves it so much he dedicates his life to it. He commits full-time. That's what success is about. You must commit. **Pull the trigger**, remember!

13a. The Lazy Man's Way To Riches

In 1973 a man called Joe Karbo came out with what was probably the greatest advertizing catch phrase of all time: "Most people are too busy earning a living to make any real money."

It was part of a brilliant sales campaign for his book *The Lazy Mans' Way To Riches*.

Karbo's book wasn't a masterpiece by any definition; it was scruffy and cheaply printed. It cost him fifty cents and he sold it for ten dollars. But *The Lazy Man's Way To Riches* stands way ahead of most of today's books because it told you what to do. It was packed with information. There were actually chapters explaining the steps to take to get started with little or no money that could, if you did it right, make you rich. But that wasn't what was special about this book for me.

Karbo also proposed some "daily declarations". Just affirmations really. In fact let me digress a moment and tell you that after reading his book I did a list which said on it that I had a prestigious office with marble floors and wooden paneling. Eight years later I had just finished wrapping up some filming of my work for the BBC and looked around with satisfaction, when it suddenly dawned on me: there were marble panels on the walls and polished parquet wood floors! I'd made it! Just got the details a little wrong, that's all.

But Karbo wasn't just proposing the usual trite affirmations stuff. He thought it was valuable to declare what personal characteristics you needed for success. It was part of what he called *mental well-being* and I guess that's what I'm referring to all along in this segment. It's probably the most important list you'll write on your way to success. To be sure of a good start, Karbo even put the first three on the list for us.

1. Each and every day that I follow these procedures set out for my improvement, I become more effective and better able to function without limitation.

2. I pursue my goals free of any ill will or animosity towards others. I am a warm, friendly, well-liked person. My success is assured and does not require me to take advantage of any

other person. Rather, it obliges me to help others, without telling anyone about my "good deeds".

3. I see myself with the success-eye of NOW. I have discarded the failure-eye of my infancy. I am free at last of failure or limitations.

Nowadays we wouldn't word declarations like number 3. There is too much negative "I don't have [bad trait]" doesn't seem to work. Nevertheless, it's a great little book and still on sale.

And the strangest, saddest thing about Karbo's book is that it has sold millions of copies and yet almost nobody follows his plan for success. They just read it and put it down.

So let's work on Karbo's proposition.

Certain mental characteristics will be essential in the pursuit of success and achievement. I'm sure you can list some of these straight off the wall:

- Determination, especially when the going gets tough

- Energy, especially when the going gets tough!

- Self-belief, especially when the going gets tough!

- Commitment, especially when the going gets tough!

- Confidence, especially when the going gets tough!

- Focus, especially when the going gets tough!

- Clarity, most especially when the going gets tough!

- Intelligence helps, of course

- and persistence

Using declarations to instill these important qualities of mind I consider far more valuable than phoney affirmations, such as "I am rich", when you know damned well you're broke.

A daily declaration that "I'm strong, confident, wise, industrious, brave, determined..." etc. etc. will help bring about these necessary traits and they work directly because these are about you, not about what's in the bank or other worldly possessions that you don't really have.

14. Shift vs. Clear

There are two valuable but distinct ways to improve a person's state of mind and abilities. Acquiring new and valuable information about the mechanics of life and living is one... plenty of that in this little volume. That's about quality learning.

But we can also take the individual on a journey of inner exploration, locate areas that are stressed, confused or horribly painful to face up to, and clean them up so they are no longer troublesome in mind. We call this approach "piloting", so likening it to the process of guidance and steering.

We take our client to the precise moments of snarl up and soften them to the point of dissolving the pain and re-classification as harmless. In other words, it's a question of melting away hostile areas of the mind.

We return memory to a fond garden or a favorite pathway, rather than the usual onboard "Jurassic Park" of emotions! This too is a kind of learning, if you think about it.

There isn't space here to describe *how* we do this. But I would like to share some thoughts about the aim in doing this...

The Object In View

In Supernoetics™ we are seeking shift. This is not an absolute state but an alteration in view point; we see things newly. Things have moved; hence the term *shift*.

Contrast that with the New Age therapists' concept of "clearing", which in computer terms implies dumping everything out of the system, all gone, all nice and fresh and... well, clear. It's a good sounding analogy in the popular mode of comparing the human mind to a computer. But it's an absolute. Absolutes are un-attainable in practice anyway.

But you can Google clearing and find plenty of references to it, like Maya Cointreau's book *Grounding And Clearing*. Even the Feng Sui people talk now of "clearing" spaces of toxic energies. The concept is found in Tibetan Buddhism and it is referred to by the term "clearing" in Alexandra David-Neel's beautiful 1932 book *Magic and Mystery In Tibet* (p. 270 in my 1971 Dover edition).

The concept is also explicitly described by Freud, though not using the term as such.

However, an absolutely clear mind or a state of "clear" is demonstrably not practicable. It's a destination you can never reach. Maybe we don't even want it? I firmly believe that an unpleasant person, such as Hitler, could have been worked on and theoretically "cleared". But would that have made him a nicer person? Or would he have become a more efficient, cleverer and more ruthless person, with more "Hitler-ness"?

That's a question which need not trouble us in Supernoetics™, even if clearing were actually attainable (which I don't believe). Because what we are seeking is not "clearing" as such, but meaningful change for an individual; evolution of mind.

Clearing was originally a bright, sharp term but it has gradually become hazy. It has lost its lustre. I think that is because nobody is getting there! Being and consciousness, which interests me far more, is a swirling, soft-edged thing as I have written elsewhere. It doesn't lend itself well to comparisons with a computer, where all the edges are hard (limit of file size, limit of screen resolution, limit of capacity, limit of RAM, limit of program capability, download speed... and so on).

No Hard Edges

Shift, on the other hand, comes from the flow of mind spaces. It's a new way of seeing things; specifically, a new way of seeing OLD things; how you once were becomes transformed into a new you by altered perspectives. To have that happen, things have to be deleted and what remains is then re-aligned with the new north.

Shift is not the act of getting rid of "stuff". *Shift is what happens as a result of getting rid of stuff.* So again, we don't share the clear/clearing syntax. Nor do I want to see the verb shifting in use (verb). It's experiencing shift.

The way we see it in Supernoetics™, with educational programs and personal coaching and piloting, is that there are lots of Aha! Moments (our term is: *cognosis*), which build into shifts. Shift can come at you in spades or it can be gradual. We value it highly; the more of it the better!

As the term implies, shift is movement. That's how personal growth comes about; we improve how a person sees things; we improve abilities, attitudes and emotions; we handle (diminish) a person's case until he or she sheds unwanted layers of confusion, inability and compromise.

Then in time there is real transformation where the person is majorly new in outlook, emotional tone, attitudes and abilities. It's like being a new person but really the individual is more his or her own self, the deeper persona that always resides within, but gets overlaid by troubles and stress.

That's a key point: it might seem like a "new" state but it's more a throwback to something much older and wiser, not seen on Earth these days. But it's there, innate within us all. We were, in times long past, beings of vastly greater capabilities than we exhibit today. That being the case, shift is finding our way back. Transformation is getting there.

But none of this is an absolute; there is no portal where this side of it you are "human" and beyond it we become gods. It's a gradual transition. One day you suddenly wake up to the fact that's it has happened.

Haunted By Our Unpleasant Past

There is nothing wrong with memory, in principle. It's experience. It's knowledge of a kind. But the way it works against us is when we accumulate bad experience and negatives, which create adverse mental charge. Charge is an electrical engineer's term but we use it here to denote negative energy in the mind.

It's energy alright, because it creates change in us; energy is the universal agency of change. We notice it most when charge is stirred up: we feel bad, we act irrationally, we do and say things we later regret. It leads to negative emotions, like fear, sadness and rage. We are indeed changed.

In fact you can see emotional charges reading on an psycho-feedback meter, like the eMind Sensor™ or Clarity Meter. That's how piloting proceeds: we locate the areas of most charge and reduce or "release" the adverse energies, until the person feels different. Eventually, a river of small insights turns into a tidal flow and then, inevitably, there is a major shift. The person sees everything in a new light, from a new viewpoint, freed, energized and intelligent in that area.

The special benefit of using a meter is that we can see very clearly what to run on a case. That prevents us falling into the hubris of "knowing" what's wrong with a person, when we don't at all. By simply transforming the charged memories offered by the mind and recovered by the meter, we don't have to think hard or "interpret" a case, as the psychoanalysts like to do. We just accept the gift and address that!

Thing is, when we remove charge, the person UN-changes. In other words they generally experience shift by going back to an *earlier better place* before there was pain or hurt. Yet we get to keep our memories and experiential learning; brilliant, isn't it?

Deletion Not Addition

It's important to understand that this model means we do not add anything to the basic personality. We are not gifting, persuading or indoctrinating. We are deleting the adverse energies, beliefs, postulations and attitudes which lead to a distorted viewpoint. We can't foresee what shifts the person's viewpoint will move through—after all, everyone is unique—but by removing the negatives, we restore and enhance the person's clarity and freedom of view.

That's done by eliminating negative charges on memories. We don't lose those memories, they are reclassified in conscious view, instead of being buried. In fact memory grows and improves. For instance someone with a history of childhood abuse might have buried the whole thing and be completely unable to recall their unfortunate experiences.

But after Supernoetics™ piloting, the person is then able to accept the unpleasant memories, review them and come to terms with what happened. Examining the past in this way, from a position of stability and emotional clarity, and with the help of a skilled pilot, leads to major changes in perspective.

For example, I have seen a case with a strong hatred of his deceased mother and a firm belief that, "She messed up my life; she was a bitch" within less than an hour move to, "She tried her best, I guess; there was no money, but she got us through," to "I love you Mom" (tears); I forgive you... I love you, I love you... I wish you were here..." (sobbing).

The case was a tough hard-hat construction site manager, weighing over 260 pounds. He sobbed for an hour after this release. That was shift! And that's how fast it can be, with our focused and efficient techniques.

In another case, a woman was dealing with unhappiness about her education. She had passed an important exam but the school refused to promote her to the class above, saying she would be happier among her existing friends and being top of the class, rather than becoming a mediocre student in the stream above.

This had always irked and operated as a severe negation of her abilities as a child. Despite all, the woman had gone on to study at one of the world's leading colleges and obtained two degrees (BA and Masters). Her designs have appeared on TV and in top magazines. She was in every sense very clever at what she did.

Nevertheless, the childhood stigma and humiliation of being kept in a class below where she felt she should have been had always rankled; partly, it emerged, because she never really understood why this was enforced on her. Floods of tears were released in revisiting this time, using our techniques, showing clearly the upset was still there, some forty years later.

Yet in just one hour this woman came to realize that the misfortune she wailed about was actually a very good thing. In revisiting and discharging memories of the time, she recognized that her friends had been important and she would almost certainly have felt displaced in joining the stream above. Even more importantly, by being promoted she would have lost access to studying her favorite subjects, including the one that eventually carried her to university and an international career.

Her life would probably have been ruined by being promoted to an unsuitable class full of nerdy academics! Now she could see it differently and was thankful. She could even allow that maybe the teachers had foreseen that a different class wouldn't have been right for her. Now that's a major shift!

Missing Capabilities

My own text *The Propositions Of Being*, lays out the potential abilities of a fully ascended Being. These would be formidable indeed and approximate a god-like state. It goes even beyond the condition Abram Maslow famously described as self-actualized. It's bigger.

A fully realized, ascended individual would have no trouble with the laws of space and time. Since consciousness is, by definition outside the space-time continuum (Proposition 1), there are no fixities of location in space or time. The Being would be able to "be" anywhere it considers it wants to be. In fact the Being isn't anywhere but can assume a viewpoint, which gives the illusion of location.

So one of the important stages on the way home to Native Being is not being fixed to a body identity. Being out-of-body is an important marker to the rising ability to be nearer the truth of Being. This state would not emerge, except by accident, until the advanced levels of

Supernoetics™ have been mastered. Being out-of-body or exterior at will is a sign of greatly increased spiritual ability but it is not always accompanied by insight and wisdom. Piloting brings the wisdom.

More high-end abilities would include the ability to make things appear and disappear at will. Also the ability to ride above time. Notice I do not say "time travel", which is an Earth-side concept. If you accept time and are in it, then you can't violate it. You can only step outside it.

The Native Being state would not include the ability to make other beings disappear and does not include the right of infringement. In Supernoetics™ we define infringement as taking over and altering or controlling time, space, objects and energy which are strictly speaking not ours to manipulate in this way. Infringement means taking something away from somebody else.

It cannot be overemphasized that the primary rule of living in this plane is agreement. Agreement leads to tolerance. We are here because we all agreed to be here. Vain efforts to override this basic agreement can be seen to fail, always, except in the very short term.

Our trick is to learn to change those agreements!

Learning and Shift

Let us not overlook that significant shift can come from full and proper learning too, as I remarked above. Pilots in training have many an aha! or cognosis as they begin to see, from the inside out, how they are creating the reality that they experience.

The truth is that embodiment learning is a state change too. Wisdom, growth and insight are all about perception and understanding. We can come to those by reducing or eliminating charge, as described; that's the slightly passive route, with others assisting our progress.

Or we can do it by learning new concepts, new thought structures and new mind mechanisms. I've seen it happen to people, time and again. I should guess as much as 50% of recovery and growth comes from learning the nature of Being and the new evolved reality that comes from absorbing Supernoetics™ science and method into our hearts and minds.

You can get quite a lot of shift from learning something you didn't know before, such as discovering truths about the mechanics of the mind and the drivers of emotion and behavior. Supernoetics™ is a far-advanced teaching system in that respect.

But the most complete and exciting shift comes from releasing charge in piloting. The sudden amazing changes when the gates of freedom burst open is exhilarating and life-changing.

Do join us for a new life "up there", among the lesser gods, at least!

History of this document:
Partially written in 1994
Revized and completed 3 Sep 2014

15. Today Is The (Only) Day!

Happiness is here NOW, today; it is not in the future, or the past. If you don't find it here, you won't find it anywhere!

Carpe Diem: "Seize The Day!"

No, this isn't a lesson in Latin but in the joy of living. The present is all you've got. Rejoice in it. More broadly translated, *carpe diem* could mean, "enjoy what you've got!" which we now often slang down into simply: "enjoy!"

John Ruskin had on his desk a piece of rock carved with the word: TODAY.

Here is a famous poem by 5th Century Indian playwright, Kalidasa, said to be kept on the desk of the famous English doctor Sir William Osler:

> Look to this day!
> For it is the very life of life.
> In its brief course
> Lie all the varieties and realities of your existence:
> The bliss of growth
> The glory of action
> The splendor of achievement
> For yesterday is but a dream
> And tomorrow is only a vision,
> But today well lived makes
> Yesterday a dream of happiness
> And every tomorrow a vision of hope.
> Look well, therefore to this day!
> Such is the salutation to the dawn.

Time: The Biggest Hoax Of All

Most of us have been brought up on the idea of finding something outside ourselves that will make us happy. It's a hoax, of course.

This is something foisted on us by the Church and other major religions, wanting to usurp natural values and substitute their own particular cuckoo's egg instead. By far the worst hoax they peddle is that happiness is some other time, some remote future, an after-life, some other dimension, "Heaven", whatever. I think we have been stuck with this one far too long and it is now difficult to shake off. It has become what we call a cultural implant.

We grow up constantly brainwashed to the belief that some time hence we will get what we desire. As a child, we yearn only to grow up. We go through school wishing for it to end and looking forward to freedom. In our teens we want to be men and women, who can marry, have kids and settle down. But life is never quite as we pictured it and we end up subscribing to the idea that we'll feel great on weekends and holidays. Eventually, when the burden of work and living seems cemented in place, we start to dream that all will be roses and delight when we retire.

But when it isn't, what is left? Time has all but run out before we discover for ourselves the fraud that the future is no place. When we reach it we have only NOW, which we had all along --but failed to notice or cherish, as it fleeted by.

Regard the warning words of Oliver Wendell Holmes "Too many people die with their music still in them. Why is it so? Too often it is because they are always getting ready to live. Before they know it, time has run out."

Read Kalidasa's poem again: there is no tomorrow; it is only a potentiality. It is what you make it. The past is gone (only we insist on dragging it around with us, to hurt ourselves with painful memories).

Change
As Heraclitus said, the only thing that never changes is change. It is with us all the time. But it is never exactly the same. "You cannot step into the same river twice", Heraclitus told his pupils.

Life is ceaseless change. The only certainty is NOW because you have it in your hand.

We feel pressured by the accumulating burden of painful yesterdays and fearful tomorrows. But what is all that about, when you start to think about it logically?

As Dale Carnegie put it so well in his book *How To Stop Worrying And Start Living*: "You and I are standing this very second at the meeting-place of two eternities: the vast past that has endured for ever, and the future that is plunging on to the last syllable of recorded time". He goes on to make his real point: "We can't possibly live in either of these eternities--no, not even for one split second. But, by trying to do so, we can wreck both our bodies and minds".

So now let's be content to live in our allotted time span--which is not "four score years and ten", but from NOW until bedtime!

"Anyone can carry his burden, however hard, until nightfall," wrote Robert Louis Stevenson. "Anyone can do his work, however hard, for one day. Anyone can live sweetly, patiently, lovingly, purely, till the sun goes down. And this is all that life really means".

The NOW

NOW is the great engine of life, the workshop, the factory that generates all our tomorrows.

What you put into today is what you get out in the future. The raw materials for fabrication of the days are energy, concentration, commitment and honesty. And above all LOVE.

If you want a brilliant future full of love, light, beauty, grace and passion then you must put all these qualities into TODAY.

Now is here. Tomorrow is what you get.

Treat the day well!

Live In Exhilaration

Live life with a furious joy and fearless, bloody-minded determination!

Nothing can hurt you but that you let yourself believe it can.

It is possible to live life in this exalted state of energy and thrill, without needing a sense of frenzy or excess, profligacy or lack of control.

There are no "disasters". There are spills aplenty. We cannot live the perfect life but we can live with near-perfect willingness to experience it all!

Remember the sweet epigram that goes round and round...

Sing as if no-one was listening,
Dance as if no-one was watching,
Love as if it could never hurt.
That's the true meaning of life!

At the peak is what I call the cold fire or fury of living! It's glorious. I never want to slow down or die!

Time Is Your Capital

Time is probably our most precious asset. The whole secret to personal success is how you "spend" your time (see: we even talk of it like it was money!)

If you are in business, time is the key to profits. Think about it: if it were not for time, you could do all the tasks yourself; you wouldn't need the expense of employees. Then leverage, the real key to great success, is also a function of time: how to get the most action out of a given unit of time. Leverage simply means to multiply the result that could be obtained by one person alone.

Residual income is another function of time: the idea of doing a task only once and then being able to sell or profit from it many times over, through time.

OK, if I've got your attention a little, let me introduce...

Thomas Carlyle (1795 – 1881) was a bit of a grumpy old fart. But he wrote some good stuff; some very good stuff! Here's one of his famous maxims, "Our main business is not to see what lies dimly at a distance, but to do what lies clearly at hand."

You could argue this was a Victorian version of "living in the now"!

Sir William Osler, a Canadian physician who rose to be Britain's leading doctor of the Empire and therefore, arguably, one of the most important figures of his time, attributes his success to that one saying of Carlyle's. Osler organized the world-famous Johns Hopkins School of Medicine. He became Regius Professor of Medicine at Oxford - the highest honor that can be bestowed upon any medical man in the British Empire and eventually he was knighted by the King of England. When Osler died, two huge volumes containing 1,466 pages were required to tell the story of his life.

But what of Carlyle? Coming from a strict Scottish Calvinist family, young Thomas was expected to become a preacher by his parents, but while at the University of Edinburgh he lost his Christian faith. Instead he became writer and orator of great skill. His combination of a religious temperament with loss of faith in traditional Christianity, made Carlyle's work appealing to many Victorians who were grappling with scientific and political changes that threatened the traditional social and religious order.

He understood so well the Supernoetics™ 10th Channel of Being: "In books lies the soul of the whole Past Time; the articulate audible voice of the Past, when the body and material substance of it has altogether vanished like a dream." Today we have the Internet and electronic retrieval but, for Carlyle, books were the investiture of our history and Being.

Carlyle was a flawed genius. While being the most high-minded devotee of the ideal, he was nevertheless, at times, churlish and uncharitable to the work and personalities of others — even to such a great writer as Charles Lamb. He was the most vociferous and ungracious of grumblers and, apparently, despite loving his wife, he made her life with him a torment. He was against emancipation: didn't want slaves to be freed and considered democracy a waste of time!

Even so, his reputation remains fast. He was a great thinker in a truly great age.

Vocabulary

Carlyle invented some good words and phrases. I like this one especially: "Centre of Immensities", an expression of his to signify that wherever anyone is, he or she is in touch with the whole universe of being, and is, if he or she knew it, as near the heart of it there as anywhere else a person can be.

And what about: "Present Time" or "The Now", defined by Carlyle as "the youngest born of Eternity, child and heir of all the past times, with their good and evil, and parent of all the future with new questions and significance, on the right or wrong understanding of which depend the issues of life or death."

Actually, this last is a derivative of another monstrously vast idea: "The Conflux of Eternities" and it obviously influenced Dale Carnegie's choice of words (above). This is Carlyle's expressive phrase for the now time, in which the vast eternity of the past meets—or becomes confluent with—the even vaster eternity of the future. But this moment, the now, for Carlyle, is not just a fleeting evanescent experience; it is a vast edifice, standing at the confluence of All-Times and on which all our lives are built and the world shaped.

Living the Now to the fullest possible expression is accordingly the first and most sacred duty of every successive age, and especially the leaders of it. He bows to the future and honors the past but speaks from the present, which is the only cord or link by which we are attached to eternity.

Daytight Compartments

Those of you who know much of my mind power and spiritual writings will have met the term "mini day" or "process loops" (see "Slices Of Eternity" #7). There is the germ of that idea in the writings of Sir William Osler.

The secret of Osler's success he attributed to living in what he called "daytight compartments." What did he mean by that?

Shutting out distractions and focusing on just one day at a time: today! Osler compared it to ship technology. At sea, the master of the vessel can operate watertight bulkheads, which seal off parts of the ship. It didn't work with the Titanic because the designer, foolishly, did not have bulkheads all the way up to the next deck above: water was able to spill over the bulkheads into the next compartment, then the next, and so on...

In fact, in a way, the Titanic is a reverse example of this principle. If you don't live by daytight compartments, you may sink! See what you think when you've finished reading!

Using this model, you will see that raising the aft bulkhead against past miseries and defeats will insulate you for your work today; raising the forward bulkhead against the blurry, unfocused future will stop you being distracted and your energy dispersed by too many attractive possibilities, most of which will never come to pass, no matter how appealing.

There's a time for reflection and dreaming about the future. But when you are supposed to be in action, making stuff happen, is not that time!

When you need to act—do it! Just do it!

16. Brushstrokes

Attention to detail

Many a big concept is made up of small details, much as a painting is the sum of numerous tiny brushstrokes. If you want to change your life, to succeed with issues where you have been failing, then you need to start paying attention to the details.

To wish for a better relationship is too vague to work – it will (probably) only ever remain a wish. You need to get re-involved at a new level in each tiny brushstroke of the relationship, every sentence of communication exchange (touch, gift, service, word or gesture). Make the details conform to your desired painting (outcome) and you will start to see a new picture emerge from the dismay.

You goofed?

No problem. Just re-do the brushstroke. It does not violate the picture! Don't let it. You can overpaint a patch of the wrong paint on a canvas; you can do the same with your life. But trying to re-do the entire picture from the same perspective would be too difficult.

Get a mind brush and start painting sweeter detail in your life, from today.

Morale

There is another aspect of working in small chunks: morale.

If you have a totally scruffy garden where you can't keep on top of growth, weeds, pests, and untidiness, that is demoralizing. But if you take one small portion of that garden and prune, clean, weed and tidy it up, so that it looks very nice, your morale will improve just a little. Maybe a lot, because you can see to the next phase and tidying that up too. By planning, phase by phase, to remedy the situation you can enjoy the morale of having matters under control, while not yet finished!

See how the logic works?

A small piece done well brings much higher morale than hard-to-measure progress along many fronts. If you are musician, this takes on a different aspect. It is far more satisfying to learn one piece of music and play it really well than to learn dozens of tunes to an mediocre standard. You know that's true, even if you are not a musician.

The Scots have an oaty saying: Many a mickle makes a muckle. In plain English, lots of little things go to make up big things. The proverb has a lot to do with economy, meaning if you waste pennies, soon you will waste much more; conversely, if you save the pennies, you'll soon have a lot of money.

But it is a broad proverb with a lot of wisdom. It applies to life. A superb painting is made up of lots of brush strokes, none of which in themselves are interesting or special. But the overall picture can be magnificent.

Warren Buffet

Buffet is one of the richest man in the world at the time of writing and without doubt the most successful investor of all time. He is quoted as saying: "I don't look for seven-foot bars to leap over; I look for one-foot bars to step over". To me that is yet another restatement of the brushstroke principle.

Women have always known this! You can dye your hair a different color and totally change how you feel about yourself. Even flat shoes to high heels – you feel more elegant, sexier, your posture changes into something that makes you sassy. These are just brush strokes. But they work!

Men change their ties! Sometimes we change our shoes or jacket but not much. Male clothing is conservative compared to womens' flamboyant fashions. We are not as daring as women, who will change anything to alter how they feel about themselves.

Work with this practical and powerful philosophy in your life.

Along Similar Lines, We Can Talk About Tidyness

Wealthy and successful people are, in the main, tidy and orderly. If you visit their homes or office, what you find is neatness, space, cleanliness and aesthetic charm. It would be going too far to say that only rich people are neat and tidy. But it is almost a rule that untidy and scruffy individuals, with their belongings in chaos, appointment book out of date or non-existent, house needing repair etc. are not making any impact on the physical world. In other words they are broke.

The one apparent exception, which rather proves the rule, is the world of pop-stars. The most bizarre and disorderly individuals can become rich. But they are nevertheless far from successful and many end up on life's scrap heap, or dead of drugs and drink. So perhaps, after all, they do not violate the principle described here.

This actually comes from an important law of the physical universe. Scientists call it entropy. The whole of existence is gradually running down, like a watch. It is changing from orderly and advanced into something random and chaotic. This cold non-functioning dispersal is known as entropy. The problem is that this gives up energy and order. As we fall from a highly energetic states, the orderliness vanishes and so chaos is best seen as a loss of energy. It certainly feels that way when you are in confused and untidy surroundings or when your schedule is in disarray.

The uniqueness of life is that it is an energy system which overcomes the drag of entropy. Somehow (and scientists do not know how), life manages to retain a high degree of order in a universe which tends only to disorder. Life energies can fight against the degradation of entropy. Thus there are pretty high-level reasons why order is important to conquering the barriers of physical limitation. Since money is energy, we need to keep order to keep control of money, indeed to stand any chance of having any, long term.

Order and success are the same. Disorder and confusion are the enemies of good life and success.

Put order into your life!

Order has many forms: tidiness, good files, cleanliness, mental harmony and comfortable surroundings which are set out for Feng Shui is a version of this. But probably the most important order is in the head. A person who is dispersed by many, many cycles of activity, stacking up incomplete units from the past, is getting into a state of major mental disorder.

If You Want To Change The World, Start Off By Making Your Bed

Here are some apt words of wisdom given from the 2014 commencement address to the graduates of the University of Texas by Naval Admiral William H. McRaven.

> Every morning in basic SEAL training, my instructors, who at the time were all Vietnam veterans, would show up in my barracks room and the first thing they would inspect was your bed.

> If you did it right, the corners would be square, the covers pulled tight, the pillow centered just under the headboard and the extra blanket folded neatly at the foot of the rack — rack — that's Navy talk for bed.

It was a simple task – mundane at best. But every morning we were required to make our bed to perfection. It seemed a little ridiculous at the time, particularly in light of the fact that we were aspiring to be real warriors, tough battle-hardened SEALs – but the wisdom of this simple act has been proven to me many times over.

If you make your bed every morning you will have accomplished the first task of the day. It will give you a small sense of pride and it will encourage you to do another task and another and another.

By the end of the day, that one task completed will have turned into many tasks completed. Making your bed will also reinforce the fact that little things in life matter.

If you can't do the little things right, you will never do the big things right.

And, if by chance you have a miserable day, you will come home to a bed that is made — that you made — and a made bed gives you encouragement that tomorrow will be better.

So... If you want to change the world, start off by making your bed!

Handling.
Start with the simple things. Clear up your desk. Even better, deal with it, as per section 24. Clean up the house. Renovate the physical structure of your home. If not, you'll have to do it sooner or later anyway. Then is will be a major disorder and very likely an aggravated expense.

Schedules are half way between the mental and physical domain.

Set some schedules. Structure your day into *production syllables*.

17. Fail As Fast As You Can!

The More Mistakes You Make The Better!
A lot of you may have heard of the teaching, often glibly delivered by on-the-make wannabe gurus, that "the faster you fail, the quicker you reach success" and so forth.

Well, it's not wrong. In fact it follows an information theory principle called "Dancoff's Law. Want to know more?

In the late 1940s, Dancoff began a collaboration with the Viennese-refugee physician and radiologist Henry Quastler in the new field of cybernetics and information theory. Their work led to the publication of what is now commonly called Dancoff's Law. A non-mathematical statement of this law is, "the greatest growth occurs when the greatest number of mistakes are made consistent with survival".

[S. M. Dancoff and H. Quastler (1953). "The Information Content and Error Rate of Living Things". In Henry Quastler (Ed.). *Essays on the Use of Information Theory in Biology*. Urbana: University of Illinois Press]

What does this law actually mean? You might enjoy a slightly deeper look at the mechanics. This idea is part of a much bigger principle of science and philosophy. In fact it's quite scholarly.

First let's put in the basics. Entropy is the process of slow decay, decline and death in this universe. It's the natural outcome of the so-called Second Law Of Thermodynamics (which may or may not be a law). Sometimes referred to as "heat death", ultimate entropy is the state of a dead universe where there is no more energy transfer possible. It's still, cold, dead and silent.

Heat death used to trouble intellectuals, who thought it made everything about human life empty and pointless. William Inge, Dean of St Paul's Cathedral London, wrote about it extensively in his 1934 book *God and The Astronomers*:

> Modernist philosophy is, as I maintain, wrecked on the Second Law of Thermodynamics; it is no wonder that it finds the situation intolerable, and wriggles piteously to escape from its toils.

For Inge, as for most Christians, God is the creator of the universe, and distinct from it. The universe, as God's creation, may be subject to the Heat Death, but he is beyond its reach. Christianity has also always spoken of an end of the world, a Day of the Lord, a *Dies Irae* (day of wrath). While the Heat Death is properly described in mathematics outcomes, rather than the Apocalypse, the conclusion is the same: all things of this world will pass away. [http://home.comcast. net/~gmcdavid/html_dir/anderson.html accessed 1.36 pm BST, 24th Sept, 2012]

But—and it's a very large BUT—the Second Law Of Thermodynamics may not be a law, after all; at least not a law which envelopes everything. If the life force and consciousness are not actually part of the physical process, it would not affect them, would it?

That does seem to be the case.

Entropy states that everything is gradually breaking down, decaying. There is less and less order as time progresses. But life doesn't obey that pattern. Life goes on learning, adapting and getting more organized and complex. It's a process we call evolution and, whether you give it anti-religious significance or not, nobody can argue that evolution is taking place.

Negative Entropy
So life, as we know it, seems to be going in the opposite direction to entropy. In fact, as Erwin Schrödinger, founder of quantum mechanics, put it: "Life eats negative entropy" (life thrives by drawing in the opposite of entropy).

What is this "negative entropy"? Let's move over the Claude Shannon (1916-2001).

Shannon is famous for having founded, single-handed, Information Theory, with one landmark paper that he published in 1948. He is also credited with founding both digital computer and digital circuit design theory in 1937, when, as a 21-year-old master's degree student at the Massachusetts Institute of Technology (MIT), he wrote his thesis demonstrating that electrical applications of boolean algebra could construct and resolve any logical, numerical relationship. It has been claimed that this was the most important master's thesis of all time.

What we want Shannon for is to quote his evolution of theory that states that information overcomes entropy. This is so startling that some scientists have trouble accepting it (even though Shannon was a lot smarter than they are!)

This is often very confused in the literature. I have seen it written in many tracts and books that Shannon said the opposite (information = entropy). Not true! What he said was that Information is always a measure of the decrease of uncertainty at a receiver. Since uncertainty, or chaos, is the nature of entropy, information overcomes entropy. The more information you have, the better (the longer) you survive.

Shannon called the uncertainty which is subtracted by information the 'equivocation'.

The Nun's Research

A few years ago I read an article about an Alzheimer's disease study started in 1986, where a population of nuns volunteered for lifelong participation, including giving their brains after death for study. The nuns, among the School Sisters of Notre Dame, were ideal for scientific study because their stable, relatively similar lives preclude certain factors from contributing to illness. They do not smoke, hardly drink and do not experience physical changes related to pregnancy.

Well, what did the researchers actually learn, under Richard Suzman, chief of demography and population epidemiology at the National Institute on Aging, and University of Kentucky scientist David Snowdon? They found that a number of those individuals who had brains that were badly deteriorated, supposedly due to Alzheimer's, had never exhibited any symptoms of dementia while living.

Why? Because they were educated, active in their work and mental life, watched very little television, and were constantly involved in educational pursuits that expanded their knowledge base well into old age!

In other words, they had never stopped thinking and learning and working with their minds. They were beating the entropy of decay and senility!

Researchers could predict, with 85% to 90% accuracy, which ones would show the brain damage typical of Alzheimer's disease about 60 years later.

The physical state of the brain allowed no such prediction. So much for the "mind is brain" theory!

Among the documents reviewed as sources were autobiographical essays that had been written by the nuns upon joining the Sisterhood; it was found that an essay's lack of linguistic density (e.g., complexity, vivacity, fluency) functioned as a significant predictor of its author's risk for developing Alzheimer's disease in old age.

In other words, this Alzheimer's study was interesting in that it demonstrated that persons with "low word use density" were more likely to manifest early symptoms. People who had used their minds very little and who, therefore, had no "deep thoughts" and were, in effect, shallow, who had lived their lives based solely on "faith", were more likely to develop Alzheimer's.

[Suzanne L. Tyas, David A. Snowdon, Mark F. Desrosiers, Kathryn P. Riley and William R. Markesbery (2007). Healthy ageing in the Nun Study: Definition and neuropathologic correlates. *Age and Ageing*, 36(6), 650-655]

So, if learning, exercising the mind, working with difficult concepts, and continuously expanding the knowledge and awareness base can have such effects as this, what else might it do?

Strokes

So much for the background, back to learning and gathering information.

If you couple this with Dancoff's Law, that failing is a great way to accumulate information, then it all starts to come together as a scientific and spiritual principle, easily stated: do nothing is the road to death; take action and evolve is the road to infinite survival!

In fact this could sum up the history of the human race!

Let's make it even simpler and drop the word "failure"; it's emotive and probably not all that accurate a word. If you don't get what you wanted but accumulate information that makes you stronger, should that be considered a failure?

Let's call it "strokes".

Definition: stroke. An act or feat, as in "stroke of genius"; or a single complete movement or one of a series of complete movements.

The key word is act.

Speed Of Strokes

Now we can introduce another key principle of success: speed of strokes. It's another way of saying momentum and there is probably no more powerful factor in achievement.

Take a bullet. If you just threw it at someone, it would do nothing. But if projected from a gun with a muzzle velocity of 4,000 ft per sec (1,200 m per sec) it would do its wicked job.

So speed, fluidity, adaptability and momentum are all part of success. They boil down to movement: speed, direction, being able to change trajectory rapidly when something isn't working, or when an even better opening shows up, are all critical to the question of power and being able to get and hold what it is you need or want.

I can't emphasize this speed thing enough.

If you do sales calls and make ten calls a day, you are not nearly as powerful or likely to succeed as someone who makes ten calls an hour. That might seem obvious.

But what about a pop star who gives a concert every night? He (or she) is going to sell more records and chart more often than a performer who only goes on stage once a week. If you are thinking maybe the once-a-week person could have more talent, you are missing the point. A person's own actions will outperform his or her own results, if there are more and faster strokes.

So if you are a once a week or a ten times a day person, get into gear and become a seven times a week or a hundred times a day super-achiever instead.

Power is everything. Speed is power. *The number of strokes in a unit time governs your power (and success).*

And while we are on the subject, classy performance and classy results are gunned down, every time, by speed and quantity. It's not how good your sales calls are, or your guitar playing, it's how often you make calls or perform that most influences your outcomes.

Follow that up with improved quality and performance, then you'll win at whatever it is you choose to do.

Spiritual Information Against Entropy

One of the reasons people on a spiritual quest appear very special to us, especially when they approach mastery, is that they are imbued with a special light and energy. Coherent light is the exact opposite of the chaos and disorder that defines entropy.

The knowledge they have acquired releases them from the downward trend of physical life. In fact this is also the real answer to karma; a person clears their karma, to the degree they agree to share in beauty, healing, love and compassion. Knowledge and practice, when related to the 12 Channels Of Being (chapter 9) I have defined does this too. It's just another layer of knowledge.

The 12 Channels is another way to beat mind and spirit entropy.

The individuals who are well along on the path to mastery are in an increasing state of grace, because of accumulations of spiritual energy, often over vast aeons of time. Their condition is one of lowered spiritual entropy and increased grace.

In fact, as I write this, I think I see grace as meaning just that: the person has low spiritual entropy. It's wonderful to be with such people. In accord with the laws of physics, their coherent, ordered energies can cohere and straighten out our own! You know that happens; whenever you have been with a master, or someone close to it, you felt better; you saw deeper; gazed further than ever before.

So pain heals, disease saves, setbacks redeem and failure is, after all, just learning.

My Enemy Makes Me Stronger
I saw a great B-movie once (around 1974). I've never been able to trace it (please help if you can). In it, a man with fabulous psychic powers—literally a wizard in a suit and tie—was able to telekinetically manipulate objects. He does a demonstration, with a group of people sat around a table, by spinning a blade, just by staring at it and using intention.

Then, one by one, those who were in the room and witnessed this ability began to be killed off. One of witnesses (lets call him X) gradually emerges as the chief target. He's on the run. But why are they all being killed?

Weird inexplicable events keep occurring. Suddenly it dawns on X! Wow!

The man with psychic powers didn't spin the blade at all. One of the other people in the room must have done it unintentionally. The wizard realized right away there was a threat to his powers in the room. Now the wizard wants to kill all of them, to eliminate the potential challenger. He doesn't know who spun the blade but he knew it wasn't him. The answer is to kill them all.

Almost right away, X realizes he must be the one! The weird things that keep happening around him are from his psyche. He must have latent psychic powers of great magnitude.

X starts developing and practicing the powers and as the ensuing duel of wits progresses, he gets better and better at manipulating time and space. When X is finally trapped and faces off with the evil wizard, he has developed just enough power to actually defeat the killer on his own terms. The wizard is just a day too late to stamp out his rival. He is vanquished.

Great story. It's a classic "my enemy makes me stronger" story and I loved it.

It's a theme you will encounter again and again, in life and in story books: struggle and defeat develops your skills and powers. You should welcome the contests. The more you fight and lose, the more you develop your latent medical powers.

German philosopher Friedrich Nietzche stated the principle in these words: That which does not kill me, makes me stronger (from *Twilight of the Idols*, 1888).

Also, Hollywood actor Heath Ledger says in the movie *The Dark Knight* (2008) "I believe whatever doesn't kill you simply makes you stronger." So it must be true, right? (joke: please don't write to me)

The Persistent Spider

Forget the animal images you see of a defeated old alpha male, his a** whipped by an upcoming stronger rival, who then crawls off into the jungle to die because he's beaten. Wrong model! We are humans and don't do the animal herd story.

Take instead something like the Robert "The Bruce" legend. Despite the idiotic portrayal of Scotland's great hero as a skunk in Braveheart, The Bruce, as he was called (1274 – 1329), is said to have persisted because, while in hiding in a cave, he watched a spider trying over and over to fasten its web, never giving up.

So he emerged from hiding one more time; raised his standard yet again; and finally, in 1314, overwhelmed the English army at Bannockburn, to win independence for Scotland. Robert The Bruce is buried in Dunfermline Abbey.

Practical Aspects

So it's corny old teaching, "If at first you don't succeed, try, try, try again!" It sounds glib. Yet it's something that people violate all the time.

Mere persistence won't bring you success. Doing the right thing is what brings success. But you will eventually figure out what needs to be done, if you keep going. The value of persistence is that it keeps you in the game.

But there is another, deeper, value to persistence which I have outlined here. You gain information; you beat the entropy of failure and death. You live again to fight another day (OK, lots of clichés cover this space).

So, the more strokes you make, the nearer guaranteed success you come. I would re-substantiate Winston Churchill's famous admonition: never, never, never give up. Now remember, Churchill was a monstrous failure in many ways. He was a disaster at school; he goofed shockingly in WWI, wasting many men's lives in the Dardanelles campaign (Turkey); same again in Norway in WWII; he almost messed up the successful campaign against Rommel in Africa, by trying to interfere; he did mess up again with the invasion of Greece, which also wasted many lives. Constantly he kept pushing inept military ideas, against the advice of experts, in order to further his political machinations.

Yet Churchill is revered as one of the greatest British statesmen of all time. Even in the USA I often see photos of him and the famous cigar, along with quotations from his fiery, thrilling rhetoric. The famous speeches inspired more than just the Brits holding out against Hitler, I can tell you. Sixty years on, the Americans still see him as the iconic British bulldog, who would never, never quit and lie down, unless you literally put a bullet in his head.

So I hope this raises your courage in the question of taking action: with this impetus it becomes a divine duty to test, learn, fail and thus acquire knowledge. Far from being embarrassing, a failure is a step closer to God or to the divine, whatever you conceive that to be.

But only if you keep going. To fail and then quit is the ultimate insult to the gift of our lives. Like suicide, it is a deplorable cop out, a retreat without honor, from the task of creating ourselves and evidencing our Being.

18. The Thunder Of Knowledge

The Rise of Embodiment Learning

You may grow old and trembling in your anatomies, you may lie awake at night listening to the disorder of your veins, you may miss your only love, you may see the world about you devastated by evil lunatics, or know your honor trampled in the sewers of baser minds. There is only one thing for it then — to learn. Learn why the world wags and what wags it. That is the only thing which the mind can never exhaust, never alienate, never be tortured by, never fear or distrust, and never dream of regretting."

- T.H. White, The Once and Future King (Merlin is speaking)

Knowledge is sacred. It interlocks with our Being. It's been a saying of mine for decades that we are what we know. Think about this: a doctor is a doctor because of what he or she knows.

Not all knowledge is equal, to be sure. It matters little if we know the kings and queens of England or how to work the calculus. The latter may be useful, whereas the former is not, but neither are of much importance when it comes to our own Nature. The present educational system is not geared to knowledge of any practical value. Schooling is all about grades and passing exams. It's a false standard of learning. In fact it's been said that schooling and education is geared only to those who want to be university professors.

Doris Lessing is worth quoting here:

"Ideally, what should be said to every child, repeatedly, throughout his or her school life is something like this: 'You are in the process of being indoctrinated. We have not yet evolved a system of education that is not a system of indoctrination. We are sorry, but it is the best we can do. What you are being taught here is an amalgam of current prejudice and the choices of this particular culture. The slightest look at history will show how impermanent these must be. You are being taught by people who have been able to accommodate themselves to a regime of thought laid down by their predecessors. It is a self-perpetuating system. Those of you who are more robust and indi-

vidual than others will be encouraged to leave and find ways of educating yourself — educating your own judgements. Those that stay must remember, always, and all the time, that they are being moulded and patterned to fit into the narrow and particular needs of this particular society."

- The Golden Notebook

I'm talking about knowledge with purpose and, in terms of value, knowledge at a far deeper level. My standard of learning is full integration with the materials; knowing which becomes part of the structure of our mind and Being. It is all so involved with the nature of spirit and what it means to be, that in Supernoetics™, knowledge is looked upon as the highest possible evolution of mind.

But then, what do I really mean by "knowledge"? Let's take a look.

The Short Hierarchy of Knowledge
You are probably familiar with an elementary evolution of knowledge, often attributed to the 13th century Persian poet and mystic philosopher Jalaluddin Rumi, which progresses as follows:

I.   Knowing and knowing you know.

II. Knowing but not knowing you know.

III. Not knowing but knowing you don't know.

IV. Not knowing and not knowing you don't know.

Level 4, of course, is a dangerous degree of ignorance. It could get you into trouble, whereas level 3 might not. When a person knows what they don't know, at least they can take steps to remedy the deficit. But generals in battle, who think they know what they are doing when they don't, can get a lot of soldiers killed unnecessarily.

Thanks to the current education system, which teaches meaningless "realities" that cover up ignorance of actuality and life, most people complete their schooling at level 4, rather than level 1, which is where they should be.

This is the truth level of Simple-IS in our panoply of knowledge and the people stuck in that misery are IS-people.

My Own Hierarchy
In Supernoetics™, we go better than Rumi. Degrees of knowledge can be expanded considerably, to become a series of gradations that could

be considered a true Hierarchy Of Knowledge and this brilliant scale is vital to the full understanding of study and learning. It can also be studied in conjunction with my masterful Rising Scale Of Learning, which is a breakthrough in psychology.

From the full spectrum, I select the following identifiable valuable levels;

- Being
- Integration
- Understanding
- Look
- Thinking
- Know About
- Symbols
- Memorizing
- Naming
- Recognition
- Unknown

Remember to read this list in reverse: top is better, not last is better. You'll soon learn to "think" in scales, when you delve into the magic of Supernoetics™! Scales are far more useful than yes-no standards (dichotomy). Almost everything shades from one thing to another; it's the way the fabric of the universe is built.

The Lowest State of Knowing and Learning is Unknowing

I could have started this scale with false knowledge. It's something we have to live with in today's world. Lies and spin-doctoring are a way of life for many. That's learning in reverse. It takes you away from knowledge.

But the first real step on the way up is: unknowing.

As I have written elsewhere, all problems in life and living are essentially unknowns. An unknown is a disability.

As powerful beings, akin to gods who have lost their way, we know everything. In order to function in this plane of existence, we choose to selectively unknow certain things.

But we know everything is Source and that is why Plato famously said that all learning is "remembering". We knew it anyway!

You'll get that feeling often in Supernoetics™, by the way. You will feel yourself on familiar ground; a sort of learning déjà vu. The best kind of knowledge is that which fits what you already know. Then you know you are good ground.

Unknowing, then, is just a pretense. Don't forget that!

Recognition

This level is perception: seeing something is there. You have to make contact, to connect, to learn anything. So recognition is an essential first step. Perception is even the undercut of recognition. It's fundamental to knowing.

Naming

Naming is the next crucial step in knowledge. Words and language were the critical step in the evolution of human consciousness. Hans-Georg Gadamer's view (see below for more on this man) was that Being is not constituted as such by race and nationality, but, in his celebrated dictum: "Being that can be understood is language." If I have no word for something, it does not "exist" for me, so existence, or failure to exist, happens within language. Without language, there is no understanding, and language is a product of history and culture.

Language is about communication. It is about transferring, aggregating and processing information. As such, language is the gateway to all learning.

Labels are a good start in learning. But they can also be a curse. To label someone a "racist" for example could be far from the truth and a verbal convenience that does no justice to either the target or to the utterer of the word.

Categorizing is a skill at this level. Categorizing is an abstraction and based on verbal representations. Even the famous set theory of Boolean algebra is not purely abstract symbolism. It is verbal categorization into sets. You couldn't have a set of "All my past acquaintances", or "Dogs without collars", without the words to go with that, could you?

Example of a label: pen. Example of a category: writing instruments. We are learning a little at this stage.

Memorizing

Now we come to the level of knowing which is so prized by the educational establishment that it considers this all of learning! If you can memorize data, facts, figures and phrases, you have "learned" it! Can you write down "20 different kinds of writing instruments?" type knowledge.

Compared to understanding, memorizing is as nothing. You can understand something very well, without even memorizing it. You may have had this experience with, say, a language. You can speak it; you can get the right food when you order in a restaurant or ask for and receive good directions to where you are going. Yet when somebody tests you on your memorizing skills, it feels like you can't remember half the words or what they mean!

Symbols

There's a whole science of symbols and thinking, called semiotics. It's fascinating. Certainly it falls above naming and labels.

In Supernoetics™, we view symbols as substitutes; therefore really as fakes or not the real thing.

Symbols are just a substitute for true knowledge; they represent something but are not actually that thing. An example would be a chemical formula. It depicts certain items of content and appears to represent structure but it is easy to lose sight of the fact that we don't really know the nature of atoms and compounds properly. Chemical symbols are a guess. Religious ritual and symbols are supposed to be a substitute for transcendent knowledge of God or the Supreme Being, which factually is lacking. The problem is, that the ritual and symbolism gets in the way. We have divisions because we are divided by our symbols. You cannot have an Islamic God or a Christian God. Such ideas are foolish. It's only the symbolism that divides us and leads to conflict.

Real knowing of God would never allow such a thing. So divisive symbolism, by definition almost, is a very lowly standard of religious faith. What is called gnosis, which direct experience of God, is probably the same in all religions. How could it not be?

Knowing About

To know something exists is not a high standard of learning. To be able to quote facts and figures by the yard is still not true knowledge, in any sense.

A man who has read about Africa and can quote all the travelogue data but has never been there cannot rise above this level till he has. Music critics sometimes know about composers and their works but they do not know how to play an instrument or absorb themselves into a rendition of music.

Celibate priests advising married couples about the mechanisms of sex and procreation is an absurdity but well illustrates the weakness of this level of engagement with truth.

Unfortunately, knowing about tends to be the peak of knowledge in an academic setting. You can become a professor or don with enough knowing about!

Alfred Korzybski brought this whole issue into focus with has famous saying "The map is not the territory" or: the representation is not the thing. The maps of things, the lists of things, the essays about things, the teaching of things is not any of the things that amount to knowledge. It's *instead of* the knowledge.

In a very real sense, the map is a distraction, especially when it carries the illusion you know the geography of something, whether on land or in the mind.

Thinking

Until a person reaches a certain level of competence with data, he or she cannot think with it. It's "there" and he or she can trot it out but is not yet fluent with it, like learning a language. But it's important to be able to think flexibly and comprehensively with what one knows. This is the difference between merely knowing about something and it being useful learning. If you've really grasped it, you will be able to think with it.

However, it's important to realize that thinking is a far lower level of knowledge than being integrated with it. Let's continue to explore upwards.

Look

This is the first level of separation, coming down the scale. To look (at), you need to be disengaged. Therefore the person is not on the highest rungs of the ladder any longer. He or she is not integrated with the material but apart from it. From here on down, the more distance comes between the pupil and the knowledge, the less he or she grasps it. Mere memorizing does nothing to help really learn.

On the way up, it means the person is at last beginning to "get it", he or she can "see it", as we say. A wise or knowledgeable person will say, "Yes, I see!" notice, rather than "Yes, I hear" or "Yes, I feel it".

Remember the old metaphor of stroking with the eyes. Ida Rolfe, one of the great somatic teachers of the 20th century, pointed out that looking was in a sense touching with the eyes. Thinking this through, then "Looking" is a level of knowing which connects on to things. That's the sense in which I introduce it here. Connecting. "Aha!" That's a moment of sudden seeing!

Understanding
Above that, we rise to a higher standard that's real understanding. It's the true frontier of knowledge. It's the boundary condition between real knowing and academic knowing. Beyond this point, you've arrived, so to speak!

Know and understand is far more than know about. It means to have total certainty on data that is owned but not a very part of one. Familiarity is key. Missing aspects are not a part of this level. Knowledge is comprehensive, though knowing what is still to be learned is implicit in this knowledge level. A learned foreign language or a subject studied to expertise and easy understanding would come into this class. An instrument competently or expressively played but not with artistic mastery would represent this class of knowledge.

Integration
To fully integrate knowledge into one's Being is about the highest standard of knowledge there is (but not quite). It means one thinks it, thinks with it, feels with it, speaks it like a language, can expand outwards from existing concepts, solve problems and teach fluidly. In other words, what we would call competence. True wisdom, on the way to full mastery.

Once integrated, the person is really on their own knowledge cycle. Once you have it, it grows. Knowledge takes on a life of its own. At this level you begin to transcend your sources of learning. You become your own source.

Mother tongue would be a good example of this order of knowledge. A musical instrument can be learned to this level and this is the essence of artistic mastery.

That's not to say that outside sources have no further value. Of course they do. But the learner knows what's to be done anyway and will seek out their missing knowledge.

In other words, he or she has truly arrived at knowing and knowing what you know from Rumi's short hierarchy!

Being
Highest in this system of knowledge is "being" something. It would become, quite literally, a part of one's Being. The virtuoso performer IS his instrument. People in love we often say are being "as one" and this certainly entails a very high degree of togetherness and under-

standing. Zen is a knowledge-acquisition system, which is really a kind of psychology. The adept becomes as one with whatever he or she is doing in life.

All is for the present and there is no room for intellectualizing and think, think, think. In fact it's often said, "Don't think." If you think, you lose it!

See the archery example below for knowing at the level of Being.

Summary

To sum up then, it's not just a question of acquiring facts or memorizing by rote. The conscientious learner must first get past the difference between the words and the actuality; between what is real and what is just the map; between knowing about and being able to think with the materials. The process of learning is not just piling data on top of more data. It is one of obtaining new understandings and better ways to do things.

He or she must engage with the data or skills to the point of being able to look, see and think with them; then onwards to action. That's real learning and is synonymous with full understanding, which is what we teach in Supernoetics™. True capability (doing) comes from the levels of knowing and integration with self.

As for "being" the knowledge, if you've ever watched a recording of Jacqueline Du Pre playing the cello, you will know that she is fully and consciously being her instrument and speaking the music from her very Being.

A story from the annals of Zen may also be useful to illustrate this; or at least from a modern interpretation of Zen. Eugen Herrigel, in his book *Zen In The Art Of Archery* (which sparked a whole run of Zen in the Art of... books) describes an event of knowing and Being which almost defies rationality.

He was learning archery from a Japanese master teacher Awa Kenzo. Being the typical Westerner, Herrigel was impatient, stubborn, wanting to "know" (without understanding the implications of this scale) and he pestered his teacher until finally, one day, the master had had enough.

Via the interpreter, Herrigel was invited to attend a demonstration; it took place after dark. When he arrived, Master Kenzo was already present. The target was in complete darkness. A small point of light lit a faintly glowing stick of incense, so small it was practically impossible to make out, marked the target. The master agreed to be blind-folded.

After some time in silence, the master took up his bow and shot the first arrow. From the sound of it, Herrigel knew it had hit the target. The second arrow also made a sound as it hit the target. The master motioned to Herrigel to verify the condition of the two arrows that had been shot. The first arrow was cleanly lodged in the center of the target. The second arrow had struck the nock of the first one and split it in two (the notch at the rear end of an arrow).

It was a masterful demonstration of skill. It was also a demonstration of knowing and Being; knowledge at the highest level, as described here.

It was true knowing in a context.

Hermeneutic Learning
All knowledge has a context and that is most deplorably ignored by the current educational system. Teachers would do well to spend less time on Piaget and trying to make the children fit an imagined universal schema and put more time into trying to associate data and learning with its unique personal context.

Every student is a context. Each one is different.

There are two particular flaws with existing teaching methods, described and rejected by Hans-Georg Gadamer in his seminal book *Truth and Method*.

One is to pretend learning fits an exact science, where every particle is the same as every other particle. This may work in quantum physics or cosmology but not with human learning. Every individual is unique.

The other mistake is to believe that learning is 100% a question grasping what the source teacher or doctrine wants copied. This doesn't work either. The student is an individual with a history. He or she has needs, as well as the demands of the originator.

True learning is integrating with the self, not making the self into some robot copy of whatever else is out there. The goal is full and integrated understanding, not memorizing and rote. It could (and should) be called hermeneutic learning—not to be confused with another hermeneutics, meaning the New Age mystical theories about Hermes Trismegistus, such as the Rosicrucian movement (they just hijacked the word, though it's true they have a good grip on it now).

Our term for this full learning absorption, integrating into body-mind-spirit, is **embodiment learning**. Interestingly, there is recent science on lower layers of this idea: they call it embodied cognition and it means "learning in the body" as well as in the mind.

True hermeneutics, historically, was about learning and interpretation of religious, spiritual and wisdom texts. Hermes (Roman Mercury) was the messenger of the gods, which just goes to reinforce the sacred nature of true learning. Hermeneutics dates back to Aristotle at least. Today, the meaning is broadened to include not just the problem of deciphering sacred texts but to all human texts and modes of communication. We are a type of hermeneutic learning, for sure.

Definition: embodiment learning means to fully integrate knowledge with body, mind and self, in the context of our Being.

Since, by this definition, full understanding requires the state of integrating and becoming what one knows, the true science of learning is, inevitably, a study of the mind and the spirit. It is not merely an offshoot of psychology and behavior, which is where the educational system places it. The coexistence of Being (oneness) is the purest form of knowledge there is. Since Being is also love, as we teach in Supernoetics™, it means true knowledge is love. That nicely closes the loop and leads us back to the term philosophy which, as you know, means love of wisdom or love of knowledge!

Embodiment learning techniques are probably the biggest property of Supernoetics™ and something which can change the world the most. Personal growth is great but we would have to wait a long time to get major shift on enough people to alter the world.

Embodiment learning can do it from the ground up! To achieve that we are going to have to approach things very differently. As anthropologist Margaret Meade put it succinctly:

"Children must be taught how to think, not what to think."

18a. Thunder Of Knowledge Hacks

OK, here come the hacks...

1. Terminology.
Look up Hermes, Hermeneutic and be able to rattle off the Supernoetics™ definition of Hermeneutic given above.

2. Memorize the levels.
Be able to recite them from top to bottom and bottom to top.

Then work with someone who can jump around and ask you questions like "What's below understanding?" and "What comes above memorizing?"

3. Get a grasp of each level from your own or others' experience.
Take each level and ask yourself: where am I with this in respect of any subject? You should be able to find an example of each. Keep notes.

You intermix that with asking others where they lie in respect of topics and learning levels. Don't try to share the whole scale; it's too daunting except to dedicated Supernoetics™ learners and tutors. Just pick something like "know about" explain it and then ask, "Can you think how this applies to you?"

Of course you can go past tense. A person might very well remember being in the struggle state with something, confused about the terminology (words, labels and categories), unable to apply any of what they studies. But then they since learned enough to be able to work with or think with the data. You might even find someone with complete understanding, despite the educational system!

4. Top Of The Scale.
Try to isolate a story that illustrates knowing as complete Being, as with the archery story I have shared. This has to be more than a flash in the plan. It must be clear to you that this person lives and IS what they are skilled at.

You can use fiction as a last resort (I hope you don't need to). But stay away from corny examples like Yoda from Star Wars.

19. The Thunder Of Competence

Strengths and Talents are highways that flow through you. You grow much quicker when you try to reinforce them than by trying to correct weaknesses.

—William Kent Larkin

This chapter is really part 2 of *The Thunder of Knowledge*!

In that issue I told the story of a master archer, who has his "knowing" of the art of archery so integrated and so truly part of his Being, that he was able to shoot out a small incense candle many yards away, and send a second shot which split the first arrow, while blindfolded.

That's true mastery. Something we all aspire to—or say that we do. But have we patience to learn at that level?

Competence could be said to be the minimum standard of mastery. It's the least to which we should aspire. Competence is the more "everyday face" of mastery. Being competent means you are good. Mastery, in truth, is really a spiritual path.

As George Leonard, author of the book *The Way Of Aikido*, wrote, "There is a human striving for self-transcendence. It's part of what makes us human. With all of our flaws we want to go a little bit further than we've gone before and maybe even further than anyone else has gone before."

I vote for that! Mastery is going just that little bit beyond what is normally required.

But competence too is far from ordinary, in its way. It's a great gift for us to treasure. It's one of the wonderful experiences of Being. Ancient Greeks used the term *areté*, which meant virtue/excellence/expressing your highest potential and considered it the only route to true, sustainable flourishing and happiness.

Makes a lot more sense than reading scriptures over and over, as if that will bring you closer to holiness!

Morale

Nothing beats competence for building morale. The reverse is also true: nothing brings a person down in shame so fast or so far as the realization one is not really able to do anything particularly well.

When we are competent and can display our competence, we get a buzz. It's valuable to us.

Competence is really teaching you that you have causative power, control and understanding. That's a great trio for a start. It also shades into values like pride and persistence, art and integrity.

All these nuances are great for boosting morale. And that's something we can observe anywhere, any time: when we see someone doing a job well or performing a task competently, we see pride and smiles.

Pity the dope then; he or she is not going to have much satisfaction in life, until choosing to gain competence at something. Because it IS a choice... Anyone can actually build competence; even those we may choose to label disadvantaged in some way. We all know the stories of children who are (supposedly) mentally handicapped and yet exhibit the genius traits of a savant. So instead of being miserable with frustration and failure, as you may expect, these youngsters are remarkably self-sustaining and complete, unaware of any sense of lack.

They just enjoy being who they are and doing what they are so brilliant at. That's about all there is to the feeling of competence.

Logic

Logic too is a species of competence. It is one of Humankind's greatest attainments. With it, Western society was transformed forever. Today we could not use our handy computers and smartphones without it. Logic is here to stay.

It burst on the world stage in an amazing time and place: Greece in the Classical period. Plato (late 5th century BC) and Aristotle (late 4th century) are the two names we most associate with the foundations of logic. But all of Greek society at that time was blessed with great thinkers, from Pythagoras and Parmenides (late 6th century BC), to Socrates (late 4th) and Archimedes (late 3rd).

Plus, I must not omit to mention Thales of Miletus. Many, most notably Aristotle, regarded him as the first philosopher in the Greek tradition. According to Bertrand Russell, "Western philosophy begins with Thales." Thales attempted to explain natural phenomena logically, without reference to mythology, and was tremendously influential. He is credited with the first use of deductive reasoning applied to geometry. Also, Thales was the first person known to have studied electricity.

Despite the intervening millennia it's true to say that no modern thinkers have surpassed the level of logical skill and competence of these men. Modern philosophers may know more, because there has been more research, but they are tangled in their own disputations and, in a very real sense, lack the logical clarity of their Hellenistic forebears!

We have a great deal to thank them for. There is no question that a person with a high command of logic feels competent; he or she knows that his or her reasoning powers are solid and cannot be deflected by fluff, opinion, criticism or fashion.

In a way logic is self-confirming; when you use it, it speaks to you of exactness and reason.

Competence and a Sense of Worth
Self-worth does not come to a child when he or she is endlessly told, "You are wonderful...", "You are fabulous....", "Everything you do is just perfect..." This is a stupid and illogical approach which seems to have taken root in Western society, most notably in the USA.

A child's sense of worth comes from accomplishment—being able to do things. Competence is the key to self-worth, not flattery!

The child, like anyone else, knows the deep-down truth about his or her skills and abilities. He or she knows that a result is a result and that it stands for the measure of what you can do. The effete philosophy of TRY does not wash with honest people, including our youngsters. To glibly say that the outcome doesn't matter, it's how hard you tried that counts, doesn't cut it. The child wants to know that he or she can perform.

In a sense this "try" philosophy is a watered down version of the old British spirit of cricket (that is, cricket as a philosophy, not just a sport). We Brits gave the world the belief that the important part of cricket is to play well, with good humor and an energetic sense of self; this counts for more than the number of runs (the score). Who wins doesn't matter so much as how well you strived.

But if we gave the idea that losing meant feeling you a poor player, that's a mistake. To enjoy cricket and play it truly as a "sport", you need to feel you are good at it; that even if you didn't win, you played well; in other words competence is the pleasure, not the final score card.

So it is with study and learning. A child knows what it knows. Pretence is not a valid part of learning; just to "try" is not a valid part of learning. Only duplication and embodiment of the knowledge is valid learning. You know it or you don't. You can't even measure that with grades and tests; only the possessor of the knowledge can grade or score it meaningfully. That measure comes from competence at using the knowledge, not memorization of facts and figures.

The Irreducible Minimum

Trouble is today, there is a poison at work in the workplace. It is death to competence and morale. It detracts from any product, good or bad. I call it the idea of the irreducible minimum. It is the attitude of doing as little as possible just to avoid being fired. Nowadays the frame of mind is all too often, "Near enough is good enough", meaning no more care is taken on the job than it requires to produce a result which will escape criticism.

But that can be a million miles from what it takes to carry out an assignment properly. Asked to clean the office, an individual with this attitude will probably clean only what is visibly dirty, without attempting to move the furniture in order to scour and clean everywhere.

The worst of it is that the workman (or professional) involved in this kind of mentality knows very well when they are giving less than their best and the slow erosion of integrity this sort of cheating brings about is very damaging to self-esteem, work enjoyment and above all competence.

It is an easily observed fact that someone who is cheating their own standards, as well as the customer, will probably subconsciously sabotage their own success.

That's no road to competence and achievement.

Your dream will have no value to others and serve nobody, not even you, if you try to just get by. In fact chess teacher Orrin C. Hudson, who founded BeSomeone.org for kids, says to be really good is not enough, even to be exceptional is not good enough: to succeed you have to be amazing.

Try to live your life by that creed and you won't have to wait too long for success! Your morale will soar.

Deliberately Performing Badly
There is another twist on this. It's amazing what the human mind can come up with. It's negative creation, negative exchange and worse than the irreducible minimum – but it is kinda creative!

That's to do things badly on purpose. Not for revenge but to make sure nobody asks you to do it again! Some kids are great at this: asked to cut the lawn or do the washing up, they do it so badly they make a worse mess than was there to start with.

They try and duck competence because they want to remain somewhat invisible.

The trouble is it can hang over into adult life as an unexamined pattern. You get the lazy slob who doesn't want to do anything and sure does it badly if asked.

Well I'm sure nobody on the road to success in the Supernoetics™ tribe would be guilty of this. But it's something you need to be on your guard against – there are people trying to do it to you. You fire or teach.

The Tall Poppy Syndrome
There is another undermining of competence, which has been named the "tall poppy" syndrome. I have encountered it often in my field of holistic medicine. If you get great results and really heal people, instead of letting them die miserably while getting rich selling them worthless medicines, you become a target.

Being even half decent as a doctor shows up the criminal incompetence of most of your colleagues and they don't like it. No, not at all. They may pull your license, sure. But it could be far worse. They may try to get you jailed. Dr. Immanuel Revici, possibly the most outstandingly successful cancer doctor of all time, found himself being shot at as he drove along.

But it's far from just a medical thing. You meet it everywhere: at work, on the streets, among friends, in clubs and societies, in schools and at college... people just don't like others to stand out. It makes them uncomfortable and insecure.

So an exceptional individual is not as liked and admired as you might think. In fact the opposite. There is even language to go with this hostility and someone is labeled "arrogant", "cocky" or "big-headed".

It's partly a religious thing, at least among Christians. We are supposed to be meek; "The meek shall inherit the Earth" goes the saying...

Oh no it doesn't! Meek is a mis-translation of the Greek word *praos*, which means disciplined, not wimpy. A classic case of a formalized religion perverting facts to suppress people and gain control over them. Disciplined is a whole different take on success, happiness and religious perfection.

Discipline, of course, can mean will power: determination, persistence, not giving up. True. But it also means a degree of competence and capability. To have a discipline is to have a skill and knowledge base.

In any case, we admire tall poppies in Supernoetics™ and hope everyone who wants to can fulfill their innate potential and learn to outshine all others. We have the knowledge and skills to make it happen for each and every member, after all.

Talent Is Meaningless
Finally, let me put to rest an old, a very old, myth: that some people are born with talent and that is what makes them competent. They don't have to strive to learn, it "comes naturally" to him or her.

Wrong!

Apart from exceptional cases—who are probably born with a full-on past life memory bank which makes them a prodigy—the so-called talented people are no different form the rest of us. This has been researched at length in recent years and it has emerged that really "gifted" people have simply practiced their particular discipline more than the rest of us.

In fact we can put a number on the amount of practice needed to be exceptional in any field and that is 10,000 hours. To be merely very good, you need to put in at least 5,000 hours! This is all documented fact.

When people think talent, they think of Tiger Woods, winning the Golf Masters at an exceptionally young age. He is cited as one of the most successful golfers of all time and the highest-paid athlete. But the part of the story you don't hear often is that Woods began playing golf at the age of 2 and had easily put in his 10,000 hours of development while yet a teenager!

What about Mozart? (my first thought) Nope, he fits in here too. It's true he wrote symphonies from an early age but they are trite and were probably finished off by his father, who was certainly not shy of exploiting his young child for money. By the time Mozart was writing decent music as a teen, he too had put in his 10,000 practice hours.

Even the Beatles hold to it. Their years in Hamburg, performing every night, writing new songs continuously, soon racked up their 10,000 hours, when added to the early years spent performing in Liverpool. The result we all know; they became the most talented and successful pop group of all time. Their song writing and performing skills are legendary.

So forget talent. It is not the key to success. It may not even exist. Competence racked up by repeated practice and honing of skills is the real key to competence. If you have not done your 10,000 hours yet, no worries: that's a mere 5 years at the rate of 40 hours a week! Not so long to become a Tiger Woods, a Mozart or a Beatle!

There's one other qualifier: you have to practice in the proper sense, meaning to work out the bugs in your capabilities; hone and improve what you are doing. Just to put in time without purpose doesn't work; you'll just repeat your mistakes. It has to be creative practice time.

For more on this 10,000 hours thing, read *Talent Is Overrated* by Geoff Colvin (Penguin Group (USA), New York, 2008).

20. Honesty, The Surprise Tool

It may seem strange to many readers to bill honesty as a tool. Some people consider the very opposite to be their best weapon. More commonly honesty is thought of as the "luxury" option, an affected and decorative add-on, which is the first to go when times get tough and the chips are down.

That's where philosophy can change things and why integrated rational thinking is a must for big dreamers. Only by looking at the bigger issue is it obvious to those not bound by the hoaxes of self-delusion and greed that dishonesty, lies, cheating, short cuts and negative exchange are short-term solutions at best.

They cannot sustain.

If you have understood anything from this introductory manual, let it be that proper exchange (added value) is the only way to enhance your life, earn riches and fulfill those dreams you have promised yourself.

Rationality and integration in all zones of responsibility (12 Channels of Being, chapter 9) we have seen really defines sanity. It is also a new and comprehensive overview of the definition of "integrity" itself. Notice that integrity means "whole and entire, complete or balanced". It grows out of a sensible integrated life in all 12 channels.

Integrated rational thinking cannot exist without the accompaniment of honesty. Complete truth is the only way to endure and conquer because if you are misled about any aspect of your life, you are put in danger. You wouldn't want that from others; so you must not dish it out yourself.

To repeat: honesty and rationality is the same thing. Lies are madness and achieve nothing except in the short term and, even then, are of any doubtful merit.

When we tell lies we are admitting we are incompetent. We are also admitting fear. It is not so much that we are telling the world something it doesn't want to know but the pain is from telling ourselves we are no good and cowardly. No matter how much we sell the lie to other people, we cannot sell it to ourselves.

Self-Esteem
Anyone who has ever told a lie, and that is everyone, knows that self-esteem gets hurt.

So you will observe people who tell a lie go just a little bit sad. They know they just sold themselves down the river. Those who tell lies habitually become chronically sad. Compulsive liars destroy themselves. It's kind of horrible.

Apathetic people who are hard to help often have lives filled with so much untruth and dishonesty, they can't let themselves participate in Life. They withdraw for fear of the consequences. Here at least is one reason for the "lazy" individual.

One of the first truths to face then is that telling fewer lies means more survival, more pleasure - a greater sense of self worth.

Effect On Others
Consider also the effect on the people you lie to. To lie to a person is to treat them with mockery and contempt; you are in effect saying they are not worth telling the truth to.

It can hurt them considerably and also put them at risk - a person being denied the truth can come up with some pretty weird and unworkable solutions for the situations they believe themselves to be in.

If you want to get to really hate someone, just tell them lies and watch them flounder and look stupid. The chances are, they'll get to hate you too. They may not know what is happening from the other end of the communication line but they will instinctively know it feels sick and strange. Every time the truth is approached, it is forced to veer off on another track.

It can drive one crazy, frankly.

Blaming Others
Sometimes we blame others for our lies. "It's their fault", we tell ourselves, "Because if they were not the way they are, we wouldn't need to lie to them," (so we fondly imagine).

It is a hoax, of course. Trying to shift blame won't work because it is yet another lie - so our position is weakened more than ever.

We damage ourselves greatly by trying to pretend we are not responsible for our own integrity.

Digging Yourself In

There is another problem with lies. They multiply trouble. First there is the well-known effect that when you tell one lie, you generally need to defend it by telling others. You can be drawn into a web of deceit most alarmingly.

But lies also seem to attract other kinds of trouble. Bad things start to happen to people who lie a lot. They don't get the breaks. They suffer "bad luck". They get injured by "accident"; the "lose" things; they become inexplicably ill.

Honesty, then, is a question of husbandry. You tell the truth and problems recede; speak lies and you get trouble. The harvest from truth is more freedom, less danger and reduced counter-survival. Tell lies and the crop goes bad; you put yourself in danger; there is blight and dismay.

Luck

Forget the movies and cheap novels. Really there is no such thing as "luck" or "bad luck".

You get back according to what you put out. It's just another statement of the Buddhist principle of karma or the Christian aphorism "as ye sow, so shall ye reap". Look, this is a simple law of living that is so basic and so obvious that everyone has spotted it! Philosophies throughout the Ages have referred to its immutable justice and dressed it up in all kinds of fancy words and phrases.

It all boils down to the one simple reciprocal mechanical principle Outflow = Inflow.

Consequently, we can infer that if you haven't had the breaks you wanted and that life could be much better for you, you must have put out something that is now holding you back. To be more exact, the truth is that you subconsciously hold yourself back, because you don't feel good about what you have done - you know you don't deserve success. The result is the same: less optimum living.

The Inactivator

When a basically good person transgresses dishonestly in one or more zones of life, he or she naturally feels regret. This may be at some deeper unconscious level, while outwardly the individual is manifesting bravura and a couldn't-care-less attitude at what he or she has done. But we all know the subconscious has deadly force which can influence our apparently conscious reactions. So if the sub-conscious isn't happy with what we are doing, how do you suppose it will respond to "help" us?

It cuts our power. We have an automatic aversion to further activity. As it goes on and the transgressions continue or get worse, we become steadily more paralyzed for action. This is usually what lies at the bottom of the phenomenon of self-sabotage. Now you can understand it better.

This diminution of power, out-reach and effectiveness we call the "in-activator effect". It's a kind of withhold phenomenon. You can see it at work all around you, once you know what to look for. So if you are ineffective in some aspect of life, take note. You have probably trans-gressed for a considerable time, probably without questioning any longer what you are doing, and have paralyzed your performance in this respect.

It can be quite specific in focus, meaning an individual could perform well in many areas but singles out certain types of interaction to self-sabotage as a subconscious "inactivator".

Redemption
This begs the powerful question, Can anything be done to rectify this? Is it possible to restore the balance, perhaps make restitution for past wrongs, and so unblock the flows you need for success and happiness?

The answer is Yes. Indeed this is what religious confessional is sup-posed to be all about. Not that we espouse religious doctrine; there are too many hoaxes and too many unhappy collective experiences. One of the biggest hoaxes of all, taught by the Church, is that another can release or "absolve" your wrong-doings. This is nonsense. Even if it were true, why would you want to allow such an abrogation of responsibility?

Happily you can absolve yourself!

It requires mainly that you take responsibility for what you have done. Just own up to yourself; you'll be glad you did and feel better right away. The expression "coming clean" has particular signifi-cance here. That's exactly how it feels - like a cleansing. You keep listing your transgressions and misdeeds until you find that clean open feeling that speaks of a sweet conscience. It's a kind of transpar-ency and is characterized by a big resurgence and revitalization of psychological energy.

Remarkably, it isn't usually necessary to make restitution for all that one has done. Often it simply isn't possible. But where it is obvious that something could and should be put right then, if you are truly contrite, you will fix it up with the people you infringed against.

Enriching

Look, this isn't a sack-cloth and ashes trip. It is an enriching and innervating clean up. You are moving away from the shady tactics of the skunk or shark and saying "I am better than that. I am worth more. I don't have to deal with people this way. It isn't natural to me".

Do not allow yourself to feel degraded about what you have done. Yes, you may have skunked a few people; pulled some dirty tricks; shucked a few suckers. But by making this stand and repudiating your own behavior you are elevating yourself above the herd. You are admitting responsibility; it's something most people don't like to do.

It's a much bigger issue we call "Agency". It means you are admitting you are at cause. You rule. So it's no bad thing to own up!

From the point of view of expanded thinking and self-guidance you need to do this. Because it's all about cause. If you pretend to yourself that you weren't to blame for your own bad actions as well as the worthy ones you are saying, in effect. "I am less causative" or "I'm weak in at least one dimension".

These are not the words you would expect from a successful and integrated person. Do not enjoin yourself to this attitude. Even if you are uncomfortable with your admissions in the short-term, the long-term perspective is what counts. If you are striving towards something better, you have to accept what is NOW. You can't get at the truth by moving outwards from a position which is fundamentally a lie. Your map to fame, fortune and happiness can only help you if you know where you are presently standing.

Laziness

Laziness is really just another face of dishonesty. When an individual is chronically dishonest, he or she becomes inert and often sad as well. Humans are fundamentally good and do not like to transgress. The result is a self-imposed attempt to restrain bad behavior; the "In-activator" I have already referred to. He or she does not want to harm any more than hitherto and feels subconsciously that no action is better than continued dishonesty.

That's why the criminal is basically lazy. Hard working energetic crooks simply don't exist. The glamorized Hollywood image of the witty sophisticated urbane gangster is a myth. Any one of them would sell their own sister for gain. They are a sick and sorry mob. This shared insight is not to encourage you to come down on lazy offspring or colleagues from a position of conceited supercilious antagonism. That would merely be hypocrisy. This phenomenon is something we all suffer from to a degree. Look around your own life; you will find areas where you are definitely uncomfortable with the idea of involvement - people you can't talk to comfortably, topics that annoy you unreasonably or activity you can't bring yourself to engage in. The chances are that dishonesty lies behind this retreat from life energies.

You have been "inactivated"!

It is all about restraining self. The wife who can't be bothered cooking and cleaning her home as she once did has transgressed against her husband and kids so many times, she has become reflexly inert. Similarly, the husband who is the proverbial couch-potato has lost his drive because of numerous small daily infringements - lies, neglect and petty thefts - and probably some pretty big transgressions that his spouse or colleagues don't know about.

If you find yourself holding back in any area of endeavor, this is why we call it the Inactivator. You need to recognize the possibility of this phenomenon in yourself. Step back and challenge yourself; get it cleaned up. You will know you have when the excitement and energy for activity returns in relation to that area, topic, person or activity.

The truly aware self-managed individual will not be tolerant of something as destructive as this reserve and the point about this effect is that is it completely reversible. It is as easy to do as it is for you to coach yourself into being fully honest and integrated.

But we also have piloting and the release program called "The Golden Path" to help.

Getting The Breaks
However, for the would-be world-winner and dynamic dreamer, the important issue with dishonesty is that you don't get the breaks. You are holding yourself back; nobody else is doing it. This again is a question of self-restraint or "sabotage". There are numerous little unconscious "slip ups" and examples of bad luck and wrong turnings. But in truth they are all deliberate and fed into the conscious mind by the subconscious.

This leads onto another issue, which is self-worth.

190

When someone has a bad self-image, he or she acts as if it isn't quite possible to believe in personal success. The individual won't allow it to happen. Once very fast way to kill your own estimation of yourself is to cheat and lie. You know it is wrong.

If you have been suffering from that intractable nothing-will-go-right syndrome, then beware. It could be self-sabotage and you may have some integrity issues to work through. You had better do it, fast.

Here's a true example of what could happen:

A man develops an exciting and novel board game. Market testing, and what the computer people call beta-trials (limited release), show every indication this is going to be a winner.

But the breaks don't come. Sales are poor. The industry, and most especially the public, aren't noticing.

Then he meets and is counseled by someone who knows Supernoetics™ techniques intimately. She tells him to write up all his transgressions, especially in connection with business and honesty with money. After much anguish and coaching, he does so.

Bingo! Within days, the orders start to march. Within weeks the game is given rave reviews in the press and on local TV and sales soar. A coincidence? Well, that's what the brickhead analysts and business consultants would say. But students of Supernoetics™ know better.

Now you will understand the meaning of honesty as a tool.

Supercharge that dream!
Get down to writing your own transgression list now. Why hesitate? If you want to get things turned around and positively, productively moving your way, then you have no choice. This is a vital instrument. Any delay is costing you heavily in wealth, success and happiness.

Don't kid yourself you have been good. That's delusion - self-hoaxing. You'll have no problem coming up with transgressions, once you get started owning up meaningfully and writing them down. Do not be tempted to merely think about past misdeeds in your head; that won't work. Commit them to paper. This is your future you are playing with, do not fool around. Extended thinking is hard, realistic and merciless: fudging won't do if you want to triumph. Remember the reward, which is to gain even more control over your life, your prosperity and you future goals.

You must be honest with yourself, first and foremost, because if you can't be that, you have no chance of taking on life on your own terms. You'll be ducking and weaving, with justifications and excuses, rather than clean-focused.

Focus especially on the topic of business, family, or whatever dream it is you want to supercharge. Make sure you include the people you are or will be involved with, where you have a track record with them.

Look for the desire to criticize or reluctance to be involved in activity ("laziness" in any form) that may be flags to an underlying transgression. Prompt yourself with the general case qualifiers of:

1. "What value did I steal from that person?"

2. "What lie did I tell?"

3. "What am I holding back from them?"

4. "What did I force on that person that he or she didn't want?"

Note: it would be a good idea to get your write up checked on an electro-psychometer, by a competent Supernoetics™ pilot, peer mentor or coach, just to make sure nothing is left "hung up".

21. On Rightness

This is very powerful: grab a cup of coffee, sit down and read slowly and carefully...

> *A man should never be ashamed to own he has been in the wrong, which is by saying, in other words, that he is wiser to-day than he was yesterday.*

—Alexander Pope (1688-1744)

There's a great paradox here: people in good shape feel they are right. We have a joyful saying, "All's right with the world." But there is a murky side to being right, which is a ridiculous and destructive obsession. We call it rightness. It means I am right, even when I am wrong and others are wrong, even if they are right.

If this rings any bells with you (it had better), then read on...

You need to be able to admit to yourself when things are not right. To justify yourself instead of admitting you are wrong is to defend failure and unhappiness.

Rational thinking is mankind's most potent weapon. We rely on it utterly to overcome factors in our environment that would otherwise reduce our survival. Yet we can, by nature, be hideously irrational in our thoughts and deeds.

One question is always puzzling to any intelligent aware individual: why is it that people doing the most awful things certain to lead to succumb, hurting themselves and others around them still believe they are right? Despite all evidence to the contrary, even bright and capable people it seems, are unable to admit being wrong. But few people are more "right" than those who are getting it wrong all the way down the line.

Crooks, perverts, murderers, terrorists, fanatics, madmen, fundamentalists, devious politicians, and other undesirables all have in common the fact that, no matter what they have done to hurt themselves or others, they believe in their own invincible rightness.

The last thing a conscious being can cling to on the way to failure, death and oblivion is being "right".

It seems at times that the more wrong a person is, the more stridently they will yell about being right. Such people also strive to make others wrong. Nobody wants to be wrong or admit they are wrong and especially nobody likes to be told they are wrong.

The look-what-you-did-to-me case can be very uncomfortable to live with; it's all your fault. You did wrong. We too have our rightness and we want to assert it and these people antagonize our desire to be right.

You Cannot Choose "Wrong"

It is a fundamental teaching of Supernoetics™ that no being can choose to be deliberately wrong. This is a core precept wrapped up in my "Propositions Of Being". It's at the core of a procedure I developed called The Tri-Partite Theorem, taught to our life and living coaches.

You see, even choosing to be "wrong" (if there is a need to do so) is right!

It is highly probably that it is impossible for any organism or individual to override the survival instinct and try to deliberately succumb. Whatever anyone does, it is always with the intention of surviving better. No matter how stupid an action, the person does it because of the belief that it helps achieve a desirable outcome.

Even Hitler and Pohl Pot were stuck on this. Evil as they were, their intention computed as "better" from their aberrated point of view. They didn't see the consequences of their acts and the inevitable disaster, only the gain they were seeking short term.

Even "admitting you are wrong" is really stating you are right to change and improve. Often it is nothing more than a desire to escape retribution.

But what about suicides, you say? Well, they are trying to be right and make everyone else wrong to the point of personal extinction. That's how batty this subject of "rightness" can get.

Asserting

What is the mechanism? It's simple. A person does something wrong by accident: a mistake or mere oversight. They avoid feeling bad by making themselves right. They thus begin to assert it was the right thing to do and start to do it compulsively, to justify their actions.

They try to make themselves right by repeatedly committing the mistake or bad act. Nutty? Of course. This is so fundamental, I have even seen it in animals. Scold a cat for doing something wrong and it will do it all the more, to assert to you that it was OK. If you want to get someone to do something, just imply they are wrong for doing it.

We even have a bit of kitchen sink philosophy for manipulating people that we call reverse psychology. It is a way of getting someone to do what we really want, by pretending we want the opposite and making them wrong for doing what we actually want.

With luck, they will go out and do it, just as we intended.

Dichotomy

Right-wrong is one of the fundamental dichotomies of our existence (but all that changes with my *Incremental Scale of Logic*). It seems that it is a universal hoax of some considerable force that if you can make others wrong, it somehow makes you automatically right. This is fatally flawed, of course, but a curiously intractable logic. Most of us suffer from it; and yes, I do mean suffer.

The ability to discriminate between right and wrong is said in law to be what separates the insane from the normal person. Yet the standards that most people try to apply are based on nothing more than opinion that is, social mores or just plain prejudice. Unfortunately, without clear thinking on this subject it is very difficult to live harmoniously with others.

The real answer lies in our 12 Channels of Being. An act is right to the degree it is favorable in one or more of these Channels or zones of responsibility. An act would be considered wrong which caused harm to more Channels than were benefited by it.

A truly rational act is the one which contains the most index of right. This also defines sanity incidentally.

A quality "good" act would simply be one which did the greatest good in the greatest number of Channels. Such an act could be doing something, or not doing something. For example, an act which supported several of the Channels would be good (if it harmed none); to not do something which harmed many Channels would equally be right and good. Not putting your foot in it may be more beneficial than what you actually did do! Hippocrates had the term masterful inaction for this (doing nothing may be better than doing something).

Even destructive acts can be right, if for example it is to destroy or overthrow something which is broadly speaking harmful. Pacifism can be very wrong from the point of view of survival, if it means doing nothing while a madman like Hitler runs around killing millions. Destruction can be right if the overall situation is improved.

It is doubtful if even avowed pacifists would stop at killing bacteria and viruses, where these are harmful.

Dead Wrong!
To be as right as possible would be survival into infinity and be perfectly happy; to be totally wrong would be no survival (dead). It has some of the characteristics of a game: to be right is to win, to be wrong is to lose.

Infinite abundance, endless survival and the ultimate happiness which ensued are obviously somewhat theoretical concepts. But being dead isn't theoretical! So we have a strong drive to avoid being wrong. This causes people to want to be right obsessively and at times irrationally.

Interestingly, you don't have to be totally right to survive. You only have to be right more often than wrong. But the righter you are, the more you succeed.

Intelligence and knowledge have a great deal to do with successful survival, as you will discover as you probe deeper into Supernoetics™. Mental skills are all about being right, or as right as possible within your means, in a given computation for a given situation. People with poor reasoning faculties often make difficulties for others; they just can't see the best solutions for a problem.

Let me remind you we are talking about the issue of rightness here; to live to the full is being right. We cherish it in our self-improvement and ascension programs!

Rightness is something we recalibrate and help you find a true north in Act II (*Trans-humanoid Abilities*), milestones 12 and 13 along the Golden Path (*Justifications, Patterns, Stubborn Self-Serving Computations* and their allied mind mechanisms).

Trying To Help
Here's the queer thing: it is more important to a person it seems, to assert rightness, than to actually be right. In other words, an individual will persist with their blatant wrongness, rather than admit something is bad and change it for something better.

This can be very frustrating when you want to help someone change their life. You can't begin to improve something while the person is convinced there is nothing wrong.

Social workers, reformists and even the penal system come up against this one a lot. People don't want to be reformed when it means admitting they have been wrong. Those who abuse the welfare system do so because they believe they are right in doing it; the drunk thinks he is right and everyone else wrong, he wants to drink to show he is right and prove all the people who are wrong have done bad things to him; the criminal only pretends to admit he or she is wrong, to escape the wrath of the system. It is to appease others in the hope of reducing punishment, not because they really believe they were wrong to do it.

TIME OUT: take a few moments to think of a time when you could clearly see how to improve something but the person at the center of things refused to admit there was a problem. Did you get them to admit they were wrong? Did it do any good to try?

Save yourself the trouble if you want to change someone's behavior by trying to convince them they have "hurt" you or done wrong by you. You will never get it across that way. First of all, you are probably dramatizing this trap yourself and you should review why you want to let yourself feel that way. But more importantly, the suffering you show will only reinforce the other person's rightness.

Work Only With Rightness

All this leads to an important principle therefore. If you want to change someone, to help them and better conditions surrounding them, you must respect their rightness.

Work around the positive view and showing what could be done that is better. If all you get is "Yes, but..." in response to such efforts, you know you have a person who:

a. can't see the truth objectively, only their own opinions and

b. is dramatizing being right.

In this case, get them to explain at length what is right about themselves and what they have been doing in life. After all, it may be the first time for him or her that anyone has listened and been interested in their rightness.

And of course they are right. But what you want is for them to get off the compulsiveness and relax about it, not to be so defensive. This can take minutes or weeks to attain. Once you reach this point, you can make rapid strides in betterment.

A Simple Transformational Procedure

When a person is overwhelmed by life, having got just about everything wrong, he or she is still "being right", you may be sure, no matter how desperate. It's axiomatic.

To win trust and be able to help, you must tread very carefully and avoid this particular button. The last thing you want to try and do is point out where the person has gone wrong. It would not be accepted because, to be wrong, would be the final extinction. So you cannot succeed. That route is blocked.

The answer is simple though: address the rightness!

Just ask: "What is right about what you are doing?" or "What is right about your recent actions?". To relate it to a particular topic: "What is right about what you are doing with the children?" or (past tense) "What was right about what you did in your marriage?" The chances are you will get lots of answers and release buckets of negative emotional charge off the case.

For a person in better shape, or as the client recovers, you can broaden this out into general "What is right about what you have done?" but keep it to this lifetime, for sure.

We Are Always Right!
The power of this procedure is that it does, in fact, hit out at the wrongness and charge on the case but only obliquely, so it is not accusative. As the client insists it was right to dent the car, he or she gets off the charge caused by what is, deep down, a harmful act.

Instead of feeling threatened and defensive, the individual feels thoroughly validated. You can see some very timid, cautious or scared people turning into real tigers as you run it. It is wonderful to watch the person expand as they begin to think "Yeah, I am right... really!"

The irony is, whatever the person did, he or she was not wrong; it was right to do it at the time. It computed, otherwise he or she would have been incapable of over riding that intractable survival urge. Even a wicked act must have been right at some level! Think about it.

So you can always find the rightness of the conscious being and harness that, with good effect.

The end result would be a person who came to understand that there was no need to assert rightness, that it was better to spot source and admit the causation of one's own condition. And that is no mean level of ability to reach. Of course we have procedures, like Revelation Processing to help with this.

Overwhelm
Long-time worker in the self-development field, my friend Mike Davidson, confided in me that he believed that there was a power cate-

gory below even "Confusion" and he didn't know what to call it but the formula for digging yourself out was something like "Figure out what you are doing that is right".

Let's call that state "Overwhelm". But you need to wait to read my Power Categories to see how this integrates. Suffice it to say that, for someone out the bottom, this is as good a place as any to start them. Here we have one of the deepest undercuts of a case from any philosophy, any era. Its bite is awesome.

Below this is probably psychosis and then oblivion. Even the psychotic is right, in his own inner world. The outer reality threatens to make him wrong and so he stays out of it!

No One Is Immune To This Disease

Truth is only attained by those with the courage and strength of mind to admit where they are wrong. This is why progress and discovery takes teamwork, sometimes. A person gets an idea but can't progress far with it, because of his attitude of complete rightness. His or her innovation cannot be questioned. It takes someone else to follow along and get the bugs out of it, then someone to work out what was wrong with his achievement, and so on. Thus human knowledge can progress.

This is the answer to stubborn gurus and their self-delusional follies!

Even great intellects can stumble on this. You get people like Sir Isaac Newton, probably the greatest mind of all time, squabbling and being nasty with Gottfried Liebniz about priority over the discovery of calculus. Newton was clearly first but the truth is Liebniz published first. For some, it's the action of publication that establishes priority. If Newton had been able, he could have admitted objectively, that his long delay in publication gave Liebniz the chance to catch up with his own developments. Instead he preferred to accuse Liebniz of stealing his research, which was clearly ridiculous.

But Newton was incapable of admitting he'd been wrong!

Survival Patterns

Coming from some of the recent research in our *Transformational Psychology* is the concept of a "stubborn self-serving patterns". This is something the individual has adopted as a behavior pattern as a kind of "safe solution" to difficulties in life; it's a modus operandi. The individual brings it up time and time again, regardless of its inappropriateness or lack of workability.

We have a technique for eliminating these unwanted patterns we call The Pattern Breaker. Its efficacy rests on detecting what outcome the person is actually seeking and establishing a better way to come to the same result.

In developing this work, I came to realize the answer to what was puzzling me about rightness! It is simply that the value of the action takes its power from the perceived value of the intended outcome. It does not take its force from how clever or correct it is. A person may be doing something completely daft but he or she is so fixed on the desired outcome, which is valuable, that he or she cannot back off and will not even contemplating giving up what they are doing.

Not, that is, unless you can show them a better way to get the same outcome.

If you attack the action as crazy or point out it is "wrong" the individual feels your attack is really directed at the desirable outcome and goes into the defensive overdrive. Whatever is wrong with irrational and destructive behaviors, there is never anything crazy about the hidden desired outcomes that we have been able to unearth at the deepest levels.

These winning outcomes mean true survival: love, abundance, joy, companionship, or whatever. It is a good outcome and for this reason the mind can over ride or rationalize away the stupidity that is supposed to attain it and which is evident to everyone else. The rational mind isn't being exactly stupid but rather clinging too hard to the outcome it is seeking and paying too little attention to the faults in the road taken to get there.

This is another version of short-term vs. long-term happiness. It is also a considerable new insight into behavior, I believe.

You'll encounter its powerful enhancement changes further down the Golden Path, as you progress in piloting and experience our Transformational Mind Dynamics™.

Admitting Mistakes

To conclude then, one can re-evaluate behavior at any time, realize it is unsuccessful and decide to change it. This can only happen if we can bypass the mechanisms of "rightness". This in turn means being willing to be really honest and truthfully look at what we are doing and the mental landscape that leads to all destructive patterns.

This is not admitting one is "wrong". Get rid of this foolish and self-defeating limitation. Embrace change! How else can one correct mistakes and injustices? If one can move towards a better outcome, one can start to win in life and help ourselves to more happiness.

Let us avoid some of the strife by changing the vocabulary of wrongness to speak in terms of new levels of rightness.

Rather say, "I see the need for change" instead of, "I wuz wrong"!

22. We Are All Talking About Ourselves

People who go banging on about things they don't like, what's wrong with the world, my wife is a bitch because... are actually voicing what's stuck in their own psychological space. They are, "Talking about themselves."

> Everything that irritates us about others can lead us to an understanding of ourselves. - Carl Jung

Here's a brilliant application of the outflow equals inflow principle you can use right away!

Situation Encountered:
Friends, relatives, acquaintances with endless carping about the same stuck complaints and aggravations, which never seem to go away. Dwelling just a bit too long and being just that little too self-righteous about things!

Background
Shakespeare first said it with "Action speaks loudly in accusation", meaning what people tend to rant about reflects their own guilt about doing the very thing they are complaining of.

David Hume, Scottish philosopher, got hold of it with: "We never remark any passion or principle in others, of which, in some degree or other, we may not find a parallel in ourselves" (*Treatise Of Human Nature*, 1738)

I think it was Emerson who quipped "The louder he talked about honesty the more I was inclined to hide the family spoons".

Freud revisited the idea in modern times with a book called *The Psychopathology Of Everyday Speech*. In it he explains how what we talk about, especially when it is repetitive, is a reflection of our own negative aspects of case or "stuff".

From this book we got the term "Freudian slip", meaning some verbal marker to our real hidden feelings. It is rather like a flag sticking up in the sand; when you dig down, underneath is a buried sewer.

In fact Freudian slips have come to mean only smutty innuendos, but as originally used, Freud intended any revealing talk.

A more fundamental principle is that what we give out is what we find coming back to us. We create our own reality, through creative conscious thought, and thus what we see "out there" is a reflection of what lies within ourselves.

The bits we are free and easy on cause no trouble; it is the parts with negative mental energy or "charge" which we tend to hang up on. We get stuck to the unknownness that represents the difference between what we thought we wanted and what we actually got.

A reverse or complementary aspect of the same phenomenon is that what you reject, you get.

The Law Of Similars

My friend Susan Fludd, who has taken an active interest in the development of Supernoetics™, and suggested the title for this key strategy, calls attention to the homeopathic Law of Similars - Like tends to resonate with like.

What all this amounts to is that we are all talking about ourselves. Our language reflects our case; our thoughts and ideas are more than a little to do with where the charge lies in the memory and personality. The more we blame others, the more we admit our own guilt.

Understanding this principle leads to one of the most powerful remedies in this article; one which undercuts most entries to a person's REAL problems.

It shows you where the person's case starts and thus: what to handle first.

What You Do Speaks So Loudly, I Cannot Hear You

We've all heard this saying and it's a wise one. It too belongs here. People talk about things but what they do often doesn't match or reflect what they say.

In a way it's the reverse of "We're all talking about ourselves." What we do is more important than what we say. But it still comes down to the same thing: people obsess about their own stuff. If you see a person behaving a certain way, that's their case, no matter what they say by way of explanation of their actions.

In fact Earl Schoaff suggested a variation of this maxim: What I am speaks so loudly I cannot hear what you say and what you are speaks so loudly, I cannot hear what you say.

That's more akin to my saying. What we are being is given off loud and clear, both in actions, body language and speech itself.

Learn to read other people: they generally make it easy!

How Serious Does It Get?
Consider this: on 13th September 1996 *The Guardian* newspaper carried an article reporting that an Indian womens' activist group Mahila Jagran or "Woman's Awakening" were opposing the staging of the "Miss World" contest in the town of Bangalore by threatening to commit ritual suicide by burning. Ask yourself what could be more degrading to a woman than self-immolation as a protest? Then think who is talking about themselves!

It seem a cliche that many womens' rights workers are somewhat harming the case for their sex. But judged in terms of this revealing knowledge it would be predicted that those who complain the most are women who themselves are failures, trouble-makers and somewhat less than complete in the feminine virtues.

Or perhaps there is no gender issue at all; merely that those who complain of being held back by society's prejudices are those who most sabotage their own prospects of achievement in life. Is it not true that the majority of activists are at the odd end of society?

Research Proof
Now a study, published in the July 2010 issue of the *Journal of Personality and Social Psychology* seems to finally nail what I have said all these years.

The study participants, who were college students, were asked to rate positive and negative characteristics of other students with whom they were acquainted.

The researchers discovered that a person's tendency to describe other people in positive terms is an important indicator of the positivity of the person's own personality traits.

Strong associations were found between positively judging others and how enthusiastic, happy, kind-hearted, courteous, emotionally stable, and capable the person describes his or her self and is described by others.

On the other hand, negative perceptions of other people are linked to higher levels of narcissism and antisocial behavior. A huge suite of negative personality traits was associated with viewing others negatively, indicating a greater likelihood of depression, antisocial traits and various personality disorders.

Being overly negative may be a tip-off that the person describing someone else is disagreeable, unhappy, neurotic, or has other negative personality traits, the researchers say and concluded that how positively we tend to perceive others in our social environment is a highly stable trait that does not change substantially over time.

[Wood, D. *Journal of Personality and Social Psychology*, 2010; vol 99: pp 174-190.]

So - What Action To Take

If someone is griping bitterly, stuck obsessively on a topic, carps about another individual, blames partner or in any other way is dwelling a bit too long on one topic, then recognize that he or she is dramatizing some case.

Instead of listening to him or her complain, get the person to make a complete list of groans. Then turn it round on him or her and say "this is your list; this is what you are doing". A word of warning however- this is tough! Choose the time and your manner carefully, otherwise you can lose a friend.

If a wife complains her husband is abusive, get her to work out what she is doing to make him that way; if the husband says the wife is cold and distant, let him work out why that is his own failure; if the boss is a bully, what is he or she doing to provoke him; if the children are unruly, how did the parents make them that way?

This is a question of assuming full responsibility for a situation, if you like. One of the hardest things to do in a relationship is to take responsibility for the other person and what they do. Yet to accept less, flies in the face of truth.

Conversely, to show you understand this rule and to live by it is to manifest kindness, love, wisdom and tolerance.

Quickie:

A quicker version of this remedy, which doesn't truly handle but at least gets the person out of your hair, is to point out "Look-- that's your stuff, not mine. Now please drop it. I won't be drawn!"

It Applies To You

If you can live by this tough standard, you can save yourself a great deal of grief.

You need to practice the difficult art of self-observation. Basically, whatever you get mad about and makes you steamy under the collar, does so only because you have case on this topic.

It actually is not true that what other people do cause you pain. It's what you do to yourself. You hurt because is reflects something in yourself.

The trick then, is being able to peel back the layers. Sooner or later, you will get down to the point where you are at cause.

In that instant, all hurt and upset will vanish! This is remarkable but true.

Try it if you dare!

23. Quantum Loving!

Years ago, I wrote one of my most popular essays; it's called "Find The Love In Everything". I suggest you download yourself a copy and read it in conjunction with this section. I'll make it available as a download (some of you, I know, have already read it. Well, read it again!)

In it I remark that one of the greatest sayings I ever encountered and which changed my life the most at the time was that 'True freedom is liking what you do, not doing what you like'. It came from a text on Zen Buddhism, which appealed to my heart and intellect a great deal in the 1960s. As a number one unruly individual who hated authority and conformity, it was a completely new way of looking at the balance between independence and involvement in life.

Peter Caddy, one of the founders of the Findhorn community in northern Scotland, you may have heard of it, was fond of quoting his Rosicrucian teacher Dr. Sullivan: 'Learn to love the place you are in, the people you are with and the work you have to do.' The point is of course to find something you can love about the place you are in, the people you are with and the work you are doing. Just forget the negatives and smile. This seems to me to encompass much the same philosophy.

But we can go further than that and say that everything in life becomes wonderful, worthwhile, pleasurable and meaningful if we put love into it. If you find that you cannot flow love into what you are doing, then it isn't worth being involved with. If your task isn't something you love doing, then it isn't spiritually valuable to you.

The computer people have the term GI-GO. It stands for 'garbage in-garbage out'. In other words, what you get out is only a reflection of what you put in. Life is exactly the same as a computer in this respect. If you can pour love into whatever you have your attention on, it comes back to you. By that I don't just mean the old idea of someone will love you or the boss will give you a raise, though that's possible and a valid part of the formula. But what is overlooked - and it spoils the beauty of this bit of wisdom - is that: you get it back inside yourself. Something lifts and glows inside that gives one a tremendous feeling of lightness, joy and involvement that simply never comes if you're in a grumbling just-a-job mood.

What then of the mundane tasks, like washing up and shopping for groceries? Well, they have to be done. So why not put love into these too. You have a perfect opportunity to develop spiritually, so these moments can become a sort of exercise in personal growth. Instead of wasting precious moments of your life complaining and trying to avoid needful assignments, why not cultivate the skill of putting love into these too?

Of course it does help to know that your life is focused. If you are drifting from day to day, with no true purpose, then you cannot see the web-like inter-relationships between each simple task of the moment and your big life picture. If you haven't got a bigger picture, nothing makes sense any way.

So experiencing boredom, laziness and lack of involvement is a very good pointer to the fact that you need to shape up your life and make something of it; work out some meaningful goals and start to work towards them.

The reverse of this is equally true: when you know what you want to do and are working for it, every act becomes a statement of commitment, achievement, satisfaction and SUCCESS! Every small task becomes delightful as well as necessary, because it is taking you to where you want to be.

It's easy to "feel the love", if we put passion into what we do. That's the standard to aim for.

Food
One of the great times to discover love is while you are preparing food. There is a saying that the food tastes better if the chef puts some love into it. Well, you can test this out for yourself and you will find it is true! More than that: mealtimes are those moments of the day when there is time to take a little pause and feel relaxed, gentle and human. You can share it with friends where possible. If you all involve yourselves in the meal preparation, that's even better: someone to cook, someone to prepare food, someone to lay the table, put out candles, crockery etc, with LOVE. It all adds a great deal to the pleasure of eating.

If all this is new to you, try one or two simple alterations in your style while cooking. Put on music and dance while you peel vegetables; or swirl round once, like a dancer, as you move from place to place in the kitchen; or just make one or two graceful gestures with your hands as you fling in the condiments!

Here's A Simple Practical Exercise ///
If you are tired, inactive, lacking involvement or feeling resentful about what you are doing, stop and look for love. It is vital for the peace of your soul and the good of your heart and mind that you find it. Sourness and hating what you do is the very opposite of life's true principle of happiness. It will lead to trouble in the long run, and it can be BIG trouble - such as heart disease, cancer and an early death. I'm speaking now as a doctor.

If you can't find love in what you do and who you are doing it with, then it is time for a change. In the meantime, find something that you love; something to make you get up and do it before work; something to rush home for at night, so that you can get started with it. A really good hobby might fulfill this requirement.

Love That Problem! //
Again, to reverse the view, if one flows love at a problem, it will tend to vanish. Each individual must support the other and be part of the solution, not part of the problem. There is nothing more powerful about a loving relationship than the way that the two together can conquer seemingly insurmountable difficulties. It is a version of Buckminster Fuller's Synergy; two people acting in one accord are much MUCH more powerful than just the sum of the two separate energies.

There is scientific truth to the saying 'Love conquers all'.

Love is like life, it could be the same as the life energy itself. As beings, our spirit nature is love. You will never see a spiritual person who doesn't emanate considerable love and tolerance. So to love what we are doing and who we are with is simply to give life and expression to our deeper nature. By the same terms, to not feel love or have an expression of it is to shrivel and die as persons. We are depriving our inner being.

I can sum all this up in fewer words than either of the key quotes above by saying: being really truly alive is loving everything that you experience.

The doctor in me is prescribing you love; lots and lots of it. Have an abundance of this blessed feeling in your lives, so that you know the true happiness that love can bring.

Quantum Loving ///
But here's an interesting thing. This is from my friend Buryl Payne. He talks about his quantum theory of love. I like it!

A lot of people bandy about the word quantum, without having the faintest idea what it means. A quantum (plural quanta) is a tiny packet of energy, the smallest "something" you can have almost. Except it isn't a something, like a particle, it's a wave. No, it's a particle! No it's a wave. It's both! Even the physicists can't sort it out.

But start with the idea of a quantum as the tiniest packet of anything. In the quantum theory of love, what's the smallest particle of love? You decide. But Buryl suggested a smile maybe. Could it be a kiss? A hug?

Well, to me, it would be a thought wave. A little flicker or feeling that sent love and positiveness towards something. If an atom bomb of love goes off, of course, $e=mc^2$ means that there will be gushings of love energy. I'm sure you've had that feeling, where love grips you to the depths of your soul or, as Elizabeth Barret Browning put it so beautifully: *to the depth and breadth and height the soul can reach, when feeling out of sight for the ends of being and ideal grace...*

But—back to the smallest particle of love—go figure and let me know what you think.

The Mathematics Of Love
This is a bit tongue in cheek. Again it's from Buryl Payne. He talks about "gain", a physics term that radio buffs use. It's a knob on your amplifier. Most of us would call it volume but gain isn't quite the same. Never mind.

For the most part, well balanced human beings act like love amplifiers. In electronics, amplifiers convert an input current to an output current. With a given input current, the gain, or volume, determines how large the output current will be.

In interactions with each other, most human beings seem to operate with a gain of about one. That is, they do as asked, sometimes a little more, and sometimes a little less. Extremes exist, of course. We all know and feel uncomfortable around the minus 2 and 3s. It's wonderful to be with a plus 2 or 3 or 5 even!

But when we look around at people in general, we see that some people are operating with a love gain factor just slightly less than one. That is, they often are a little bit unfriendly, don't return a smile, and leave a place a little bit dirtier than when they came, or are apt to take advantage of a situation in a selfish way. They usually do not do this deliberately; just unconsciously.

Let's turn this into some phoney but delicious math!

The process can be described by the difference between 1 x 1 x 1 x 1..., which is always equal to 1, no matter how many times the multiplication is carried out, and 0.9 x 0.9 x 0.9 x 0.9..., which equals 0.66 after only four times. If there are a lot of .9 people, the result of continued interactions will soon be close to zero.

And that's what we experience, isn't it? If we are surrounded by lots of people who may be only a little off positive, the combined effect soon multiplies rapidly and we find ourselves down to zero energy. Inertia. That's what committees do; fusty groups.

One key rule to success is plough your own furrow. It doesn't mean do it alone. But it does mean you have to be king (or queen) or your own domain. Too many decision makers and there are no decisions at all, just dissent.

Buryl's math is very compelling: even if there are millions of people operating at a gain of only 0.9999999—very, very slightly negative—the eventual outcome of millions of interactions will still approach zero—and that's what planet earth is suffering from right now.

On the other hand if each transaction has a gain of only 0.01—a really tiny amount—after just 200 transactions the total of love has DOUBLED. The Earth needs lots of 1.01s, not 0.9s, to survive.

Buryl's formula even I can follow and I'm lousy at math. Let q = a quantum (smidge) of love. If it's a negative quantity that means a little bit of love subtracted.

So $(1+q)n$ just gets bigger and bigger; while $(1-q)n$ just gets smaller and smaller and will eventually become zero. It doesn't matter what size n is. N is just the number of negative interactions.

So to start this formula working for the good of all, for your own good, for your own success, for the happiness of self and others AND the survival of our fragile world: just add a minimum tiny quantum of extra love AND TEACH EVERYONE ELSE YOU COME ACROSS TO DO THE SAME.

You'll be surprised what comes back to you. And remember, as Buryl says: we are designers of the Earth-Park. We are also caretakers of it. Not just idle public walking through it.

Shoot For A 2.0!
Let everything be a gain of more than 1.01. Shoot for a 2.0!

When engaging with anyone, whether at work or in private life, focus on what you can do to benefit the other person, not vice versa. Your positive, genuine efforts will have a lasting impact.

Some people use the word 'Karma' in referring to this sort of concept. It's a complex Buddhist and Hindu ideology. But we can adapt it for our use. Think of it as kindness, going around and coming around. People who do good things generally find that they experience good things as a result. The universe - or whatever life force is out there - does seem to keep checks and balances.

But don't keep score. That's mercenary and doesn't work. Give to others and care for them because it doesn't matter if you get your turn. Remember what I said a few moments ago: expressing love rewards you NOW, immediately, in how you feel, not in some nebulous future reward.

Give people more hugs. Not every culture and environment is given to physical contact but it is an immensely powerful thing. Many people really enjoy a good hug - in fact sometimes it's the only cure when people are upset or angry.

We are born to love. Love is our being. Love is what you are. Don't settle for less than being your full potential.

And don't let people hurt you who do not understand. Hurtful people just need more love, so turn it around.

Do The Right Thing
Positive gain also translates into "doing the right thing". That's integrity, rather than love, you might think. But it is SELF-LOVE. Don't worry about what other people are thinking. It's what you think (about yourself) that counts. If you love yourself, don't allow yourself to degenerate into cheap, crude lies and cheating.

Sometimes it's very difficult indeed to do the right thing, especially if the whole organization and all the people around you are advocating and accepting something that's wrong. But often all it takes is one brave soul to ask a sensible question, "Do we all really believe that this is the right thing to do? - I mean is this really ethical and good?" Or to say, "I'm really sorry but actually I can't go along with that because to me it's not right."

And then lots more people will feel strong enough to say they don't agree either, and then you have a real basis for building something good and ethical. Sometimes all it takes is one brave soul, and that can be anyone. It can be you.

At the root of any successful change in life you will increasingly find the qualities of love and integrity will focus power like a laser. Don't sell yourself short. Remember, your reputation is the most valuable asset you have. Character is critical.

No matter what the financial temptation, never say anything you don't believe to be true; never commit an act you cannot defend as being entirely the right thing to do.

The "Love" Generation

I'm a 60s Boomer. We believed in love. We thought it would change the world. It didn't... or hasn't yet. But I still believe it can. The Love Movement got itself corrupted by drugs and crazy behaviors, notably among celebrities and leaders. Drugs take away freedom and awareness, they do not create it where it does not exist. And it's a fact, no matter how good your core philosophy, if people are left stupid, dysfunctional, ignorant and emotionally inept, your social philosophy will not work.

That's why in my Transformational Psychology we have a strong emphasis on freeing people from their automatic, subconscious, self-destruct behaviors. That's another story for another training.

But you could have a week long "love fest"! You don't have to take any clothes off, as we did as kids during the "Summer Of Love" years. But pour it out for seven whole days, non-stop, and see what comes back. You'll be amazed!

And if you get a good result, why stop? They say it takes 30 days to create a new habit. Keep it up for that long and enjoy a new life. Ebenezer Scrooge from Charles Dickens' "Christmas Carol" did!

Try a version of Anne Herbert's *Random Acts Of Kindness And Senseless Beauty* [you'll find that beauty isn't very far away, when love is around, by the way, but that's a whole different talk!].

Do something outrageously kind for others with no expectation of anything in return. Maybe unexpectedly treat the colleague ahead of you in the cafeteria line to lunch. Just for the heck of it. Throw surprise parties for people. Buy flowers for the office and share them. Let someone cut in before of you in traffic.

Workplace

All this can be practiced in the workplace too. Individuals at all levels of an organization welcome being treated as a full person, not just a workmate or a phone extension, or an email address. People are not inventory items! Show them love and respect. They'll respect and love you for it, in return.

I feel sad for many people at work because hugging is seen as a potentially dangerous signal. That's how love-starved and hostile our world has become. If in doubt don't use it; express yourself some other way (but see *10. The King Of All Communications*).

Nevertheless there are times when you can trust your instincts and reach out to people in this way, even if it's a gentle touch on the arm, or a pat on the back. Just don't single out one person to do this with and it should be safe from misinterpretation.

But you can always be plain friendly. Be the first to say hello. Never ignore someone because you think they ignored you first - they probably never even noticed you because their mind was on something else.

Take the generous view always and assume that the other person didn't intend to slight or upset you at all. Maybe it was just you reacting and not the fact that he or she is a so-and-so.

Love And Success

But now let's talk about giving. Everyone knows that giving and love go together. Getting doesn't work so well. But one of the universal laws of success is to give freely. If you give in plenty, it will come back to you in abundance. And, no, this isn't an accountancy thing, where you measure it out and what you give you get. It always comes back in surprising ways and from the least expected directions.

So love and giving coincide with our target: success!

Smart marketers know that people will only do business with you if they know, like and trust you. If you give freely, they are more inclined to like and trust you. That's obvious. Perhaps love is too strong a word. But then, maybe not. It's all about definitions.

I can tell you from experience in Internet marketing, that if you give people stuff for free, they like you and then want to do business with you. It's easier on the Internet because you really can give away lots of stuff for free, without going broke. Digital books and instructive videos don't cost a thing, beyond your time in preparing them. But people value these gifts. If they are good, of course they are valuable.

Knowledge, or what I call *remedial knowledge*, is almost priceless.

I recommend you read the works of professor Arthur Brooks. He's author of several books and introduced the term *Gross National Happiness*, or rather he took it from the little country of Bhutan. The term was coined in 1972 by Bhutan's former King Wangchuck, who brought Bhutan into the modern world after the death of his old-fashioned father. The new king used the phrase at first as just a casual, offhand remark, to signal his commitment to building an economy that would serve Bhutan's Buddhist spiritual values. But soon it was taken seriously and entered our dictionary! It's a pun on gross national product, of course, but more about love and happiness than mere money.

Brooks has presented some interesting research showing that giving freely (time and/or money) creates personal and communal wealth and, not surprisingly, happiness. By that I mean Brook's evidence showed the relationship wasn't just a correlation, which means very little. It was causative, meaning *giving creates wealth*.

Part of it, I'm sure, is the impact of altruism on our emotional state. Giving creates that nice warm fuzzy feeling, associated with the release of endorphins and it makes us happier. Additionally and perhaps more importantly, those who give their resources and time to others are perceived as leaders, and leaders attract success.

So if you want success, GIVE! Give till you bleed! It'll come back to you.

24. Don't Recycle Work

Do you have work backlogging? Do you find it difficult to make time for leisure activities (golf, nice dinners, museums)? Does heavy workload cause you stress? Are you tired and miserable at the end of a typical day?

Do you work hard and yet the results often do not reflect this?

You are probably recycling work. It's a common fault and so easy to miss what is really happening. Incredibly, people make unnecessary work for themselves. The most typical reason is the failure to terminatedly finish off what has been started. Take dealing with correspondence: the individual will read a letter and then put it down! Later, he or she has to pick it up and read it again. The loop was not closed (see 7).

Or the person is badly organized and spends time wandering around looking for key files, the stapler or something they had in their hand a moment ago.... Sound familiar?

This is all recycling work.

It's time to get a grip and correct these bad habits, which are so destructive to the proper frame of mind for enjoyable, comfortable working. Success comes through improved general work habits. The Program begins with one's own local environment, one's desk and office. The remedy to the above problems is a simple one and often overlooked with people searching elsewhere for the "solution".

Why It Is Successful?
Authorities on the subject of one's attention tell us that a human being is capable of thinking and dealing with six or, at the most, seven thoughts at any given time. So the ideal working scene would have the individual with these six attention units addressing the work in hand. When we have full concentration on what we are doing it is done better, quicker, and more creatively. Sadly, few people are able to use all of their concentration capacity at once.

Attention units for most people are consumed by their many incomplete actions or open loops. It is very easy to "trigger" a memory from the mind. When doing one piece of work a word it contains brings back a memory not often connected to the current work and there goes the attention. The more open loops, the easier attention disperses.

The most amazing aspects of this concept is that it is the small incomplete actions that prevent a person from being able to put all his concentration on his work! It is not the big incomplete actions! It is the small ones! Most of these small, incomplete actions require only a few minutes each to complete.

Stop Re-Cycling Work!

The best way to double your work is to pick up a letter, read it and put it down to do later. When you pick it up again you will have to re-read it *again*. Ouch! This is doing work twice.

The way to lessen your work by half is not to do it twice. If you receive a message to call someone, deal with it right away. If you use a file and it needs to be refilled, do it right away.

Peter Caddy, the real founder of The Findhorn Foundation, along with two women to help him, was fond of the maxim: do it now. In the moment. In fact he titled his autobiography *In Perfect Timing* (Findohrn Press, 1996). To Caddy, the perfect time to act was when the subject first surfaced.

Stop recycling work! Complete it first time! Do it right away! This should be the motto. Get it blazed across your forehead and keep it in mind. Do it NOW!

Otherwise you are constantly living in the history of your job, instead of in the present. Work becomes a chore and you cannot enjoy what you are doing with that feeling hanging around.

Older schools of thought on efficiency have either not recognized or not stressed the importance of this revolutionary work concept. Some have even contradicted it. They want you to be "more efficient", so you can pack more work into a day. Not much of an incentive, is it? But I want you to do everything at the timely moment, right away if possible, so you have more leisure time! So you can relax! Isn't that a more inspiring goal?

Organize Your Work Area

In order to ensure that all the work done to wrap up incomplete actions (closing loops) from the past does not go to waste, you must organize your work area for maximum efficiency. Otherwise the confusion just starts again.

Never cure the symptom without first curing the cause of the disease (that's the doctor in me talking!)

Start with a three-basket organizing system on your desk or in your work area:

1. One basket is marked IN and receives incoming correspondence

2. The second is marked TO DO or PENDING and holds any correspondence or projects not yet complete, usually awaiting further data

3. The third basket is marked DONE or OUT, which is where you place all outgoing correspondence when you are DONE with it.

You will need these, as described later.

A file system must also be established. Usually office desks have one drawer large enough to put in a file system. If not, file-holder systems with wheels at the bottom exist which can be placed near your desk. The file system is used to file papers and materials you refer to in doing your work. They can also hold outstanding projects. They can be used to keep the papers you refer to regularly in a convenient handy place.

The file system is put in alphabetical order so things can be found again easily. The best time to put the system together is at the same time you are going through all the papers in your work space and cleaning up the area

Layout

The next thing to check is: Do you have at hand all the tools you need to do your job? Order can be defined as having everything in its proper place. Do you have paper, pens, stapler, hole punch, plastic files, paper clips, scotch tape, eraser, etc., all in easy reach? Do you know where they are? Or do you have to get up and leave your chair to get a paper clip every time you need one?

Do you have the forms you use or letterhead, envelopes, correction fluid etc. all to hand? To organize this, you look for everything you need to do your job and ensure it is put within immediate reach.

The reason you organize your work area is to make it easier to complete actions in the present and future. Simply speaking, if you do things now and keep your area organized you will not waste time. If you don't waste time, you will have more of it spare, to do what you want with!

Priorities

Lack of agreement on priorities can create a great deal of work and confusion. The establishment of proper priorities is essential to work efficiency.

1. Nearly every piece of work is someone's priority. An internal memorandum arrives in your office from a colleague requesting some information. You read it and decide it is not a priority for you. You put it aside... But to your colleague, the information requested was a priority. So, some days later he arrives in your office or phones you. This interrupts what you are doing. You will now waste time explaining why you haven't answered his memo. You will probably have to provide him with the information he requested anyway, so you are just doubling your work load, right there.

    When your colleague departs you will return to your work and spend some time retracing your thought pattern, which had been interrupted. So that slows you down too.

    It would have been smarter (and more efficient) to just do it, in the first place.

2. "Priorities" can be used as an excuse to put things off - procrastination. This is frequently the case with work we don't like to do. Procrastination wastes your time. You will find yourself worrying about things you haven't done. Some of your attention units will be tied up on the things you haven't done. You will not have as much concentration on the piece of work you are attempting to deal with. Therefore, it will take longer to complete... and you might make mistakes you otherwise wouldn't.

Quick tip: here is a piece of advice worth mentioning to help keep procrastination at bay. Each morning when you begin work, select the task you hate the most and do that first. With that out of the way, you will now have the rest of the day to look forward to. The worst aspect of the distasteful task is the contemplation of doing it. The best aspect is having completed it.

Develop the habit of dealing with every piece of work that comes your way when it comes your way. When you complete it, you will not have to deal with it again. Once that work habit exists, and you are not using "priorities" as an excuse to put things off, then you can begin to effectively use planning to organize your work.

Individual intelligence enters, of course, figuring out the best sequence for how to do it all as quickly as possible. Just avoid re-cycling. It's madness!

If you need to phone someone external to your organization but cannot make contact, call the other party, or send a text, or an email, alerting them to the fact that you are awaiting a reply. He will receive your communication. Once put in writing or in the form of a voicemail, for you it's over. You don't have to tie up attention units with "I must remember to contact John".

Delegation
Definition. To delegate (v.) 1. to give or commit duties or powers to another as agent or representative; depute. 2. to send, authorize, or elect (a person) as agent or representative.

A primary function for any executive, is the correct delegation and routing of work. An executive is responsible for ensuring those under his care get the work done. A key to this is ensuring they receive the work to do. His job is to issue the order (make sure they write it down), send the memo, client, materials, mail etc to the proper person to deal with the matter. Executives can fail to send the work on and try to do it all themselves. They also can send the wrong work to the wrong person. Either causes confusion and inefficiency.

Executives and administrators, who have subordinates working for them must be alert to the mistake of retaining work that rightfully belongs with the subordinate. This is frequently caused by fear of overloading the subordinate. But then you overload the executive! Do not retain the work in such an instance. Pass it on to the proper person. It is normally the person at the top who is most overloaded. Nothing ties up a business faster than overload at the top.

Route and delegate the workload.

Action
Ready? Here's a major catch-up step. You need your 3-basket system set up: IN, TO DO, and DONE.

Then do the following, alone or with the help of an assistant:

A. Go through your desk and gather together all papers. Put all papers from in and on top of your desk into your "IN" basket (or on desk if basket too small).

B. Take any notes from the wall and any papers filed on side tables, bookcase or cabinets. Put these into your "IN" basket.

C. Empty out your briefcase (look under the desk blotter too!).

D. Gather everything you can find that is not totally and utterly finished with (if it really is finished with, file it or trash it).

Now... Pick up the top paper and deal with it now!

With each particle you pick up you can:

1. Deal with it to completion. No more recycling.

2. Delegate it if you have personnel under you to do the job. No more recycling.

3. File it if it is information you need and doesn't require that you do anything. No more recycling.

4. Throw it away if it is trivial, already dealt with, or of no use. No more recycling.

5. If it is a long project, or requires extensive work to complete, or you need to gather more information - move it to the TO DO basket. Do what you can; get something moving on it. Create a nudge file for it to be followed up and completed when the needed information is received. No more recycling.

6. Keep all papers from the same project together in one file. No more recycling.

7. Set aside time each day to do your paperwork, mail, memos etc. Do it once a day in that time. No more recycling.

As you deal with your papers put a working file system together:

I. File those papers you refer to and work with in your job.

II. Categorize the papers so they are easy to remember and locate.

III. Put the categories in alphabetical order.

Planning

Once one has completed the past incomplete actions, has organized the work area, and applied the *No More Recycling* philosophy to the workplace, only then planning then comes into the picture.

Because other efficiency courses stressed planning without placing the correct importance on correcting the underlying principle that led to the mess, these efficiency courses often failed. Having planning books is convenient and impressive, but if all they are used for is writing down all the things one is inevitably going to put off doing, it's all a waste of time!

Planning comes into use when one is organized enough to be able to effectively execute the planning.

Work At Home

All this advice applies, of course, to work at home and running the home office.

But don't forget it can also apply to running the home itself! There are bills to pay or file, shopping lists, outstanding jobs, errands and improvements that are all in some stage or other: IN (not started), TO DO (pending) or DONE!

You might even find bringing in the 3-basket system helps bring calm in the household too! Not re-cycling at home doesn't mean more time to work; it means more time with the kids, out hiking, at the ball game or a concert.

Summary

No more recycling is a means to have more time and leisure. It does not mean you have to work harder.

Normal time and motion approaches from the so-called business consultants means (usually) better schedules, lists of targets, fitting more in the day....

But we don't want to fit more work into the day! We want to work less. Don't we?

We want to get the results we are paid for or require, in order to earn our living. So putting an end to unnecessary re-cycling or work is a means of doing that with less effort. You can be more efficient and have bags more free time. Less stress. Happier working conditions. That's what we would all like to see.

Once more:

Don't recycle work. Just do it!

APPENDIX

What Comes Next?

If you have enjoyed reading this book so far, you'll want to know more about our Supernoetics™ powerful life and living transformation techniques.

In particular you will want to know more about piloting which, as has been hinted, is a deep psychological cleansing of unwanted and disempowering thoughts and old energies (no, not "brain-washing"!) It's a nice mental detox and a gentle spiritual refresh. But really, it's much more than that. We effectively modify the interface between your mind and the world, so you find much more delight in living and you are more at the cause of things. As a long-time member of MENSA, the high-IQ club, I have naturally been interested in development along the lines of improving human capability and avoiding destructive irrationality. What we have now, I believe, is something very special; in fact, quite amazing.

Once in a while something turns up which is truly revolutionary; different from anything which has gone before and in every sense a "new" approach to matters. Sadly, there have been few such developments in the field of the mind. Probably the most pivotal breakthrough of all time was the recognition of the power of the subconscious mind, so named by French psychiatrist Pierre Janet and later, rather unfairly, attributed to Freud.

Certainly Freud has a place in history, justly deserved. His seminal 1895 work *Studies In Hysteria*, written jointly with Josef Breuer, showed that the subconscious mind was very powerful and capable of influencing thoughts, emotions and behavior, while remaining out of view to the patient or client. It was truly sub-conscious.

Together, Freud and Breuer took Janet's original insights and developed a whole new specialty that laid the foundations for what became known as dynamic psychiatry and clinical psychology.

Psychoanalysis held the center stage and practitioners were getting remarkable transformations and recoveries, using the simple technique of getting the client to talk about his or her problems. Indeed, the method was to be long known as "the talking cure", with a slight sneer of disapproval from those who considered it trivial.

By the 1960s we had reached the point where almost every medical affliction, other than fever and malnutrition, was seen to be a result of dysfunctionality in the mind. Doctors began to believe that everything was "psychosomatic" in origin, a word that means mind-body.

Gradually, the use of this word morphed into something more sinister: that a person was weak or inadequate and imagined their symptoms, which were not actually real.

Chemical Psychiatry
Things might have continued along those lines but for the rise of the current chemical view of mind states: the idea that every feeling—good or bad—is the result of a lack or imbalance in neurotransmitter molecules in the brain. Even happiness today is deemed to be a result of having sufficient quantities of serotonin and dopamine. This chemical model has resulted in a shift of emphasis in studying mind function away from the impact of a person's life experiences towards the idea that everything is caused by biochemical dysfunction.

It's a sterile (and dangerous) model, which has led medicine astray for decades and resulted in legions of individuals swallowing "happy pills" in the mistaken belief that their uncomfortable and unwanted feelings are the result of some deficiency state or excess. I need hardly point out the parallels between this chemical dream and the current recreational drug craze.

Somewhere along the way, the old idea that a person thought what they thought, felt what they felt and behaved as they did, because their experiences in life had led them in that direction, has disappeared in a welter of pharmacological marketing and hype. The sad truth is that this biochemical model is not working. People are not happier by taking antidepressants. Instead, the person's helplessness is being reinforced and made more inescapable.

A few struggling counselors, with no effective model on which to base their help, struggled on with the notion that life experience was important and formative. But without adequate understanding of how unpleasant memories translate into unwanted feelings and behaviors, their efforts can be seen as ill-advised and often unhelpful, merely grinding the client deeper into their misery by repetition and endless discussion.

That was the condition of well-meaning help... until recently.

New Mental Grammar
Now we have Transformational Mind Dynamics™ (TMD)! This is a breakthrough technology that I rate as second only to the discovery of the subconscious mind and its powerful automaticity.

It takes the story very significantly forward.

Through the TMD method we learn exactly how experience is internalized and why the accompanying "charge" (black energy) is able to take executive control of a person's mind.

The answer, it turns out, is really rather simple. Although the result of negative experiences is unwanted and disempowering thoughts, those thoughts are NOT the cause of the problem! The trouble comes about due to the mechanical impact of those same experiences; the force, the effort, if you like. It is this force or psychic violence which pins unpleasant emotions into place and leads to disturbing and unwelcome thoughts.

To merely process or try to eliminate those "bad thoughts" is hardly ever effective because the underlying mechanism holding them in place is not addressed at all.

My good friends and colleagues, researchers Rolf Dane and Heidrun Beer, have together evolved a method of removing what I just referred to as the psychic violence. This releases the negative emotions and then... bingo!... as if by magic, all the unwanted thoughts come tumbling out, like an unblocked water channel and they quickly vanish from view, never to disturb the client again.

The person is utterly transformed by their release from the grip of the subconscious mind. I have experienced it, seen it at work and learned to do this for myself, so I am talking to you here from direct experience, not mere theory. I am very pleased to have learned this new approach; it has totally transformed how I deal with a dysfunctional human being.

And you know what is so great about this? It's very, very easy to do.

There is a whole fresh mental grammar, which we need to chart this new territory. Many of the concepts Dane and Beer found crucial have not been described before, or at best only dimly grasped and the correct importance not given to them.

The basic mechanism is that the energy or force buries emotions and makes their origins difficult to trace; emotions in turn hold in place self-limiting or destructive thoughts. The latter appears to be what the person is suffering from but in fact thoughts are insubstantial and, in theory, should not twist and damage a person's life and living.

What's surprising and new is that we are not really concerned with "the story" at all. That's been the major distraction introduced by

Freud and taken up by New Age counselors and "therapists". We have become so accustomed to listening to the client/patient telling us what happened, that we have come to believe that the case is all about what happened.

That's just not true.

It's about the force of what happened, and the reaction to what happened, trapping encysted emotions, and building up layers of self-defeating thoughts and decisions on top of the unpleasant experience.

TMD is about thoroughly reducing the effect of each life encounter, eradicating the force, effort, emotion, thoughts and postulates surrounding the event that happened. It's actually a real sequence; we bleed off the force, which releases the emotions, which frees up thinking and allows better decisions. The future is changed, because we emerge changed, refreshed, with new awareness and new postulates to guide our future.

Other People Involved
But this isn't just about the self-viewpoint. Dane and Beer have evolved a very comprehensive procedure that also takes care of the feelings and reactions of other people involved along with us in our activities.

"No man is an island," poet John Donne (1572–1631) famously said. "Never send to know for whom the bell tolls; it tolls for thee..." It's your funeral, as well as the dead guy's burial. We are all in this together! So nothing happens to you that doesn't also happen to me, to your parents, to the local boys club, to the pooch. Everyone is in on it.

So not surprisingly, things which happen to us and because of us, affect the people around us. They are not just spectators; they are players too. We impacted them; but THEY IMPACT US. It's rather like an echo; it's our voice that shouts but the echo comes right back to us. And the sound bounces around the environment a good deal, before it finally fades.

It's astonishing that other schools of growth and development don't take these multiple-personality dynamics more seriously!

In Transformational Mind Dynamics™, we have our willing client take up the viewpoint of others, starting with the antagonist or opposition. What did the rapist feel at the moment he was carrying out the brutal assault? What in God's name was she thinking of when she walked out the door? Why did Mom always talk to me that way?

The strange thing is, we seem to know! If you occupy the viewpoint of the domineering husband, the inept boss at work, the chump who stole your first girlfriend, and find his emotions, his effort and what disastrous thought computation he was struggling with, suddenly you are released and cleansed from something you didn't even think belonged to you! It's wonderful to behold.

By having the client see the events of their lives through the eyes of others and with the others' feelings, we gain a far deeper insight into the meaning of what we jokingly call life.

It builds compassion. It builds wisdom. We grow immensely in stature as we finally learn tolerance and forgiveness. We come at last to understand, as John Donne said so beautifully, that we are all in this together!

Personalized Healing

I highly recommend you book yourself some sessions of TMD and begin exploring your psychic terrain. It is not enough to merely want to feel better or to "pull yourself together" and tell yourself you shouldn't suffer. As Freud and Breuer taught us (well, Pierre Janet, actually) the source of the pain will always remain hidden in the sub-conscious mind, unless you use a special revelation method to get at it.

Hypnotism is a bit hit and miss, athough it offends expert hypnotherapists to say so. Transformational Mind Dynamics™ on the other hand is as predictable and well worked out as quantum physics or diatonic musical scales for the mind. Please understand it's not "psychotherapy", it's explorations of mind and Being. Such a mental detox or cleansing of emotional debris is actually one of the *Three Pillars of Healing* I described in my book on cancer alternatives.

The TMD technique is now (as of July 2015) so well developed that it can be conducted in one-to-one sessions, over the phone or Internet. Members of the worldwide team help people all over the planet recover from past distresses and create a vibrant new future for themselves.

As I said, I have learned it myself and can fully vouch for its efficacy. Rates are very reasonable. You just have to learn to use skype. It's like having one of these experts in your living room!

To book a FREE introductory interview, call my executive assistant Amy on this number: +1 866 200 0456 or 001 866 200 0456 which feeds directly to her cell. (Amy has done TMD too!)

For the rest of the world, please email: piloting@supernoetics.com. She'll get you started.

Please act swiftly if you are interested; you'll appreciate there are only so many hours in a week, so it would be best to grab a place.

For health practitioners who are interested in incorporating new and exciting techniques into your methods, I especially commend this to you... A much bigger bottom line and more satisfied clients!

See you further along **The Golden Path** (see *Me To The Max*).

Keith Scott-Mumby MD, MB ChB, HMD, PhD

The 8-Step Way

I developed the Supernoetics™ 8-fold approach to change your life and change the world around you. The mind is our first environment—we should be as concerned with mind pollution as we are about contamination of our food, water and air. More so, even. Yet we don't make effective moves towards mental health and hygiene. We continue in the same old destructive rituals and patterns, even though we see clearly that they don't work and are, basically, toxic behaviors.

It's time for a change. A real change. Get involved with a wonderful and proven way forward...

STAGE 1. Sponsored FREE newsletters to help you understand why and how we are different and to inspire you to start making beneficial changes in your life.

STAGE 2. Sponsored FREE online course material. Subscribe today and work through the New Thought Horizons program. You'll be amazed and begin to see just what a revolution is on the way, with Supernoetics™. We have the protocols for change and human transformation™.

STAGE 3. Start to work on your own inner environment. We often go off the rails in life but the route back home to yourself is now well-mapped and documented by colleagues and me. What we call piloting will free you from the restraints and pain of the past. A new shining YOU emerges, energetically clean, vibrant and living in the NOW! It starts with personal one-on-one coaching. You can take a trial run, with no up-front commitment.

STAGE 4. Sponsored FREE day and half-day education programs for our kids and teens. Let's start teaching the new generation proven better behaviors. Stop them picking up the disastrous mental habits and poor performance of their parents and elders! (OK, painful to say, but it had to be said).

STAGE 5. Start the learning process by enrolling in our courses. *Ability Express* is the first step towards mastery. You will learn completely new models of reality, which have never before been divulged and explained. You will learn healing techniques you can use to help anyone get better outcomes in living.

STAGE 6. Learn to help others. Enrol on our piloting training and become an expert coach/mentor for others. In the 1990s, I developed the concept of "cascade learning", meaning everyone takes a stage in the transmission of knowledge. You learn how to learn, effectively. Then you learn. Then you teach others how to learn. Then you teach others. Then you teach others how to teach others... and so on. Pretty soon, you'll have started a wave of enthusiasm and improved living. We have saved businesses, saved marriages, got people back on their feet after a disaster and found that, as a result, these survivors want to help others to a better life too!

STAGE 7. Join our team. Become a staffer. Be a facilitator. Start your own center, running classes, retreats and seminars. You'll be taught everything you need to know to succeed at this. You can earn serious money. It could even become your main work or a new career. This is not a cult; you don't have to live on rice and beans. We pay our members well!

STAGE 8. Travel the world as a thought leader. Carry the message to all parts of the globe and start fires! A wildfire of learning, real learning, like reason, love, integrity and wisdom, would save the world right now. We want THE FLAMES to consume all ignorance, violence and injustice. The target is international accord, harmony, justice and sustainability. Nothing less will satisfy me and my upcoming leaders!

The world needs YOU! Why don't you step into the main character role of your life, which is to be spirit, love, success and joy? The path is just as much delight as the destination.

Join today. Sign up for your free inspirational letters and get to work on the New Thought Horizons course.

www.supernoetics.com/join

Index

Peter Pan days 115
Peter Shepherd 39
Pierre Janet 227
Planet Zod 92
Platinum Rule, The 35
Plato 169, 179
Plausible distractions 135
Pohl Pot 194
Priorities 220
Private Soliloquy 128
Process loop 42
Procrastination 44, 138
Production syllables 158
Propinquity 62, 72, 103
Propositions Of Being 45, 146
Pull the trigger 139
Pythagoras 179

Q

Quantum, a 211
Quantum Loving 208, 210
Quitting (study) 9

R

Random Acts Of Kindness And
    Senseless Beauty 214
Rapture 123
Rationality 98
Reality Therapy 36
Recognition 170
Redemption 188
Remedial knowledge 215
Resistance 136
Respectful silence 68
Responsibility 188
Rex Harrison 133
Richard Attenborough 87
Richard Suzman 161
Rightness 35, 193, 197
Rinky Dink Dictionaries 5
Robert Browning 30
Robert Louis Stevenson 151
Robert Ross 41
Robert Schwartz 80
Robert "The Bruce" 165

Rolf Dane 229
Romantic Sexual Urge 77
Roseto 83
Rosicrucian teacher 208
Ruler Of The Universe 132
Russell Targ 92

S

Sa'di (poet) 55
Sanity 98
Scale Of Emotional Health 116,
    126
Scale Of Loving And Connected-
    ness 61
Second Law of Thermodynamics
    51, 159
Self-Esteem 186
Self love 213
Self-restraint 190
Self-talk 128, 129
Sense of Worth 180
Serenity of Being 125
Serotonin 228
Sex 38
Shakespeare 90, 128, 139
Shamanism 93
Shift 142, 143
Showing Up 134
Show-Me Kit 17
Slices Of Eternity 42
Sly 119
Sneaky 119
Social Contract 60
Social Networking 85
Socrates 179
Somerset Maugham 138
Sondra Ray 74
Space-time continuum 146
Start Off By Making Your Bed
    157
Status 19
Stephen Pressfield 135
St John Ambulance Brigade 111
Strokes 66, 162
Stubborn Self-Serving Computa-

48907906R00136

Made in the USA
Charleston, SC
11 November 2015